CLEAN, DECLUTTER AND ORGANISE YOUR HOME

3 Books In 1.

Edit Your Home And Your Life In The Perspective Of Sustainable Minimalism And In The Ancient And Wonderful Style Of Wabi Sabi

Noelle Gill

TABLE OF CONTENTS

CLUTTER-FREE YOUR HOME

Secrets To Declutter, Clean And Organise Your Home. The Ultimate Guide With Ideas, Habits And Plans For A Perfectly Organized Life

Noelle Gill

A dirty and messy house:

WHAT IS THE CONNECTION WITH OUR PSYCHOLOGY?

CHAPTER 1 YOUR MESSY HOUSE AFFECTS YOUR WELL-BEING

The world is beautiful because it is varied and this is also true of the care of domestic spaces. If on the one hand, in fact, there are those who organize their environment in a precise and orderly way, on the other hand there are those who tend to have a less "rigid" and methodical management, if not ... chaos! Given that confusion and dirt are two different things (even if sometimes disorder can lead to a dirtier house, because it makes it more difficult to clean thoroughly), what is the link between a house in disorder and our psychology? Let's see together.

A dirty and messy house: what is the connection with our psychology?

A house can be dirty and untidy for several reasons. In addition to the "psychology" that could be hidden behind certain ways of acting, the reason why a house is neglected is often linked to the hectic pace of today's life that absorbs time and energy. This does not mean that the house should be left to itself, of course, but it is not always easy, without a doubt, to keep everything clean and "spotless" as you would like. There are also people who, compared to perfectly organized environments as with a minimalist style, instead prefer spaces rich in objects and a less set order, or who tend to give less priority to household chores in general (in this case, of course, the important thing is never neglect the healthiness and liveability of the house, which remain fundamental aspects for the well-being of the person).

Of course, as we will see, there is a limit to everything and there are circumstances in which excessive disorder is no longer a simple way of being, but can represent the symptom of a deeper discomfort.

Disorder as a synonym for creativity

In the collective imagination, disorder is often associated with creativity and imagination, a connection that has also been confirmed by research conducted by the Carlson School of Management of the University of Minnesota, according to which a disorderly environment favors creativity. How did the study take place? The participants involved were distributed in two different rooms, one tidy and the other untidy: the people who were in the untidy room were shown to develop more innovative ideas (they were asked to propose new possible uses for ping pong balls) and also a greater propensity for novelty.

Good news also for lovers of order, however: according to this experiment, an orderly environment would stimulate healthy food choices and generous behaviors. To support the advantages of order, research was carried out by Princeton University which showed that disorder would make concentration more difficult. Additionally, a study published in the journal Personality and Social Psychology Bulletin found that women who described their home as untidy showed higher levels of the stress hormone cortisol.

Although there are different personalities who prefer more or less orderly environments, there is a limit beyond which disorder and neglect can be the indicator of a problem. The domestic environment, in fact, can represent a projection of the individual's state of mind and when chaos triumphs, becoming ungovernable, it could signal an inner discomfort (for example the inability to make decisions, to leave the past behind, etc.) and also hide serious psychological problems; in the same way, too maniacal and obsessive care of the house can also be a sign of malaise.

Given that extremes never go well, therefore, trying to keep clutter in the house under control is also very important for easy cleaning. As mentioned previously, in fact, although disorder and cleanliness are two different things, excessive confusion risks demotivation and making household chores more difficult and tiring. To better manage the home, despite the work and the many commitments, a solution - if you have the possibility - can be to rely on a domestic worker (even once every 1 or 2 weeks, for example, or on the occasion of more demanding cleaning).

The dreams we have, sometimes, can reveal the state of mind we are living in a given period of life. Dreaming of a house in disorder, for example, could suggest that we are going through a moment of confusion and emotional instability, sensations that would also manifest themselves through the images of a chaotic and upside-down environment.

An untidy house "confuses" the brain and sleep is also affected

Not only does living in chaos generate more anxiety, but it also induces you to eat more with consequences on weight. Recent research has shown that those who love to tidy up usually have better cardiovascular health.

It is a law of physics, the second law of thermodynamics: all natural processes involve an increase in entropy. That is, they lead to a system in which the degree of order of the elements decreases. Translated, it is in the nature of things to tend to disorder if we do not intervene with a little effort: if we do not wash the dishes, dirty dishes will accumulate in the sink; if we do not put the books back on the shelves, piles will form on the floor, and so on. Some more, some less, we all try to oppose the chaos and do well, since order is also helpful to staying healthy. Living in a house where there are too many things piled up, for example, can compromise sleep: Pamela Thacher, a psychologist at St. Lawrence University in the United States, has shown that disorder in a room reduces the quality of rest and this can then translate into stress, anxiety, increased appetite and everything else that can result from disturbed sleep, including poorer cognitive performance. Data also confirmed by a survey by the US National Sleep Foundation, according to which those who do not tolerate seeing the bed unmade and make it carefully every morning have a 19 percent more chance of sleeping well (and if the sheets are always clean, rest is even better for 75 percent of respondents).

Cluttered kitchen, goodbye diet

Some time ago then Lenny Vartanian of the University of New South Wales in Sidney, Australia, demonstrated on a group of volunteers that having the kitchen cluttered with dirty dishes, with pans and pots lying around and bulk food on the shelves leads to eating more and choosing less healthy foods, such as chocolate chip cookies instead of fruit. On the other hand, those who find themselves in a clean and tidy kitchen resist temptation, even if they are under stress: the combination of a chaotic environment and the feeling of anxiety is fatal, and in the long run can even lead to putting on a few extra pounds. If the house is in order, however, according to data collected by psychologists at the University of Los Angeles in California, anxiety and depression, are less likely; on the contrary, living in apartments full of stacked objects increases the production of cortisol, the stress hormone.

Exercise

Lovers of order are generally in better health than those who spend their days in rooms that have not seen a broom or vacuum cleaner for some time: a research by Purdue University in Indianapolis has shown this on a thousand people followed for over ten years, noting that order was directly related to the degree of physical activity and overall cardiovascular health. "The confusion present in the rooms of the house was found to be a parameter for predicting the state of health, better than the livability of the neighborhood," says the author, Nicole Keith. "Spending part of the day cleaning, using the washing machine, dusting, and the rest is to be considered real physical exercise, which helps to keep you active and healthy". The reasons why a clean house without too many objects around makes us feel good, however, do not pass only from the calories spent on household chores, but also from the innate preferences of the brain, which loves order and regularity to the point of looking for it even when it's not there: we tend to see regular patterns everywhere, even in the absence of a "thread" that binds objects, and we don't want too many things in the visual field, because they distract us and make us waste cognitive energy.

Cognitive performance

The demonstration comes from research by the Princeton Neuroscience Institute, which by analyzing the brain activity of those in more or less chaotic environments with magnetic resonance has verified how order is accompanied by a greater ability to focus on what matters and better information processing. Corollary: if there are no piles of useless documents, blunt pencils and the like on the desk, we work better and are more productive, we do not postpone the most important tasks and cognitive performance improves thanks to more focused attention on what is really needed, rather than to the crumpled pages beside the computer screen. Confusion alarms the brain, which in fact gives the signal to produce more cortisol, and the same happens if the chaos is in one's thoughts: Jacob Hirsh, of the Rotman School of Management at the University of Toronto, coined the term psychological entropy to indicate the "uncertain" thoughts that become gradually more confused and generate anxiety.

Excess of stimuli

Chaos in the mind is favored by the excess of stimuli we are subjected to today: according to Daniel Levitin, professor of psychology and behavioral neuroscience at McGill University in Montreal, "The load of information to which we are exposed in the last twenty-five years has quintupled and today in our free time alone we process about a hundred thousand words, the equivalent of 34 gigabytes. The brain, however, has a processing capacity of 120 bits per second, listening to another person "occupies" 60. It means that we cannot really be multitasking, but we must also put order in our heads by giving priority to what is needed gradually really pay attention". Making a list of tasks to take care of in order not to waste cognitive energy or setting smartphone notifications to remind us to switch to something else when it's time to do so are therefore good methods to "clear the brain" of the disorder of thoughts, helping it to concentrate on one thing at a time and thus to work better.

CHAPTER 2 THE BENEFITS OF HAVING AN ORGANIZED AND TIDY HOME

Tidying up and cleaning the house: therapy for the body and mind.

The home is one of the places where we spend a lot of time: taking care of your home is a bit like taking care of yourself.

There is a profound link between man and the environment where he lives, both at the macro level, that is, at the level of the place in a broad sense, and at the micro level, that is our home.

Living the space

From an anthropological point of view there is a profound correlation between space and body. In fact, as the anthropologist Vanessa Maher points out, already from the verb "cure" that is used in reference to "take care of the house", it refers to an act that normally refers to the body or the self (take care of oneself).

Anthropologist Mary Douglas also talks about how dirt is seen as a symptom of disorder in any society and must be combated as such. Dirt leads to confusion and contamination, and that is why it is necessary to have order.

The categories clean / dirty, order / disorder become a metaphor to categorize not only environments, but also people and their acceptance in society.

If from a social level the space we live in is a representation, in part, of what we are, how do we experience this space and its care on a psychological level?

Tidying up the house to order the mind

On a psychological level, tidying up the house is seen as a way of tidying up and clearing our minds too. In fact, the conditions of the environment in which we live can affect our mental state: for this reason putting things in order and arranging, can help us to arrange and put order among our thoughts. Similarly, procrastinating and leaving the house in disorder can be due to a moment of mental chaos and could steal energy from our daily life, preventing us from carrying out other activities.

Two things need to be pointed out:

- in some cases the disorder can be associated with creative people who find order in their disorder.

- manic house cleaning isn't good - it could be an indicator of deeper distress related to obsessive-compulsive disorder.

Cleanliness and order, like other daily activities and behavioral traits, are not absolute truths, but everyone must find comfort and balance within a spectrum of possibilities that make them feel good.

At the level of interpersonal relationships with the people we live with, it is important to create and maintain some healthy (and non-toxic) behaviors to better enjoy the environment in which we live: our home is our refuge.

Negative relationships and toxic behaviors in the home.

The home should generally be a comfortable place, where we feel loved and where well-being prevails. This does not only mean creating a physical space in which to feel good, but also trying to avoid having toxic behaviors towards the people who are living with us, whether they are family members, partners or roommates.

It is important to have respect for others and for the space in which we live, in order not to create a toxic and negative environment.

Let's delve into some negative behaviors that would be best left outside the front door.

Shouting: Shouting means wanting to impose one's will on others and can be a form of violence and an attempt to make the other submit. On children in particular, this behavior can cause damage to the level of personality and emotional balance, but even in the case of adults this attitude certainly does not create pleasant situations. Shouting is just a symptom of a lack of control and an inability to handle the situation.

Hostility: Negativity and hostility are feelings that are palpable in the air. And if this type of behavior persists among the inhabitants of a house, it could be very difficult and distressing to spend time in our home. Above all it could be very difficult to relax and rest in such an environment, thus worsening our general living conditions. We must try to solve problems and not generate conflicts, learning to communicate and get involved, respecting others and ourselves.

Drama: We all go through dramatic moments throughout our lives. But there are people who live as if every day were a drama, living everything with negativity and creating problems where they don't exist. If we are near one of these people (or if we are the person in question) we could find ourselves in an environment that gradually becomes toxic and pessimistic, infected by the negative attitude. What can we do in these cases? Again it is important to try to communicate with these people, showing them how the attitude they have is conditioning everyone and creating a negative environment. We could try to offer them positive alternatives and a more serene atmosphere for everyday life.

Confusion. We have seen how confusion and disorder in an environment can affect or be a reflection of an equally confused state of mind. In this sense it can generate stress and our brain at the same time has more difficulty in processing information. Confusion can lead to a feeling of saturation which affects our well-being and productivity. It is important to have rules at home, which clearly define the limits and roles of coexistence, to find yourself in a positive, orderly and clean environment.

Denigration. Above all within a family, if the people who are part of it are constantly denigrated by others, it may make some difficult moments, besides the fact of causing low self-esteem and difficulties later in life. There are different types of denigration: from judging someone by assigning them a role, for example that of black sheep, or by attributing to them skills or not. This negatively affects both the person in question but also all members of the family, because no one identifies well what is right or wrong, as well as responsibilities and consequences. If we find ourselves in such a situation, to try to get out of it we can first try to understand and make it clear that each person has an intrinsic value and that each has qualities and defects that are worth knowing and experiencing.

Furnish, clean and rearrange your space to take care of yourself.

We have already said how to clean, order and beautify your home, is good for the body, spirit and mind.

We think of spring cleaning, tidying up after the cold of winter, fresh air coming in through the windows and the renewal of the wardrobe.

But how can spring cleaning make us feel better?

According to experts, cleaning the house has several beneficial effects:

Cleaning the house kills germs and bacteria, leading to a clean house that strengthens your immune system and helps avoid disease.

In addition, a tidy and clean home helps reduce stress and accidents in the home, and prevents depression.

It promotes concentration and reflection in difficult or very intense periods.

Some studies link order and cleanliness with the decision to follow an active lifestyle and a healthier diet.

ARE YOU READY TO IMPROVE YOUR WELL-BEING?

There are many ancient and traditional views, both in our culture and in the oriental one, which study and deepen the concept of reorganization and architecture as a means to foment well-being.

Below we will focus on two visions: the philosophy of feng shui and the Konmari method (whose main exponent is Marie Kondo).

We have chosen these methods because we believe there are important points for reflection and suggestions, and not necessarily because they must be followed to the letter. Let's take a closer look at them!

Seeking well-being through Feng Shui

Feng shui is an ancient art that developed in China and that starts from the study of nature and its rules to apply them to homes and architecture. Feng Shui means respectively wind and water, and they are the two main elements on which settlement choices were made in the past: they are the elements that shape life with their actions.

To apply Feng Shui within your own space, you normally resort to an expert, but we can leave some tips here:

Symmetry: the floor plan of the house should be square or rectangular (i.e. as symmetrical as possible), to avoid dead spots (although this problem can be overcome by inserting tall furniture).

Cardinal points: the internal layout of the rooms must follow the cardinal points. The entrance is preferable to the north, while the rooms for relationships are located in the south.

Colors: the colors are related to the different rooms. Warm colors will be used in south facing rooms, while cool colors will be used in north facing rooms.

Furniture: furniture and furnishings must be arranged in such a way as not to obstruct the flow (and passage) that flows into a room. So it is best to avoid sharp and bulky furniture. As for the position of the bed in FengShui, it is normally recommended to place the head of the bed facing North, but in reality it depends on some variables related to the layout of the room (for example, more or less proximity to the door).

The 5 elements: Feng Shui also recommends to include in the furniture, decorations that allow you to control the 5 elements (for example an aquarium for water, iron objects (metal), plants (wood), vases (earth), candles (fire).

Large windows with a regular shape, which should however be placed not in front of the door.

Harmonious interior and exterior. If you have an outdoor space it is important to "cultivate" it so that it is in harmony with the internal space ... and the presence of plants and a vegetable garden helps the mind and body!

Eliminate the superfluous. According to Feng Shui, objects we don't use steal our energy and transmit negative energy to us. We must leave the energy to flow freely.

The Konmari and Marie Kondo method

Marie Kondo is the author of the book "The Magic Power of Tidying" which tries to find the best way to tidy up the house (and the mind).

Some of the basics are:

Boomerang effect: tidying up the house means not only tidying up, but also getting rid of the things we don't need. Because if we accumulate things, even if we try to put them in order, sooner or later we will end up with the house being full of things scattered throughout.

Learning to throw away what we don't need. This means letting go and giving things up. Among the objects there are some that have a meaning that is visceral and makes us happy, while others leave us indifferent. If in front of an object we find ourselves uncertain whether to throw it or not, then we probably don't really care but we are victims of a neurotic impulse. Indifferent objects obstruct the house, and therefore it is important to get rid of them. But first we have to find a moment, to thank the object and greet it (so as not to feel guilty feelings and give value to the object and the effort we made to buy it).

To accomplish this task, the Marie Kondo method is developed through 9 steps, to be carried out one after the other and passing to the next only when the first is completed.

Throw away everything that is indifferent to us and that has no meaning for us (always remembering to thank and say hello).

Keep only what brings happiness and well-being to our life.

One thing at a time: sort by categories, not by area. For example, start with the closet, not with the whole room! Start with clothes: it's an easier choice, because we know what we wear and what we don't.

Organize the clothes vertically, making small triangles and then hanging them, A sort of clothing library.

Don't put it off. It is important to start and finish each category.

Keep the objects of value. Everything around you must make sense.

Carry out this work yourself, because together with others you may get confused, postpone or make you decide not to throw out objects.

Don't spend money on furniture. Very often it will be enough to order in the right way and throw away the superfluous to make the available furniture suffice.

There are many benefits to living in an orderly house, one of these is to be able to create a relaxing and welcoming environment that stimulates you to seek even interior order. Think about it, whenever you need to concentrate in a completely natural and instinctive way, you prefer to choose an orderly environment.

This is because order favors reasoning and allows you to organize ideas more easily and without distractions. While clutter often causes confusion and conveys negative feelings.

WHY PUT THE HOUSE IN ORDER?

This is because by eliminating the superfluous, you begin to put in order a little bit inside yourself too.

Ordering stimulates you to change your attitude, transform your home and

19

make it closer to what you want, it can be the starting point for a deeper and more radical change.

HOW TO SUCCEED IN ORDERING THE HOUSE

Now that you understand the reasons why you should tidy up the place where you live and the benefits it can offer you, it's time to get some practical advice.

I know how difficult it is to put the house in order, and to maintain over time the result you have achieved after so much effort, and that's why here you will find three simple steps that you can follow to put everything in its place.

Take care of your home and turn it into your refuge, a place to feel good. You will find that with the right strategies and a little good will it is not that difficult to succeed.

1. Eliminate the unnecessary

Look around and begin to notice how many superfluous things surround you, how many things you have kept over the years without any real use.

Separate them from everything else and decide whether to throw them away or donate them, but discard them. You will have more awareness of what you really need and avoid piling up unnecessary things in the future by creating more space for you and the things that really matter.

2. Organize the spaces

Organize your things so that they are functional and comfortable. Each person has a different method, look for the solution that best suits your space and your needs. It is often difficult to keep the house tidy simply because it is tiring and laziness sooner or later always takes over. It is therefore necessary to minimize the effort required. If storing your things in the space you have created for them costs you as much as leaving them scattered around the house, you will be more likely to put them away. Think about this and use boxes, dividers and binders to make tidying up your home as easy and quick as possible. Since you have to be realistic and we all know that a little clutter is inevitable, limit it only in certain areas. It will be easier this way, to keep it under control and prevent it from regaining the upper hand.

3. Don't accumulate

If you have succeeded in following steps 1 and 2 your home will now be tidy and well organized. You will have spent time and energy to fix everything, not to ruin the work done.

This hard-won order is often threatened by the inability to arrange your new purchases in the right spaces. Whenever you introduce something new into the house, store it following the organization you have adopted in a functional way, do not arrange it randomly as you would have done before. When you no longer need it, eliminate it, so as to avoid being overwhelmed again by useless things that if not managed correctly, will accumulate day after day making you return to the starting point. Get rid of superfluous things that sooner or later you will find yourself having to throw away. Make tidying up a daily habit.

If you follow all three steps you can finally feel free from clutter and enjoy your space. You've earned it, take advantage of it by filling it with what you love.

Starting to take care of the environment in which you live and spend your free time is the first step to take care of yourself.

CHAPTER 3 DISORDER TRIGGERS STRESS AND ANXIETY

Clutter in the house triggers stress and anxiety, says a psychologist.

Does it also happen to you when you return home, perhaps after a long and stressful day, to find every room completely in disorder? In a single instant, your desire to chase away the stress by closing the front door fails. At this point, usually, a nervousness emerges that lasts throughout the evening, along with stress and anxiety.

Don't worry, you are not the only one to have such a response to disorder, nor are you wrong to have it: according to psychologists. In fact, messy spaces are the trigger for stress and panic attacks.

"Clutter greatly affects how we feel in our homes, offices or elsewhere. Spaces crowded with cluttered things trigger a state of anxiety, make us feel helpless and overwhelmed. People rarely recognize that it's the clutter that is the cause of the stress in their lives," said psychologist Sherrie Bourg Carter.

Disorder, therefore, could play a much more influential role in our mental well-being than we have ever thought.

It causes mental fatigue because it exposes us to a large number of useless stimuli;

It takes our attention away from what we really want to focus on;

It tells the brain that our work is not done yet;

It leads us to think about the effort and time it will take to put everything in order.

In all this there is a solution, the simplicity of which depends both on one's willpower and on the presence or absence of other people who can contribute to the disorder.

According to the psychologist, in the event that the house is inhabited by a family, it is good to involve all the family members in the tidying process. You can think of assigning a room each or of establishing one day a week dedicated to cleaning the rooms.

One way to prevent clutter from amassing is to avoid all'open and "exposed" furniture; you have to get containers, wardrobes and furniture with doors, which eventually allow you to temporarily "hide" the disorder.

The other secrets to keeping chaos out are:

Establish rules, such as always putting things away in the place and in the way they were found;

Throw away anything you don't need or arrange to donate it to someone who might need it;

Distribute cleaning and tidying over time, avoiding doing everything together.

As a final trick, the psychologist recommends adding a pinch of fun; while you tidy up the house you can put on some music or turn on the comedy program you like best!

CHAPTER 4 WHY TIDYING UP AND CLEANING THE HOUSE MAKES US SO HAPPY

A clean and tidy home contributes to our emotional and mental well-being.

Tidying up and cleaning the house can make us happier. Indeed, there is nothing more relaxing and satisfying than entering an organized home, where a kind of peace and calm reigns. But have you ever wondered why this happens? According to scientific and psychiatric studies, a clean home also contributes to our emotional and mental well-being.

All experts agree that a little discipline and order can work as therapy and contribute to a happier life. How?

Reduces anxiety

Swati Mittal, a consultant psychiatrist for Fortis Noida and Swastik Assist Homes, says that, in addition to burning calories, our body releases endorphins and chemicals that make us feel good. This means that these types of activities can reduce anxiety and positively contribute to our mental health.

Increase happiness

"An orderly and organized environment affects our mental and physical state in ways we cannot imagine. From having more family time to creating a stress-free life, good organization contributes to a happier life," confirms Gayatri Gandhi, organizer by profession.

Improve concentration and performance

The feeling of living in a clean environment also increases confidence and provides a sense of satisfaction and motivation. "If our environment is in order, so will we be, and we will perform better," says psychiatrist Jinesh Shah.

Cleanup and the pandemic

Jinesh Shah recalls that "focusing on cleaning and disinfecting surfaces during the pandemic was stressful and created anxiety for many people." Stressing, "The pandemic has had a particularly negative impact on people with OCD who are obsessed with cleanliness, as it has aggravated their symptoms."

Here's a tip: We should never ignore cluttered spaces, unsanitary living conditions, poor personal hygiene or a listless approach to life, "as it is a clear sign of depression that requires immediate medical attention."

CHAPTER 5 COUPLES ARE CLOSER AND HAPPIER IN A CLEAN AND TIDY HOUSE

The holidays are over; putting everything back in its place was challenging and, little by little, we resume the daily routine, made up of a daily dose of order and organization. Many couples do not find the balance between household chores and personal needs.

Some experts suggest dedicating at least half an hour a day to tidying up the house, but not everyone is able to make that time or maybe get up earlier in the morning to dedicate themselves to their nest. Yet, it is enough to imagine the pleasure of returning to a loved and tidy home to already feel involved.

Have you already experienced the pleasure of sharing the daily chores as a couple?

In reality, a few tricks, organized and divided, are enough and everything will magically flow faster. From the bedroom to the bathroom, without neglecting the kitchen and what was not put away the night before, a healthy couple organization will allow us to leave the house ready for our return.

If as soon as you wake up, before escaping to the bathroom, we open the bedroom window for just 5 minutes, we are already doing a small fundamental action: ventilating! Removing germs and bacteria re-oxygenates the room and protects us from allergies. In addition, leaving the bed open to let out the humidity allows you to find it healthier in the evening. A few minutes and, making the bed together, it will seem that we have already carried out a first important task to bring order to the room with our partner.

If one of the two is dedicated to preparing breakfast, the other can arrange the living room, tidying up the blankets, pillows and other things left around, the trick is to start with what catches the eye first and then focus on the details.

After sharing breakfast, the ideal is to do the washing up, it will only take a few seconds, and while one partner washes, the other can dry next to them, also drying the sink and taps.

A tidy kitchen makes you want to use it ... when you return. The complicity of these small gestures could give a different profile to your days, the pleasure of sharing these little things with order and organization takes a few precious moments that make our daily life richer and more powerful.

A few more minutes and together in the bathroom, folding the towels, leaving nothing lying around, putting everything away in the cabinets is a small measure to make the room even cleaner, drying the sink and taps here too.

Leaving the bulk of the work to do together for the weekend, seeing a tidier home will put us at ease when we return.

When, giving yourself a pat on the back, you turn to look at the beautiful and welcoming house that awaits you, you will be proud to have made, together with your partner, those little attentions that will make you happy to return later.

CHAPTER 6 ON DECLUTTERING

How to declutter: the secrets of this real philosophy of life.

Decluttering is not the simple elimination of unnecessary objects: it is a real attitude oriented towards the essentials. A liberation that opens up the future and new possibilities.

When avoiding the dust becomes an obstacle course and finding something in a cabinet almost a mission impossible, then comes the time to get rid of unnecessary items: declutter, and "eliminate what clutters".

In Anglo-Saxon countries this practice has now become a true philosophy of life: selecting and eliminating what is no longer used, in fact, seems to have a real benefit also on an inner level, "freeing us" from the past, opening our minds to the future and to new possibilities.

Owning less to live better: is this perhaps the secret of happy degrowth? Given this ethically correct assumption, putting it into practice is a different matter, let's see some tips.

Decluttering: practical advice

Let's start with space cleaning, or how to reorganize spaces and, consequently, your life.

The experts advise drawing up a "ranking" of the rooms with the more messy spaces, in an orderly fashion, and focus on one area at a time.

You should do a "scan" of the objects, wondering how many times you have used them in the last 12 months: if you realize you have never used them, it is time to get rid of them.

The selection of objects, of course, must be made according to eco-sustainable principles.

They must therefore be separated carefully to differentiate them in the garbage, while what can be "saved" instead, can be sold or bartered.

If you are not ready to get rid of the objects immediately, keep them in a box and give yourself a period of tim. If after the period you realize you have never used it, it is really time to throw it away.

The excuse of "I don't have time" does not apply: once you have chosen the room to tidy up you can dedicate half an hour a day to decluttering, or just one day of the weekend, depending on your availability.

Decluttering: how to proceed.

Thankfully, decluttering experts provide good advice for every circumstance.

Take 5 minutes a day.

Throw away one item a day.

Use a garbage bag: you will be amazed at the speed with which it will fill up with objects you thought you could not part with.

Compile a list of the zones / rooms to be cleaned, starting with the simplest: proceed one zone at a time, crossing it off the list.

Apply the 12-12-12 scheme, drawing up a list with 12 things to throw away, 12 to donate and 12 to return to their rightful owners: tidying up in this way will be more fun and less traumatic!

Change perspective to see your home in a new light, perhaps by taking photos of your home before and after decluttering.

Experiment with numbers, for example wearing the same 33 items of clothing for 3 months: the aim is to understand that you can live with fewer things.

When you really have a hard time separating yourself from something, try asking yourself 'If I bought it today how much would I be willing to pay for it?'

Use the 'four boxes' technique: when you have to tidy up a room, get 4 boxes and write on them 'TO THROW, TO DONATE, TO KEEP, TO REUSE', and then you will have to choose which box to put each item in; the procedure can be long, but it works!

For those items that you don't want to throw away, you can apply 3 simple 'storage' rules.

Make a selection of the chosen objects, dividing them by year or by period (old house, university, etc.).

Keep children's objects in a dedicated container and place them inside the wardrobe, where they are not cluttered: when you want, you can always take them to look for something.

Develop a functional archiving method: your children's clothes and photos, for example, can be stored in folders or albums, or you can digitize them and store them in digital folders.

We now come to the "hot" area of this period: the wardrobe. In spring and autumn, it is time for seasonal changes: let's make the most of them to tidy up our clothes and, why not, our lives. You know, deciding what to keep and what to throw away is always difficult, but with some ad hoc advice everything will be easier.

The 4 boxes rule also applies to clothes: to keep, to file, to donate, to throw away. Throw away the clothes only if you have no alternatives, otherwise do everything possible to reuse them in some way, for example organizing a barter market with friends.

A useful trick to select clothes is this: hang the dubious clothes in the opposite direction to the others, or make a mark on the hangers. Only when / if you wear the garment can you turn the hanger correctly or remove the mark. At the end of the season, garments that have never been used must be eliminated.

Throw away damaged or useless hangers, then divide the remaining ones by placing similar ones next to each other: in this way the visual impact will be better.

After the difficult selection phase, clean the inside of the wardrobe thoroughly: vacuum the bottom and dust shelves and other surfaces.

The operation is tiring, but it will pay off: seeing the wardrobe in order will make you feel lighter.

The important thing is to maintain discipline even afterwards, avoiding starting to fill it with useless items on the first shopping trip.

CHAPTER 7 THROWING AWAY THE SUPERFLUOUS

How to get rid of unnecessary things for the house: to tidy your life and learn to throw away the superfluous.

Eliminating the superfluous in the house is essential, if we do not want to find ourselves buried alive by all the objects and clothes we no longer use. However, it is not always easy to get rid of unnecessary things, indeed, for many people it is very difficult.

Some objects, although devoid of material utility, are full of precious memories and it is normal not to want to get rid of them. Many of these memories, however, lie forgotten for years in the bottom of a drawer, with the sole purpose of taking up space. Therefore, we must learn to select the things that actually should not be thrown away and those that, instead, should end up in the trash immediately. Here are 10 ways, techniques and lifestyles to do it.

10 ways to get rid of unnecessary items in the house.

• Organize your work. Tidying up the whole house, from the bedroom to the pantry, in a single day is impossible and counterproductive. It is advisable to set dates in a cleaning calendar, dividing the work into several days, so as not to miss anything.

• Don't buy new things. If you always buy and don't want to throw anything away, the best thing to do is to stop shopping, which obviously increases the things you have at home.

• Ask for help. If not enough time to do the cleaning, ask relatives and friends for help. To save space, Marie Kondo's videos can also help.

• Fill boxes. If there are things that just can't be thrown away, put them in boxes, and then store them in the garage or basement so that they leave more space in the house. Maybe the following year will be the right time to throw them away for good.

• Throw away the things you don't use. To make clean break, things and clothes that have not been used for a long time could be thrown away. There should be no regrets, as your tastes, perhaps, may have changed over time.

• Organize papers and documents. Keeping all documents is important, but often unnecessary paper ends up in the middle. It is therefore necessary to buy folders or binders with labels to keep the important things aside. The rest is to be thrown into the paper bin.

• Tidy up the pantry. When you go to the supermarket you always end up buying useless products, which end up expiring. Check the expiration dates, in order to consume the food in the right time, avoiding waste.

• Give to charity. Give the old clothes, (in good condition that you don't wear) to the poor and needy. You have to put them all in bags and boxes (making sure they are not too worn) and take them to the associations that deal with these things. Surely in your neighborhood there will also be a parish church or an association that collects used clothes for the needy.

• Save space. A good thing is to keep the house in order, so that you can find all the things you are looking for in a short time, and avoid forgetting that you have them.

• Make selections. Obviously, there are objects that you can't help but keep, because they symbolize moments in your life and create a memory. It is advisable to try to understand which are the most important objects, and the others that remain must be thrown away.

CHAPTER 8 100 USELESS THINGS TO THROW AWAY

We often have no idea how many useless objects are clogging up our rooms: here is a super useful list of useless things compiled by a space-clearing expert.

In recent years, the fashion of "decluttering" and "space clearing" have haunted us, but even if you don't like Marie Kondo, admit that having a house that is always tidy and with few objects to manage is incredibly good for the soul.

After all, the organization of the house is a real science, and even if you can not detach yourself even from the objects you no longer use, you must admit that having more free space - in addition to being comfortable and making life easier - manages to give a certain serenity.

Beginning to declutter in general is not easy, also because we often and willingly touch much deeper chords: the objects we insist on keeping are often not simply "things", but often symbols we cling to. If you don't know how to do it, know that the most important step is the first. And to do that here is a list of objectively useless things that you can start eliminating right away.

Here is the list of 100 useless things that affect both our home and our life and that we mentally struggle to get rid of

1. Dry cleaning hangers

2. Newspapers from the day before

3. Unwanted emails

4. Remote controls that do not control anything

5. Sports gadgets

6. Worn Christmas decorations

7. Expired warranties and contracts

8. Tablecloths, too large or too small

9. Mismatched socks

10. Email addresses you don't recognise

11. Broken spatulas and tools

12. Sachets of condiments

13. Empty cans, jars and bottles

14. History on the computer

15. Planters you don't use

16. Fake friends on Facebook

17. Jigsaw puzzles with missing pieces

18. Wedding gifts you don't use

19. Unused stuffed animals

20. Bad photographs

21. Unnecessary business cards

22. Difficult and laborious recipes

23. Fax machines

24. Baggy dresses

25. Manuals for item you no longer have

26. Pagers

27. Vacation memories you don't like

28. Dead plants

29. Newsletters you don't read

30. Stained, torn or frayed towels

31. Dry pens and markers

32. Food leftovers

33. Old video game accessories

34. Obsolete video games

35. Duplications of digital photographs

36. Recorded TV series you will never watch

37. Notebooks that are no longer needed

38. Too much underwear ... (we understand each other!)

39. Shopping bags of paper or plastic

40. Store catalogs now available online

41. e-books that you will not re-read

42. Ruined sweaters

43. Keys without locks

44. Chipped or damaged tableware

45. Sunglasses you don't use

46. Old school materials

47. Dry paint cans

48. Cooler bags that are too small, large or heavy

49. Shoe boxes

50. Birthday decorations

51. Uncomfortable or broken earphones

52. Invitations to past events

53. Passwords no longer in use

54. Silver jewelry you no longer wear (sell it!)

55. Broken electronic appliances

56. Stationery unused in the past 3 months

57. Cable channels (choose fewer and pay less)

58. Expired discount coupons

59. Umbrellas that don't open or that hold the wind

60. Toys for animals now unusable

61. Ugly fridge magnets

62. Trash in the computer trash can

63. Unused flower pots

64. Commitments dated on the calendar

65. Scraps of fabric

66. Cables for audio and video equipment

67. Yellow Pages

68. Paperback books you won't re-read

69. Requests for donations and charities

70. Gold jewelry you never wear (sell it!)

71. Empty candy and gift boxes

72. Useless mail

73. Trophies from your childhood

74. Cookbooks you've never used

75. Twitter contacts that communicate too much

76. Pool toys

77. Old greeting cards

78. Pajamas you don't like

79. Tourist brochures

80. Industrial foods that you do not consume

81. Stained clothes

82. Apps you don't use

83. Shoes that hurt you

84. Used plastic cups

85. Glass covers

86. Doubles of class photos

87. Car fluids that are no longer needed

88. Magazines more than three months old

89. Clotted nail polish

90. Shopping receipts

91. Shoe laces for shoes you no longer have

92. Broken or ignored toys

93. Worn doormats

94. Pins on Pinterest you don't need

95. Dishes you never use

96. Wallpaper you no longer have on the walls

97. Old pillows

98. Obsolete mobile phones

99. Bottle caps

100. Ducklings for the bath that are no longer used

The 5 "NOTs" of the superfluous object

How to know if you can get rid of something without repenting? Geralin Thomas proposes the strategy of the 5 nots. An object is to be thrown away if it falls into one of these cases:

1. You don't use it.

2. You don't want it.

3. You don't love him.

4. You have not decided or chosen.

5. You have not completed it and therefore cannot use it (applies, for example, to do-it-yourself items).

CHAPTER 9 HOW TO GET RID OF CLUTTER

The best way to keep a clean and organized home is to get rid of things that are no longer needed. Clutter can be detrimental to your home life, if only to make it easy to find things when you need them. Most of us tend to keep objects even if we have not used them for a long time, either because they recall an emotional bond, or for prudence in cases of economic difficulty, or for simple inertia. It is a wise thing to break free from old things to make room for new ones.

Part 1: Collect Things

This first part describes how to find and rearrange things. Don't waste time wondering what to do with newly recovered things; if their use is evident immediately, fix them, otherwise put them in the sorting piles.

1

Check all items that are outdated or no longer usable. Be brutal. If they clutter up the room, and you no longer have a normal place to live, put them in the pile to tidy up later. After all, do you really need those magazines you've been collecting since 1998 but rarely read?

2

Empty the closet and all drawers. Take any clothes that no longer fit you or are out of fashion now, and put them in the sorting pile.

3

Gather together all the sheets of paper and various documents that you have scattered around. Recycle or throw away the ones you don't need.

Keep the rest in organized folders.

4

First clean up any places that attract clutter, such as the bed. Then remove all objects from this area. Throw out the things you no longer need, clean up the dirty ones, and put everything else back in its place. Anything you don't know whether to keep goes in the sorting pile.

Part 2: Order

1

Put the sorting pile in a large clean area so you can see everything to organize the tidying up well.

2

Ask yourself the three basic questions about the objects that ended up in the pile:

Do you like it?

Do you use it often, or will you use it soon (within 3 months)?

Will you miss it when you get rid of it? Is it a very important memory for you?

3

Divide the pile into three distinct groups.

First group: the things you use almost every day and the things you "like".

For example, the telephone, tools, shoes, and so on. You can put the keys in a bowl near the door, you can keep the tools in a toolbox, or buy yourself a shoe cabinet. Find any solution that works for you and helps you find all the most important items with ease.

The things you are attached to, such as photos, knick-knacks, etc ... should now find a place to display them or keep them hidden, or keep them carefully, etc ...

Second group: Here you should put the things you use at least once a week or once a month. These are generally items that should be kept in closets, garages, or other out-of-the-way places. Reorder them in containers (better if they are transparent, so you can easily see the contents) and label them. Other things, like clothes, put them away on hangers.

Third group: should include things you haven't used for at least six months or a year. If you haven't used them in all this time, chances are you won't use them any more. So, get rid of them forever. Give all the items you don't use or no longer want to charities, so that they can be used by someone less fortunate.

4

Don't think you can tidy everything up in one day. Depending on how much mess there is, it could take two days or a week. If it's emotionally demanding, it may take months, and it's a good idea to call a friend or objective mate to help you morally as well.

Advice

Try tidying up one room at a time. Start from one corner and arrange it in your own style and arrange the whole room before moving on to the next one.

Treat yourself to a movie in the cinema, a new dress, or a trip once you're done. Rewards can help you get on with the project, giving you an incentive to complete the task.

If you need to tidy up after work, try doing it a little at a time. Take fifteen minutes each night to tackle a small area, drawer, or shelf.

You can donate items to charities. It could be old clothes, old shoes, old toys, old appliances, etc ...

Keep order! Working 15 minutes a day to fix a room is better than spending days tidying up a house every year or so. Remember that any improvement is better than nothing. If you get tired, take a five-minute break and then go back to work. You can listen to some music while you are busy for an hour or two.

Set a specific time to reorder. Never try to do this after a long day at work if you can avoid it.

If you live in Australia, you can enter the things you no longer need in "Free Treasure", www.freetreasure.com.au and find someone who comes to pick them up at your home; so you save time finding other things to get rid of.

Warnings

Don't try to rearrange an entire house in one day.

Before starting the task, make sure you have the energy and time to complete it. A good rule of thumb is not to take out more than you can tidy up in an hour. Set a timer for one hour, and when it's over, you can decide whether to work for another hour if you have the strength. Give yourself a 15- or 20-minute break as a reward, look at emails, have a cup of tea, or lie down on the sofa.

Remember that there is a difference between clutter and objects that create the atmosphere and environment of the areas you clean. This distinction depends on the person.

You can ask friends or relatives for help. But don't call a friend who has the soul of a junk dealer, or you will find yourself in a worse situation. And be careful not to ask for help from someone who is too tidy. If you try to get rid of all your "precious" items you could panic and end up throwing nothing away!

Don't force yourself to tidy up. Make it pleasant, or you will soon lose interest. Trust the progress you can make. You can't think of tidying up the mess, that has formed over a long time, overnight.

CHAPTER 10 ORGANIZING THE HOUSE: THE 30-DAY CHALLENGE

Blogger Ashlina Kaposta has devised a 30-day challenge to become real "domestic gods" in one month.

The purpose of this month-long commitment is to make the home more welcoming and tidier with minimal daily effort and, at the invitation of @thedecorista, to share your progress with her on Instagram with the hashtag #domesticbliss30.

This kind of challenge, especially if not too long, as in this case, can be a solution to organize life at home step by step and make changes constant over time.

Here are the daily commitments proposed:

Day 1 - Assess the situation

The blogger suggests setting some goals and drawing up a top 5 of the areas of the house that are in urgent need of refurbishment.

Day 2 - Get rid of the paper

Raise your hand if your house is not full of paper, old documents and receipts. It's time to throw away what you no longer need or put your important documents in containers and folders.

Day 3 - Aromatherapy

Diffusers, essential oils, incense: being greeted by a good scent when entering the house is essential.

Day 4 - Arrange the bathroom

Bathroom hygiene is a daily necessity, but dedicate a day entirely to this, from top to bottom. In addition to cleaning, it also takes care of order: the time has come to throw away unused samples, expired creams and broken hairpins in the drawers.

Day 5 - Clean the windows

Windows, mirrors, frames glass: spray everything mercilessly (if possible, with ecological methods, such as water and vinegar).

Day 6 - Put the books away

Organize your library, but that's not all. Gather the books scattered around the house, those on the nightstand for months or the titles left in the bathroom bin that you never read because magazines are faster...

Day 7 - Arrange the sofa

In other words: give shape to the cushions, fold any blankets in an orderly way and refresh the fabrics.

Day 8 - Starting the top 5

Review the 5 goals drawn up on day 1 and start implementing the first on the list.

Day 9 - Arrange the refrigerator

As with the bathroom, again it's time to throw out old sauces, come up with a recipe for things that are about to expire, and clean up all the shelves.

Day 10 - A touch of green

A house without plants is a sad house: adopt a floor plan. If you don't have a green thumb, you can start with succulents or hardy houseplants like

Sansevieria, Ficus and Zamia.

For each type of plant, even if not delicate, find out about its needs for watering, natural light, soil.

Day 11 - Make the bed

Making your bed every day is a good aim, but if you usually can't, today is the time to get serious.

Put on clean sheets and try to make it perfect, better than you would ever find in a hotel.

Day 12 - Landfill drawers

We all have at least one: free the drawers from all the junk accumulated over the years.

Day 13 - Clean the light fittings

Uncomfortable and boring, but every now and then, like today, it has to be done.

Day 14 - Arrange your shoes

If the shoe rack is not enough, you can take advantage of the space under the bed or resort to practical DIY solutions.

Day 15 - Take a photo

Recreate a corner of the house that you like best in the style you prefer, photograph it and then share it. It doesn't have to be perfect but it has to reflect your tastes.

Day 16 - Plan a dinner

For you, for your loved one or for friends. The important thing is that every detail is perfect: turn off the TV, light the candles and... enjoy your meal!

Day 17 - Same as day 8

Review the 5 goals drawn up on day 1 and start implementing the second and third on the list.

Day 18 - Personality

Unleash your personality and make the house represent you. Express yourself through a DIY job, a decoration, a message on the bathroom mirror!

Day 19 - Set up a studio

Or in any case a corner of the house where you usually get to work, both as a profession and as a hobby. After tidying up, getting to work will be more pleasant.

Day 20 - The coffee table

Arrange any magazines left there for months, throw away anything that survived the apocalypse of day 2 and embellish it with a nice tray or an elegant book.

Day 21 - Adding fabrics

All it takes is a new pair of colorful curtains, an upholstered pillow, an IKEA fabric. Take a look here to light up the home with textiles.

Day 22 - The drinks trolley

Even if you don't drink alcohol, insert a corner dedicated to refreshment at home, perhaps for coffee or tea.

Day 23 - Same as day 8

Review the 5 goals drawn up on day 1 and start implementing the fourth and fifth on the list.

Day 24 - New prints

Almost every home has an abandoned picture that has been waiting for its call for months, if not years. If, on the other hand, you have nothing to hang and you have no creative flair, take a trip on the internet, find a design you like, print it and frame it. A simple and clean effect, to be used in a corner of the house with empty walls.

Day 25 - Welcome guests

Organize a small reception and invite friends or relatives. Tell us about your 30-day challenge and show the changes made so far.

Day 26 - Change of scenery

In the morning open all the windows of the house, weather permitting, light a few candles and perfume the rooms. It will bring new energy and everything will immediately seem cleaner and fresher.

Day 27 - Creating a personal space

Carving out a corner of your own at home is a gift that everyone should give themselves, regardless of the space available.

All it takes is a comfortable chair in a corner with a soft cushion, ten minutes of time, a good book and a coffee to start the day in a different way.

Day 28 - Fix up the garage

If not available, the cellar or any space used as a pantry. For some garages and boxes, it would take more than a day to fix everything, but try to do what you can.

Day 29 - A gift for the home

Go out and buy a small gift for your home. After all this work, you deserve it!

Day 30 - Final thoughts

The challenge is over. Appreciate what you have done this month and, why not, thank your house.

CHAPTER 11 HOW TO ORGANIZE THE KITCHEN

A disorganized kitchen can make your life very difficult! Knowing where to find what you need in the blink of an eye saves you time and unnecessary stress. Before starting to rearrange it, divide the various objects according to use. Then arrange the shelves and organize the drawers and furniture. Finally, try to make more space if there are other products to store.

Part 1 Divide Articles

1

Eliminate unnecessary items. If the drawers are full of stuff, you won't be able to find what you need. Do not keep bulky and unused items. To determine if you need something, consider the last time you used it, if it is still in good condition, and if you have duplicates. Give unused items to a friend or to charity. If you have accumulated tons of items that you no longer want or need, consider organizing a sale in front of your house.

Maybe you want to keep some kitchen utensils you don't use often, such as party dinnerware. If you don't have enough space to store them in the kitchen, it's best to find somewhere else.

2

Clean the kitchen from top to bottom. Dust the external surfaces of cabinets, appliances and any furnishings. Use a soapy rag and a clean, dry cloth to wash and dry the inside and outside of furniture and counter tops. Sweep and wash the floor. Wash and dry any rugs or other fabric items you have in the kitchen.

Your goal is to start from scratch! Since you are removing everything in the furniture and drawers, this is the best time to clean them. It is also not recommended to put dishes and appliances on top of a layer of dust and grime!

Expert Advice

Don't forget the fridge! Donna Smallin Kuper, an expert in home organization, advises: "When you want to thoroughly clean your refrigerator, remove everything from the shelves, including any removable drawers. Use an all-purpose cleaning spray and a microfiber cloth to wipe the shelves one at a time, starting with the top one. Wash the removable parts with warm soapy water, rinse and dry them, and put them back in the refrigerator. Finally, put back the food you removed from the appliance."

3

Establish work stations. Choose them based on how you use the kitchen. This will make it easier to decide which zone to put the current in. Here are some ideas:

Coffee or tea station: place the coffee maker or kettle in an easily accessible spot. Keep cups and mugs nearby.

Food Processing Station: create enough space to prepare food. Keep the cutting board, knives, measuring cups and everything you need close at hand.

Cooking station: in other words, it rotates around the hob. Keep crockery nearby, but also pot holders and oven mitts.

Station to Serve: If you have space, you may include a point where you put the food on the plates. Choose a free shelf and keep the necessary utensils, such as the ladle and skimmer, close at hand.

4

Choose accessible places for the items you use most often. You should take them, use them, wash them and replace them easily. Keep them close at hand or near the dishwasher, sink or stove. Avoid stacking pots and pans on top of each other, or you'll have to rummage around to find what you need.

5

Group similar objects together. Sort them by category, such as glasses, pots, cutlery and containers. By storing them in the same place, it will be easier to find what you need.

Eliminate duplicates or things you don't use.

Part 2 Organize the Shelves

1

Remove utensils that you rarely use from the shelves. For example, you could leave the microwave oven if you use it every day and store the toaster if you only use it once a week.

2

Place appliances and the most useful items on the kitchen counter. Identify areas that need to remain empty, such as the food preparation station. Then, choose a spot for the dishes and appliances you need on a daily basis, such as the microwave oven, coffee pot, dish drainer, and cutting board.

Check where the power outlets are before deciding where to place the small appliances.

3

Place the kitchen utensils you use most in a container near the stove. These are the ladle, the spatula, the spoon for serving spaghetti and the skimmer. Put only the ones you use most often and keep in a drawer the ones you use most rarely.

A large jar or container is ideal for these tools.

4

Install a magnetic bar to hang knives. Put the others in a drawer.

Give away the knife block and unused knives.

5

Arrange the hand soap and sponges. Place a small tray near the sink to save space. Put on hand soap, dish sponge, and dish towel. Then, place the sink stopper and bottle cleaning brush lower.

You can buy a shelf to install over the kitchen sink. Alternatively, use your wits and use a cake stand for storage!

6

Place the oil and honey on a plate or tray. Furthermore, residues can settle inside the furniture and on the shelves, getting greasy and greasing other objects! Place them on a saucer or tray or tray that you can easily wash.

7

Group the fruit and vegetables in a basket or bowl.

Part 3 Organize Furniture and Drawers

1

Assign each cabinet and drawer to a category. So, arrange everything as you have decided. Put the items you use most often towards the front for easy picking. By grouping them by category, you can quickly find everything you need.

Put the dishes in a large cabinet, the glasses in a less spacious cabinet, the pots and pans in a low cabinet, and so on.

A drawer for tea towels and pot holders, another for cutlery and another for less used kitchen utensils

2

Keep kitchen cleaning products under the sink.

3

Use trays with compartments to organize drawers.

4

Arrange items on small, easy-to-remove trays to keep the furniture tidy. You can put them on the top shelf of the furniture

5

Place dry foods in clear containers for easy identification. Place them in special containers to eliminate clutter and keep the pantry organized. Pour the grains, flour, and ingredients for making desserts into stackable bowls. Then, arrange them nicely in the cupboards.

Group them by categories. For example, put the cereals together, collect the packets of pasta and gather the ingredients for cakes.

6

Organize the lids and baking sheets. Get a separator or magazine rack and place it inside the cabinet, then insert the lids and trays. Opt for a sturdy metal separator so that it stands upright.

To store these kitchen utensils, either a plastic or a metal magazine rack will work.

7

Use a turntable so you don't have to rummage around the cabinet for what you need.

8

Keep the junk drawer tidy by using small resealable containers. If you have a drawer in which you store a disparate set of items, optimize the space by arranging everything in small boxes. Label them so that you recognize what you put inside.

Check the contents regularly and get rid of unused items.

Part 4 Fill the refrigerator

1

Put ready-to-eat food and drinks on the top shelf. They include prepackaged foods, eggs and leftovers. The upper shelf is the one to be accessed more easily. Furthermore, by placing these foods in the upper part of the refrigerator, you will prevent them from contaminating the dishes placed on the lower levels. Arrange bottles too high for the top shelf on the middle shelf. Avoid putting them in the door area as it is not very cold.

2

Store the meat on the bottom shelf. This will prevent blood from dripping and contaminating other foods. However, make sure it is closed properly before placing it in the refrigerator, otherwise it could spread bacteria. If it leaks anywhere, pack it up again and clean the area with an antibacterial cleanser.

Place the meat in a container, even if it leaks, it will not end up contaminating the vegetables.

3

Store your fruit and vegetables on the center shelf or in the drawer. However, it is preferable to store them in the drawer as it hinders moisture and provides a better environment for these foods.

If you're using the drawer, make sure you don't overfill it.

4

Put the seasonings on the door shelves. Group them by genre to easily find what you need.

For example, combine jams and marmalades, group the marinades and put all the sauces to season sandwiches in one place.

5

Put the cheeses and cold cuts in the cheese drawer.

Part 5 Create more space

1

Use the space above the wall cabinets or the refrigerator. Do not leave the top surfaces unused. Use them to store items you don't use often. You can also take unused dishes to the basement.

Use the furthest (and least practical) surfaces to place knick-knacks.

You could use the space above the wall units to put knick-knacks or things you don't need.

2

Use a trolley if you have limited space in furniture. You can buy it at a mall, home improvement store, or on the Internet.

3

Use a shelf without doors for easy access. It can contain other dishes, small appliances that you use little, dry ingredients, recipe books and knick-knacks. Choose a kitchen wall and hang it or, if space is limited, place it on the side of the refrigerator. Arrange the objects with taste and harmony.

A shelf is perfect because it is practical and graceful at the same time!

4

Add some shelves. It is a great way to increase storage space. You can also use plastic foldable shelves. You can buy them at a mall, home improvement store, or on the Internet.

5

Install hooks on the walls or inside the cabinet doors. Attach them to the hob wall or over the sink. Mount them inside the furniture for hanging small objects. They can be used to hang pots and pans, decorations, measures, tea towels and so on.

6

Consider a fabric shoe rack to hang on the pantry door. The smaller pockets are perfect for keeping an eye on many small items. If you prefer, you can also add labels.

7

Buy a kitchen island with casters for storage and cooking. Being equipped with wheels, it can be moved comfortably according to the needs of those who use it. It will give you more space not only to prepare your dishes, but also to store utensils in the drawers, cabinets or on the open shelves at the bottom.

Sizes vary as well as prices: you can find cheap models, but also expensive ones. You can buy it at furniture and home improvement stores or on the Internet.

8

Install drawers in low cabinets to maximize space. If you want you can try to build them yourself or get help from a carpenter.

Advice

You may want to try various arrangements until you find the right one. Consider what makes your life easier and what you don't need.

If you have a "junk drawer", check the contents often to make sure you don't store any unused items. Even if the junk drawer is useless and should be eliminated, this way you gain space and get rid of the junk. That slimming herbal tea that has been there for 10 years and that you have never tried. The fillet recipe you never dared to cook. The piece of an old blender you have long since thrown away. Of all these things the best solution is: throw.

Organize everything you need in the kitchen according to your actual needs, not according to an "ideal" trend in domestic life.

Warnings

Before buying containers and shelves for kitchen organization, review all the items and try to figure out if you want to keep them or need to make a selection. If you buy something you don't really need, the clutter will tend to increase.

CHAPTER 12 CLEAN THE HOUSE NATURALLY

You can clean the house effectively and quickly, using natural products such as vinegar, denatured alcohol and more. Let's find out how.

The house is the place where we spend the most hours of the day, so it is important to take care of it, cleaning and disinfecting it in depth. It can also be done without the use of chemicals which are most often very aggressive.

The house can be cleaned with products that you certainly have available, such as white wine vinegar, bicarbonate of soda and many others, let's find out how to use them best.

1-White wine vinegar

White wine vinegar is a widely used product especially for cleaning the house. It can be defined as an ally for women, which can replace commercial products that most of the time contain too aggressive substances. The combination of vinegar with citric or lemon acid and bicarbonate enhances its effectiveness. Mixed with hydrogen peroxide, it manages to achieve even more incredible results. In particular, you can use vinegar in the kitchen and in the bathroom, let's find out how.

In the kitchen, you can degrease the oven, just pour a mixture of water and vinegar on a sponge. If the oven is very dirty and gives off an unpleasant smell, try this; in a spray bottle, put 4 tablespoons of salt, with a glass of vinegar, mix and steam directly in the oven. It is recommended to leave it on for 15 minutes, then clean with a soft sponge. Clean the fridge, after having emptied it and disconnected the power, prepare a mixture of water and vinegar, dip a sponge or microfiber cloth and wash well.

It also eliminates stains and sanitizes the gas hob, also try to clean the taps, sinks and kitchen surfaces, perhaps put the mixture of water and vinegar in a spray bottle.

If you often smell an unpleasant smell in the kitchen and bathroom, the problem could be with the drains and plumbing of the sinks. When the smell is persistent, it could spread throughout the house.

The solution to the problem can be mitigated with vinegar combined with bicarbonate. Put 1/2 liter of water to boil in a saucepan, then add about 200 ml of vinegar, in the meantime pour about 100 g of sodium bicarbonate inside the pipe giving off the bad odor. Then pour the water with vinegar into the pipe, you will have an effervescent reaction, which is completely normal. If you follow this advice, you will reduce the bad smell. Routine maintenance is important.

In the bathroom, however, vinegar can disinfect surfaces and taps, proceed as for the kitchen, prepare a solution of water and vinegar and put it in a spray bottle and spray in the tub or shower, to eliminate dirt or soap residues. In case of limescale stains or bad smell from the toilet, pour in vinegar and leave it to act, then pour in buckets of hot water.

Vinegar is perfect to eliminate the mold on tiles or shower curtain, just put a little bit of water and vinegar on a soft sponge and clean.

2-Tea tree oil

Tea tree oil is obtained from the distillation of the Malaleuca Alternifolia tree, widely used for both personal and home care. Known for its disinfectant properties, a real natural antibacterial. It is recommended for house cleaning especially if there are pets such as dogs and cats.

You can use it in different ways, cleaning ceramic, porcelain stoneware or terracotta floors, but not parquet. Just put 3 liters of warm water in a bucket, then add a glass of alcohol vinegar and 10 drops of tea tree oil. If you want to scent a little more, add 3 drops of lavender essential oil.

Clean both kitchen and bathroom tiles, even if mold is present. Prepare a mixture of 4 glasses of distilled water with 20 drops of tea tree essential oil, a little baking soda and white vinegar. Spray on a microfiber cloth and clean. In case of more stubborn dirt, proceed in this way: spray directly on the tiles and let it act, then remove with a sponge and then clean with a soft cloth.

The hob burners are a real torture; it often happens that there is stubborn dirt, which is not easily removed. Create a pasty mixture with 5 tablespoons of baking soda and 7 drops of tea tree essential oil, apply the homogeneous solution. Leave it on for a few minutes and then gently remove the dirt with a sponge.

3-Eucalyptus oil

Eucalyptus oil brings many benefits, in fact it is often used for personal care. It is obtained from Eucalyptus globulus, a plant of the Mirtaceae family. Useful for treating seasonal ailments and more, including colds, headaches, cystitis and sinusitis. But this oil can be used to clean the house, disinfecting it in a natural way, in fact it eliminates bacteria and germs. Just add 150 ml for every liter of water, then you can proceed with both the cleaning of the floors and the tiles.

4-Sodium bicarbonate

Sodium bicarbonate is a natural product, an ally for women, which can be used both for cleaning the house and for the person. But it is also used in the kitchen for the preparation of various recipes, especially for baked goods.

Bicarbonate was used by our grandmothers, it is known that it is an ecological detergent that not only deodorizes, whitens, but cleans deeply. It is called a natural disinfectant; it has the ability to eliminate bacteria and eliminates bad smells. In fact, it is often used in the fridge or oven. Let's examine in detail how to use it.

Does your fridge smell bad and you don't know how to stop it? It often happens that you open the fridge and smell a bad smell, but if you clean the fridge frequently, you can avoid the formation of unpleasant odors or mold.

Just put the baking soda and a little lemon juice in a glass. On the other hand, if the oven stinks, put water and baking soda in a bowl and create a pasty solution. Apply it to a sponge and clean the oven, even if the pans and pot have a bad smell.

Cleaning the tiles and floors can be done by mixing 2 tablespoons of baking soda in a bucket of hot water, then proceed with washing, if you want to give a little perfume, add the drops of essential oil to lavender or jasmine. Anything that smells bad can be treated with baking soda, even cat litter bins or litter boxes that often stink. Even ashtrays, after washing them, ifthey stink, put a little baking soda and let it act a little.

5-Denatured alcohol

Alcohol denatured at 90°, the one that has a pink color, can be used for house cleaning, just dilute it with water. It has the ability to break down a large number of viruses and bacteria, in no time, which is why it is an ally of women for cleaning the house. But in detail, what can be cleaned?

Floors and tiles, just pay attention because it is particularly flammable, dilute it in water and clean the surfaces with a soft cloth. Remember that in the case of parquet and terracotta floors, the use is not recommended.

As an alternative to these products, if you have a steam mop available, you can use that. In fact, the steam cleans and sanitizes all the surfaces of the house, thanks to the high temperatures, which are able to dissolve even the most stubborn dirt from floors, bathroom fixtures and tiles. In addition, the steam jet can also kill most of the germs and bacteria.

CHAPTER 13 10 HOME ORGANIZING IDEAS THAT WILL CHANGE YOUR LIFE

How many times do you happen to think: "I have to fix this, I have to fix that, but then you postpone it to the next day and you never do it.

Stop postponing with our tips

1. Less is more

What I always say in my consultancy is: "If everything is important, nothing is important", if you underline everything, in the end you do not underline anything, because you do not give value and prominence to the objects you own. The time you spend looking for things is longer than you think you will save by avoiding reordering. So, the less you have the more time you save.

2. Making lists

Not everyone loves lists, I am strongly addicted to them, because they rationalize the thousand ideas that come to my mind, so making lists helps me to make order and space in my head. If you don't love them, you can use pre-defined templates, with the days of the week. Lists are useful for families larger than one person; it is a useful method for defining roles in the home and also educating children to discipline and order. You can also consider medium-term lists, for monthly or bi-monthly activities, such as cleaning windows, cleaning the oven, defrosting the freezer and fridge (or you can also rely on your common sense!).

3. Risers for shelves

If you have very high shelves, don't underestimate the power of risers, which allow you to create space above and below to organize the furniture.

4. Focus on one environment at a time

You often get discouraged before starting because you think there are too many things to do and therefore you don't even start. If you really want to tidy up your home, divide the spaces and focus on one at a time. Do not think about the overall disorder, otherwise you will never find the urge to tidy up. One piece of furniture at a time, one corner at a time, one room at a time. You will see, once started, you will never be able to stop! Start with the smallest room.

5. Documents, archive them!

Do not pile up documents on your desk or in the hallway cabinets. Throw away unnecessary mail and unnecessary documents. Arrange important documents in filing cabinets.

6. Do not pile your clothes on chairs

After changing, put your clothes back in the closets or drawers.

7. Reuse boxes

Once again, I come back to talking about boxes! If beautiful, use them for plastic food containers in the kitchen, or for medicines or for stationery. I always prefer the square ones to the round ones, depending on the use you can make of them. I know people who have used wine containers to hold their socks and underwear, a great choice!

8. Do not stack objects on the bedside table

Having the essentials close to where you sleep is important for sleep. Loading the bedside table with too much stuff does not allow you to rest well and always leaves you in trouble. Keep the bedside table with the essentials, the bedside lamp, the alarm clock, some decorations, but nothing more. Try not to keep too many books on the bedside table, even though you are reading several at a time (also because at least they do not act as a receptacle for dust).

CHAPTER 14 HOW TO ORGANIZE A CHILD'S BEDROOM IN 3 SIMPLE STEPS

With this guide we want to help you optimize the spaces in your child's bedroom which is often the least organized space in your home by far... but it doesn't have to be!

We'll start by eliminating all that is superfluous, making sure your child's bedroom spaces are tidier and more organized. Let's begin!

3 simple steps to organize a child's bedroom

Step 1: get rid of everything that does not work, and is not useful.

Before you can actually organize your child's bedroom, chances are you need to get rid of a few things. Organize everything in the room by dividing it into two groups: useful and not useful. You can involve your child in this process, or you can choose to go through everything independently but thanks to his help you will not risk throwing away something that is really dear or useful to him. You could also take advantage of this process by using it for educational purposes: everything that is no longer needed can be donated to other less fortunate children or young people or to organizations that take care of children and young people with any kind of discomfort.

Let's start with the clothes! Sort out your child's drawers and closet by putting aside any clothing that he no longer uses or that no longer fits him. Children grow up at a frenzied pace and I imagine you will find more than a few unwrapped dresses, jeans and t-shirts.

Remember to set aside clothing items to donate. Select them from those in good and excellent condition. You cannot donate worn or torn clothing. Imagine that they must be worn by other less fortunate children / teens and that they must be as intact as possible.

Get rid of the toys your child no longer plays with. Children often have far more toys than they need to have a happy childhood. Again, you can donate the toys to charities for children most in need. Look for the institution closest to you and go to deliver them. Don't throw them away!

Is the furniture in the room still useful? Did you keep your child's old crib by putting it in a corner of his room? If your baby sleeps in his own bed, there is no point in having a cot in the room. Get rid of it!

Evaluate all the furniture in your child's room and make sure it is functional. Try to replace or eliminate anything the baby doesn't need.

Step 2: Add storage space for items and clothing in the room

If general clearing of the superfluous has not been enough to make room, you should find space-saving solutions to better organize the room. It might be time to consider some new furniture solutions that allow you to make the room more spacious and organized!

Shelving

Using the height of the room to store your baby's belongings is an easy way to optimize space. From toys to books, video games to movies, many of your child's items can be stored on shelves. You can also use containers stacked on top of each other.

If the room has a very low ceiling, using shelves is not the ideal solution but it is still possible!

You can use the space under the bed for storage.

Another easy way to maximize space under your child's bed? Get him a container bed!

You can also think about buying a container bed so that you don't have to have the task of organizing everything into boxes and containers.

Step 3: Make room organization easier by focusing on one section at a time.

Once you've got rid of everything your child no longer needs and have optimized the space inside the room with shelves and boxes to hide under the bed, it's time to rearrange the space.

The easiest way to do it? Focus on specific areas by optimizing one at a time.

Tips for organizing your child's desk

Your child's desk probably serves primarily as a homework station. Just a few items on the desk (pencils, pens and notebooks) are enough to make it look messy.

Here are a couple of tips and tricks to help you keep your toddler's desk organized:

Use containers that can be attached to the wall to hold pencils, markers, crayons, and other materials. Thus, a portion of the free space on the desk will not be occupied. There are beautiful baskets for stationery on the market.

Help your child create an organized system with labels and stickers on the drawers. It will be easier for the child / kid to know where certain items go without leaving them on the desk.

Tips for organizing your baby's toys.

Your child will have more time to keep his room organized if he can easily find the toys he is looking for. By storing items in clear plastic containers, you can keep things organized and easily accessible for your little one. You can purchase plastic containers with separate compartments to attach labels to. If the child is too young and still cannot read, use adhesive images to make him understand where to put his objects according to their type.

Make keeping order in the room fun! If you can help your child see how to sort and organize his toys, he will be much more likely to adopt the directions you gave him as a game.

CHAPTER 15 5 TRICKS TO KEEP THE CHILDREN'S ROOM TIDY AND ORGANIZED

Keeping your children's bedroom tidy for a long time can be really difficult if you don't run for cover in time. First of all, it is wrong to think that the order of the bedroom is dictated only by the desire to have the house perfectly clean.

If you consider that children spend most of their time right in the bedroom, to ensure their safety and health it is essential that this environment is tidy and clean.

In fact, having a tidy children's room positively influences the mood of the little ones, making them more predisposed to calm and serenity, reducing the stress of parents.

It is therefore important to set rules, but even before being able to design a room that is basically functional and therefore easy to organize and order. Understanding how it is more practical to arrange the furniture inside the children's environment or which are the most suitable accessories to furnish it, can help to create a well-kept space.

Taking into account the characteristics of the bedroom and the needs of your children can direct you towards furnishing solutions that help create a welcoming and well-organized environment. It is also important that children are accustomed from an early age to taking care of their bedroom, involving them in its organization and tidying up.

Does all this seem unattainable to you? In reality you will see that with a few tricks, the bedroom can become a completely tidy and clean space.

1. Separate the spaces

The children in their bedroom carry out many different activities that are the cause, very often, of the much-hated disorder.

Separating the bedroom into defined areas, providing specific spaces to be allocated to each children's activity, will allow you to avoid the accumulation of objects scattered everywhere. Having a separate sleeping area from the play area helps children to identify the various areas and use them based on the activity they have to carry out.

This undoubtedly contributes to keeping the children's bedroom tidy, as well as to having a much more functional space.

Dividing the play area from the study area, for example, prevents children from getting distracted when they are busy with their homework. The same goes for the sleeping area, which must be organized in such a way as to reconcile sleep and certainly not to favor night-time gaming sessions.

With the furnishing ideas currently on the market, it is not difficult to organize the children's bedroom. Furthermore, by choosing companies that offer tailor-made solutions, it is even easier to customize and organize the bedroom.

Do not forget that it is important to arrange the bedroom furniture to make it not only more functional but also safer: for this reason, it is vital to choose quality products.

2. Choose space-saving and order- saving furniture

The organization of the bedroom space is the prerequisite for ensuring order.

Therefore, it is better to prefer furniture that is right for the environment they have to furnish and suitable for optimizing it as much as possible.

Therefore, choosing space-saving solutions for children's bedrooms is almost a must in order to offer an environment dedicated to children suitable for their different needs, without living in absolute chaos.

3. Choose large and organized closets

It is useful to organize your children's closet in order to find the clothes easily, but also so that they can be put away quickly and methodically. With a super-organized wardrobe, it is certainly easier to have a tidy and practical children's bedroom.

Once you have chosen the most suitable wardrobe model for the bedroom, you can customize its interior to make it functional both for you and especially for your children.

4. Boxes and containers for toys.

Are you now resigned to thinking that the place for toys is in every corner of the bedroom floor?

Given that having fewer games can be an advantage for children, we certainly cannot blame you for the fact that it is practically impossible to have them all perfectly put in place.

In reality it is possible, because if you organize the bedroom with special boxes and containers in which each toy can be easily stored, at the end of the day or when the children have finished playing, order can finally be achieved.

It can be useful to organize the different containers for toys by type, perhaps by applying labels, so as to immediately identify the box / container of the game you need and keep the children's bedroom always tidy.

5. Get the children to cooperate

You have to eliminate from your head the misconception that your children are unable to order their own room.

Children from an early age must be used to collaborating and must be involved in the activities necessary to order their bedroom. In this way they will grow with the awareness of being responsible for their own things and spaces.

You can establish a few but effective rules, here are a few:

- Put away the games once you have finished playing;

- Before starting another game / activity, put away the objects you have just used;

- Each object must have its precise place.

A neat children's room makes everyone happy

Tidying up your children's bedroom is certainly a source of stress, not to mention the rest of the house!

If you can start designing a bedroom that invites you to order, in a sense the bulk of the work is done. In fact, in this way everything will have its place and it will be easier for you to rearrange.

Furthermore, having the children's bedroom tidy helps to make them feel in a welcoming and reassuring environment. Disorder, on the other hand, is a source of agitation and restlessness in children who are thus prone to generate confusion in the disorder.

To avoid this, offer your children a furniture solution that allows you to organize the space in a chaos-proof way. Contact companies specializing in children's furniture and who have developed, over the years, a whole series of solutions for bedrooms that can satisfy parents and children, in order to make everyone happy.

This means choosing those who offer you functional and practical bedrooms as well as made with quality, resistant and non-toxic materials.

Remember again that it is essential for you to have the ability to customize the bedroom, so as to be able to organize the space to get the order you want.

Once you have furnished the bedroom and adopted all the solutions to prepare it in the best possible way, do not forget that it is important to educate your children and get them used to tidying up their bedroom.

After all, tidying up the bedroom can be a fun game to play with children, as well as useful for mom and dad.

CHAPTER 16 THE RIGHT PLACE FOR EVERY OBJECT

Is the mess driving you crazy? An organized lifestyle can make your days more productive and more relaxing at the same time. When your home is tidier, it will look cleaner and you will find that you have more space at your disposal, easy to use and exploit. Follow the tips in this guide to start organizing your home!

Part 1 Eliminate Useless Things

1

Put your items in order. Examine the things in each room, dividing them according to what you intend to do: choose what you want to keep, give and throw away. Keep the items you need and cannot be separated from; throw away completely useless things, which no one would use anymore; finally, give items to charity that you cannot use, but which may prove useful for someone else.

2

Evaluate the items to keep rationally. Sometimes one gets the impression of needing something even if it is not true, but it is this attitude that pushes us to accumulate objects, leaving little space for the really important things. Once you have established what to do with each item, examine the remaining ones, think back to the last time you used them and decide if you actually need them.

3

When you decide to give an item to charity, donate it to someone who would make good use of it. Choose the charity to donate it to based on the type of item (for example, toys to the Salvation Army, clothes to the parish, and so on). Make sure you throw away any unusable items. You can't donate tattered clothes, but still functional clothes or intact kitchen tools could be very useful to other people.

Part 2 Separate Objects Based on Room and Functionality

1

Separate objects based on their function. Examine them to decide how to divide them. Group similar items together to find the best way to store them. Maybe you can stack them, or insert one inside the other. If some things don't have a particular function, you could give them to charity.

2

Separate the objects according to the zone and the room they belong to. After grouping them by function, separate them again to arrange them in the most suitable room. Although some items have similar functions, you may need to place them in different parts of the house.

For example, cooking utensils should stay in the kitchen, so you can easily use them when you need them. Things you don't use often, such as an ice cream maker or large serving trays, can be stored in less accessible places.

3

Find strategic accommodation for items that can perform more than one function. If you have several things that perform the same functions, store them in different areas if possible.

A practical example of this type of item are small towels, which may be needed in the bathroom and kitchen

Part 3 Use Archiving Methods

1

Find the right place for each item. Things left lying around make rooms appear cluttered and disorganized, so find accommodation for everything. It's worth walking into a room, grabbing whatever object is within reach and wondering if that's where it should be. If it is is out of place, find suitable accommodation.

It is advisable to find specific accommodation for objects such as keys, cell phones and wallets. For example, make it a habit to always deposit these items in the same spot at the entrance. This way, you will avoid littering them around the house and leaving them in unsuitable places.

2

Store things in a functional way. They should take up as little space as possible, but be within reach. By organizing items in this way, you will have more space available and the house will look less cluttered.

Store smaller items in metal boxes, perhaps those of mints, to avoid confusing and losing them. Use labels to distinguish the various boxes and place them all in the same drawer.

You can use slats in a kitchen drawer to divide the lids of vacuum containers and keep them in place.

Attach metal plates to the inside of the cupboard so that you can use that space to attach recipes with magnetic clips instead of using the refrigerator panel.

Arrange necklaces on a hanger, earrings in an ice cube tray, bags on hangers.

Those plastic compartments can be very useful for all the small items like watches, make-up tools, batteries or accessories of various kinds.

Organize long-life foods (such as sugar and flour) in metal containers or glass jars because they are easy to stack and take up less space. The same goes for spices, which you can arrange next to the refrigerator.

You can store laundry products in a filing cabinet; arrange the kitchen cleaning products in a shoe rack to hang on the cupboard door.

3

Create a filing system. If you have multiple copies of the same item or a series of similar items, you may want to devise an effective way to keep them and find them easily when needed. On top of that, they would take up less space and you would have a larger area to exploit.

Get a filing cabinet or boxes for folders and documents. They are indispensable for organizing this type of material that you absolutely must not lose, such as tax documents, birth certificates and other important documents that you may need to find quickly.

Create a system for clothes too. Come up with a way to organize both clothes and soiled items. The latter can be separated by color in different baskets. Instead, clean clothes should be hung neatly, or folded in drawers or laundry baskets. Take a cue from flyers - roll up your clothes as you arrange them in drawers or baskets to minimize creasing and maximize space.

4

Think of a way to take advantage of the wasted space. Often, unused areas are perfect corners to store and organize your stuff. Find a way to take advantage of the free spaces to optimize the organization of the house.

If there is some space between the refrigerator and the wall, you might want to put shelves to accommodate jars and cans.

In almost all corridors there is space to insert a shelf on which to place various objects.

The space under the bed can be used to hide boxes (or bags) containing off-season linen, coats and voluminous sweaters.

Think about vertical spaces too. This excellent solution is often overlooked. That empty space between hanging clothes and the bottom shelf in a closet can be filled with shelves or used to hang shoes, belts or ties with special holders.

Part 4 Develop Good Habits

1

Think about each new item you buy. To keep an organized home you need to cultivate good habits: for example, it is worthwhile evaluating every object we come into possession of. Don't stockpile a lot of things you don't need, or you'll end up having a messy house again. Find a place for each item you buy.

2

Put everything in its place. Get in the habit of tidying up after using something. Don't put off or find justifications, thinking that maybe someone else might need it. Simply put back everything you use. This is the best habit for keeping a tidy and clean home.

3

Get in the habit of giving something to charity. Prepare a bag or box in which to store the items you would like to donate, especially those you no longer use. It would be a good idea to put a couple of items in the donation box every time you buy or receive a new one.

Advice

If you plan to make your home more organized, start with the area you use most often: for example, if you are a student, tidy up the room where you study, or the kitchen.

Think about the actual need to store certain things: for example, CDs take up a lot of space, but now most people use only iPods, MP3s and computers to listen to music. Convert your CDs to another format.

Find ways to reuse items you have around the house. For example, do you own a candle holder, but don't use candles? Use it as a pencil holder.

Americans are avid supporters of organization, so it is possible to find on the market many useful elements for organization of the house, without sacrificing style and fashion. This way, you no longer have to worry about hiding items you don't use often, because you can keep them in plain sight!

To keep the house organized, keeping the less used items, it is advisable to invest in the purchase of CD racks, bookcases and containers to put under the bed. If Christmas or your birthday is approaching, ask your relatives to give you some gift certificates to spend at Ikea, in furniture and DIY stores.

Warning

When organizing your home, minimize the risk of fire: for example, do not overload wall sockets with extension cords, do not store huge piles of newspapers and always leave the path to the exit free, because shoes and other items could get in the way of your escape in an emergency.

Be careful when moving furniture. Do not lift weights with your back, but with your legs. If possible, ask a friend for help.

CHAPTER 17 MISTAKES TO AVOID

Control freaks or chronically disordered? Clutter is not simply about visual chaos; it is the inability to find what we need when we need it. This is usually the case with messy people: they rush out in search of an object convulsively, exploring overflowing bags or closets where clothes have been thrown in bulk, creating even more chaos. If you want to become a more orderly person, focus on organization. What surrounds you must be easily found when you need it, this will save you time and stress in unnecessary searches. True order is a matter of mind, that's why.

Fast cleaning? Start dedicating 30 minutes every day to tidying up: the house reflects our state of mind, which is why it is important to take care of the environment in which we live and improve the quality of our life through the choices made every day.

Strategies for ordering the house

Piling creates chaos

Throwing away items in bulk does not help improve organization. Start cultivating a mental attitude to order: choose where to place each object in the house. An extremely functional way is to try to think by type of use. Instead of putting the objects where there is room or where they "fit", create a specific order so that you always know how to find what you need. For example, the jackets and accessories you use the most will be ready to wear in a place near the entrance. The books still to be read in a special shelf, while the reading of the moment in the magazine rack. Bills and deadlines? In plain sight, hung on a blackboard in the kitchen or a panel with post it notes and pins. Reasoning by categories of belonging and dividing the objects is the first step to clarify even on a mental level and gain time for the order of the house.

Getting used to tidying up

Bad habits increase disorder

When you come home at the end of the day, empty your pockets and throw away what you don't need. Are you standing in line in a waiting room and don't know how to use the time? Tidy up your bag! If you usually keep your receipts, put them all together in a diary or box. Preventing clutter will save you valuable time and never make you feel overwhelmed by chaos. To optimize house cleaning, avoid the classic drawer where you end up putting what does not have a place: not knowing what it contains is almost always useless! No more dishes and empty pockets where unnecessary objects risk accumulating. Avoiding clutter will help you be less chaotic.

Living in chaos makes your mood worse.

Books like The Magical Power of Tidying Up and the Konmari Method teach that living in chaos often has a negative influence on our mental state as well. Conversely, lightening the environment and making the home more essential can also improve our well-being. Look at your home. If there are boxes full of clothes and objects around and you don't know where to put them ... it's time to renew! Today we fight against the lack of space and often live in small houses, so it is important to make peace with this aspect by learning to live with the possibilities offered by space. In the kitchen, everything must be inside the cabinets: except for appliances such as toasters and knife holders, it is a strategy to eliminate the tendency to leave objects scattered on the table and gain an uncluttered work surface. Is there no place in the closet for all the clothes? You can add a box on the wardrobe or under the bed - as for the rest, make a choice! Learning to part from objects can be difficult at first, but it makes us lighter. Chaos clutters the mind.

Tidy wardrobe

Big spaces ... big mess!

Drawers that are too large and cabinets without dividers often increase the tendency for chaos. Splitting the space into smaller portions will help you manage your things better. In the closet, add some baskets or boxes that can hold smaller items, such as belts, briefs, socks, accessories. Avoid batteries! Better to fold T-shirts and sweaters in the drawers or hang the clothes most used in a certain period with a hanger. Decluttering will allow you to have a clear home and a better organized closet. We live in a consumerist society where there is a tendency to accumulate an excessive number of objects, ending up remaining slaves to the superfluous: living in the essential not only saves you time and money, but will benefit the quality of your life. Start with the overflowing drawer or the desk covered with documents, remove the dust, eliminate, position according to the category to which it belongs and have a bag ready to throw away everything you no longer need. Your home will have a new order and your mind will acquire lightness, good humor, inspiration.

CHAPTER 18 LEARN GOOD HABITS

When there are children in the family, keeping everything neat and tidy seems like a real dream. As babies they require care and attention, when they grow up they invade spaces with their toys. How then to face the daily routine without going crazy? Having a perfect home is not possible, but organizing yourself so as not to find yourself in chaos is. Here are some tips that require little daily effort but give maximum benefits, without forgetting that everyone must work together.

When the family grows, the house changes too. If before you could choose furniture in total freedom, now practicality and comfort must prevail in every aspect. Opt for welcoming but above all functional environments.

In the entrance, arrange child-height clothes hooks, in the bedroom put containers for books and toys, for the bathroom choose comfortable drawers with the necessaries for changing and bathing. Everything must have its place, so keeping things in order will be easier for everyone.

Order comes before cleaning

It is the first sore point when the family becomes larger: a quiet and orderly place becomes noisy and chaotic. Parents lose control of spaces that end up invaded by dolls and dinosaurs, socks, bottles and so on. If you let yourself go, confusion will reign. Start changing habits by memorizing a rule: a tidy room looks cleaner, even if there are two inches of dust on the shelves!

How to do it? Proceed with a new method: small daily tasks, less effort on the weekend.

Good habits of the day.

Establish some routine tasks. Every evening, before going to bed, pick up the misplaced things, arrange the laundry, load the dishwasher.

If you are an early riser, even better, take the opportunity to tidy up and clean quickly before waking the others.

Try not to go out without making the bed. Many debates the issue, but this simple gesture will help make your day more productive.

If you are a lover of lists, grab a pen and paper and list the things to do every day. But be careful not to become a slave to it, enter only what you can really do.

Adults and children, to each his own task.

Everyone must participate in the care of the house, starting with the older ones. It will also be a great example for your children. You can entrust them with simple tasks as early as two or three years old, to move on to more complex ones, such as drying the dishes, emptying the washing machine and, of course, putting the games back in their places.

Don't be too rigid, you have to make them understand the importance of mutual help by creating pleasant moments of sharing.

Always leave them the opportunity to do creative activities, such as tempera, paint, clay, but try to protect floors and surfaces. Again, the same principle applies: after playing, you clean up together.

Cleaning: better a little a day.

There are a number of basic operations when having children, also because, as everyone knows, their presence requires more attention to hygiene. Focus on the rooms that need special care: bathroom and kitchen. Clean the bathroom fixtures, wash the shelves, sweep the floor, do some quick dusting. Remember to peek under the sofa, you will discover an endless mine of marbles, dice and crayons.

If you can clean up a little bit of dirt every day, you won't end up with a mountain of backlog on the weekend. Also keep an eye on the laundry basket. With a load of washing machine every two days you will avoid being submerged by dirty clothes. Carefully follow the entire cycle: from washing the clothes until you hang them out. So you can iron better or even not iron at all!

Try not to accumulate.

Fewer things around, less effort. Make a selection from time to time of what is not needed, check the closets, drawers. It will be useful for you but also for your children. Getting them used to the idea of having less will help them understand the value of what they have and stimulate their creativity in playing games.

The decluttering can be fun if you do it all together: you have a series of different colored baskets to select the now broken objects (to fix or throw), those with whom you do not play more (to give away), the ones to keep.

Learn not to postpone.

The drops of juice on the floor, the crumbs from the snack, the paint on the table: you really never stop cleaning! Any stain, however, must be removed immediately, without postponing. Don't let yourself be lazy; take the cloth and wash it. It will be much easier to do it at that moment than to return when the dirt is difficult to remove.

Aim for a peaceful home, not a perfect one.

Clean yes, perfect no. As the family grows, you need to be less demanding.

Especially if your children are still small, it is almost impossible for everything to work out perfectly. Better to take note of this and take on a new mentality: do not go crazy behind the frenzied rhythms of order and cleaning but try to create an atmosphere of serenity.

If you really can't do it, you can always ask for help but above all you have to learn to accept this phase of your life, and of your home, despite being full of defects.

And now, it's your turn: how do you manage to keep the clutter in the house under control? Do your children contribute to the housework? Share experiences and advice in the Comments.

CHAPTER 19 THE DECALOGUE FOR THE ORGANIZATION

Is it really possible to be organized even if you are not born with this ability, to be able to do everything effortlessly and save time? I'll reveal the 10 habits to adopt to be organized and productive!

Today I want to talk to you about the most effective habits to adopt to be more organized and productive since it is not necessary that you are an organized person from birth. Organization is something that can be learned and everyone can therefore become organized people, by simplifying their own life and reducing stress levels, yes everyone... even you! And at the end, you will have the clearest ideas on how to do it as well as the possibility of receiving a gift!

So, let's go!

1. The first habit of being organized is to WRITE EVERYTHING DOWN! In fact, relying on one's memory is really dangerous because there are so many things, life is unpredictable and it can happen that something escapes us, bringing with it the relative discomforts and a lot of stress in having to fix it.

You forgot to pay that bill and now you have a fine, you forgot to stop and buy that ingredient and now you can't prepare the dinner you planned, you forgot an appointment and maybe missed a great opportunity, you forgot to start the washing machine and now you don't have your uniform ready for work ...

Every time we forget something we should have done, we will inevitably have more or less negative consequences, we will find ourselves in difficulty, we will have to run ... why all this when you just have to write it down? You can keep a notebook with you in which you mark things on the fly or even just the notes of your cell phone.

Always mark everything: important dates, appointments, events, reminders, chores and you will discharge your mind of a great responsibility, feeling immediately lighter and less stressed. Yes, because when you keep everything in mind, you force your brain to continually think about what you have to do never allowing it to relax ... so if you want to avoid all this simply WRITE THINGS DOWN!

2.   The second habit that allows you to be more organized and above all more productive is NOT PROCRASTINATE or do not postpone things to do. In fact, many times we tend to postpone all those activities that weigh on us, that we do not like to do, perhaps using the excuse of being too busy and therefore of not having time to do them.

In fact, the procrastinator is generally a very busy person since he invents things to do in order not to do what really should be done. Very often, among other things, he postpones important things, activating also in this case negative consequences that could easily be avoided. To combat the tendency to procrastinate, you need to set specific goals with a deadline and simply START doing what you should!

Yes, because the hardest part is always getting started but once you have used your self-discipline to get started ... everything else will be downhill! And if the goal seems too big and discourages you ... divide it into small sub-goals also with precise deadlines. In fact, when the tasks are smaller it is easier to find the strength to start.

3. The third habit of organized people is to HAVE A PLACE FOR EVERYTHING AND EVERYTHING IN ITS PLACE, or to make sure

that every object you have has its exact location so that you always know where to find it when you need it and where to put it back when it is no longer used. In fact, the organized person lives in organized environments that allow them to save time on a daily basis. It is therefore inevitable if you want to start being more organized, look around and see the conditions of your home and, if necessary, start with improving this aspect.

4.   Relating to the previous point, the fourth habit of the organized person is TO AVOID ACCUMULATING DISORDER. In fact, when you tidy up what you use or in any case by the end of the day, the work to be done is very limited and can be completed in a few minutes, while if you let the mess accumulate, you will need much more time to tidy up and maybe, always having little time, you will have the tendency to postpone this task more and more until the situation becomes unmanageable.

Do not let an activity that can be solved really in a very short time, giving you the opportunity to always be organized and productive, turn into a mega work of hours and hours that maybe drags on up to lead you to negative consequences including that of living in an unwelcoming and uncomfortable environment.

5. Staying on the same theme, the fifth habit is ELIMINATING WHAT YOU DON'T NEED. It is not necessary for a person to marry the minimalist lifestyle to start decluttering, since relieving our homes of what we do not use, what is broken or that we keep for who knows what event that may never come, is something that benefits noone.

Our home must be pleasant to live in and functional to allow us to be organized and therefore why keep things that are not needed, clutter and only steal space and time uselessly? I will not add more on this point as I have talked about it extensively in all my videos on minimalism but it was essential to add it here as well as it is something extremely useful for those who want to improve their organization.

6. As for point number 5, the sixth habit of the organized person is TO BUY ONLY THE NECESSARY for several reasons: first of all, to avoid spending too much time on objects, then to keep everything in order more easily and finally to have a better management of the own money by allocating it to things that really matter.

For this reason, a good suggestion is not to give in to the temptation of SALES ... always ask yourself if you really need that thing because even if it is taken for granted, if it is useless for you, you will still have wasted your money and once brought home you will waste your space and your time managing it. So, think carefully before making any purchases!

7. The seventh good habit of the organized person is to WAKE UP EARLY to have more time to do things ... many people complain of never having time and not being able to organize themselves always doing everything in bulk and in a hurry and then maybe if ask them what time they get up and they tell you 10 minutes before leaving the house.

It is normal that when you only have 10 minutes to prepare yourself and maybe even have breakfast, you cannot devote time to anything else and in addition, you risk arriving late and forgetting things, many small gestures that instead would allow you to make things work better.

Small actions of a few minutes that would greatly improve your day by saving you time... So why not wake up a little earlier to manage everything calmly?

8. The eighth habit is IMPROVING THE CONCENTRATION... the organized person in fact tends to fit all the activities in the best possible

way and in order to carry them out in the shortest possible time he needs to keep his concentration high. There are several ways to train concentration... those that I recommend are Mindfulness meditation practiced both formally and informally during the day, and Yoga.

9. The ninth good habit of the organized person is NOT TO LEAVE THINGS HALF DONE. Each time you will have to make the effort to start over, perhaps fighting against the temptation to procrastinate ... Finally, your brain will continue to think about it until you have completed it and this will increase your stress levels or your frustration.

10. Finally, the last good habit of the organized person is to create habits or a sequence of actions that are repeated day after day. The advantage of the routines is that first of all after a few days of repeating them, the brain will carry them out on automatic pilot almost completely eliminating the effort of doing them, furthermore, you will minimize the time needed to carry them out and you will not risk forgetting anything.

It is not necessary to have a life full of routine ... you just need a really efficient one to carry out every day to improve your organization and productivity significantly.

Well, these are the things that you should implement in your life if you want to become a more organized, I suggest you do not introduce them all at once. Start gradually by inserting a few at a time and only when they have been assimilated proceed with the others.

REMEMBER YOU HAVE TO TAKE ONE STEP AT A TIME.

CHAPTER 20 WEEKLY PLANNING

We are always in a hurry and busy, the frenetic pace of life leaves us little time at the end of the day to manage the house, yet we women of today still have to manage and always do some work at home.

When I got married and found my own home to take care of, I wasn't as organized as I am now. I perfected my method over time, between experience, comparisons with friends in the same situation and various internet searches.

The bulk of the housework is always done on Saturdays when, at home from work, I am able to dedicate myself completely to my sweet home. I want it to be as tidy and clean as possible, without expecting perfection every day. It's impossible!

During the week, I always took care of the little things like using the vacuum cleaner, keeping the bedroom, bathroom and kitchen tidy.

Because I decided to draw up the housework schedule.

All worked well for quite some time until new conditions came in: two children.

Needless to say, everything changed with the arrival of the children and nothing was ever the same again.

Children require time, care, attention, there are many more things to follow and the Holy Saturday morning of before has disappeared.

Result?

Chaos! Which has decided to move to my house, albeit without my consent.

We know that when children arrive, houses change their appearance, they adapt, they are not perfect, let's say that they are re- furnished in a fun, all-to-hand style, but the cleaning of the home environments must continue, and it is essential.

I spent a first period of a few weeks without knowing which way to turn, where to start, where to continue and if I would ever reach the end. I realized that I was jumping like a top from one room to another without getting anything done.

This was on a Saturday, the day I would have to sort out most of the things.

I let you imagine what I was able to accomplish every single day ... Suffice it to say that there were days when my husband and I had dinner two hours apart to be with the children and that I didn't even have the time to vacuum the crumbs off the kitchen tablecloth.

Fortunately, this is not normal and everything can be adjusted with a minimum of organization. From here, I decided to draw up a housework schedule, a plan for when to do the housework.

Why? To be organized, to optimize time by already knowing what I have to do and how much more or less time it takes me to complete what I have to do.

How? The goal was to be able to do some housework during the week, so that I can lighten up the Saturday so I can spend more time with the kids and with my husband.

How I planned the housework.

First of all, I made a list of things to do at home, dividing them into daily, weekly, monthly and yearly.

It is essential to know how much time you have available for home care every day and how long each single item on the list takes to be completed. Only in this way can we associate the work to be carried out by evening to days.

On this basis I compiled my planning.

You can see my schedule in the photos above. I have marked it both on the notice board of the Command Station at home and on my Notebook of Lists (which I will soon tell you about), an insert from my bullet journal.

Organizing house cleaning is not easy, especially for women who have to manage a family, home and work. With this weekly planner you can plan the daily household chores for the whole week and also write down the annual and monthly cleaning.

Useful for creating a daily cleaning routine, not to forget the areas of the house, which need more attention and care.

I made this cleaning planner to better manage the time available, to organize and clean the house and to also carve out some time for myself.

How to plan weekly house cleaning

To plan your house cleaning, you need to be aware of what you want to see cleaned each week and how much time you can spend on the house. Write your to-do list on a piece of paper as you look one room at a time.

At this point, according to the time you have available, divide the cleaning you will need to do to keep what you want clean. If necessary, write the same task several times throughout the week, such as dusting or cleaning the bathroom.

Keep in mind not to write too many chores in one day, so as not to overload yourself and risk not making it. There is always time to increase them if you are faster than expected.

Some weekly cleaning:

- dusting;

- cleaning the bathroom;

- cleaning the floors;

- cleaning the kitchen,

- vacuum;

- change the sheets;

- laundry;

- ironing.

House cleaning, monthly and yearly.

As for the monthly and annual cleaning, less frequent than the weekly ones and more difficult to remember, you can organize them in the same way, listing in the appropriate sections what you want to clean less frequently.

Don't forget to maintain your appliances to keep them efficient.

Some monthly and annual cleaning:

- remove cobwebs;

- seasonal cleaning: cleaning the interior and exterior of furniture, ornaments, curtains, chandeliers and everything else you need;

- change of season of wardrobes;

- cleaning of doors and windows;

- cleaning of window frames, windowsills and mosquito nets;

- cleaning of balconies or porches.

Tips for planning house cleaning and living peacefully.

One of the tips I feel like giving you is to live in the house without being a slave to it. Yes, I know, it is the classic phrase we hear but, I too was able to find a balance after years of endless cleaning.

Try to find a compromise, the house must be cleaned as necessary without stressing ourselves too much. Don't worry if your children leave their fingerprints again after cleaning the windows. I know, you would like to go and clean them immediately but, you enter a vicious circle and you will go on forever, increasing the stress. You will clean them the next time they appear on your weekly schedule.

CHAPTER 21 THE PRINCIPLES OF MINIMALISM

The key principles of minimalism are essentially three: concentration on what is essential, removal of the superfluous and the pursuit of maximum enjoyment. Applying these principles in our life can be done in several ways, and in this chapter, I have collected some ideas to learn how to to let go of the things that do not add value to our life, to create space for us and to persevere in our principles even when it seems to us that it is impossible.

1. Focus on the whys

Living intentionally is essentially reconnecting to our whys. Asking why we do, buy, live, is the only way to discern between what is aligned with our life and what is not. And, it goes without saying, what is not aligned must not be part of it. Whenever you are called to make a decision, every time you are about to buy something, try to ask yourself why?

2. In case that... means never.

Every time we buy something or dedicate ourselves to an activity... We are just looking for an excuse to listen to the voice of the child inside us who wants to do what he likes, without listening to the adult who in our head explains that it would be useless. Every now and then it is good to listen to the child, and to dedicate ourselves to something that with the adult's hindsight we would not do, but even in these cases it is good to recognize that we are doing it because it is something that makes us feel alive. And since the world needs living people, we do it for this, ok? Does it seem inconsistent? That's life!

3. The 20/20 rule

All those times you find yourself about to buy something or say yes to an initiative, try to apply this rule coined by Joshua Fields Millburn and Ryan Nicodemus. If it takes you less than twenty minutes and less than twenty dollars to buy that thing when you need it, forget it for now.

Personally, I twisted this rule to make it valid beyond physical things as well. If something takes me less than twenty minutes and costs less than twenty dollarss, I'll let it go. Sure, then there are exceptions, but basically things of little value that require little effort are distractions.

4. One thing at a time

More than a rule for being minimalist, this is a principle of productivity good for any occasion, and fundamental for those who want to live minimally. When we are totally focused on one thing, one thing only, it is less difficult to eliminate the distractions, the superfluous, everything that does not have to do with our whys. This is why I often write with headphones on, or in conditions of total solitude. If we strive every week to eliminate a distraction, within a year we will have eliminated from our life over 50 factors that prevent us from living it to the full.

5. Take it easy

Think of quality not quantity .. It is not important to do everything in life, but to do what we do well, otherwise we will end up doing a lot of bad things, with the only result of not having done anything. If everything matters, nothing really matters. Furthermore, the only thing that matters is to progress, to advance towards the realization of one's goals. Celebrating small wins is the only way to recognize that we are progressing towards success.

6. Look at yourself

There is always someone with a more beautiful car, the latest iPhone, a more expensive dress or who simply goes on vacation to exotic countries that we have only seen in travel agency brochures. So? He may be less happy than you. As researcher Shawn Achor discovered when studying the relationship between happiness and success, there are happy people even in conditions that seem dramatic to us. If we look at what remains after we have removed what does not give us a reason, we are left alone with what gives us pleasure and is part of us. Could you be happier?

7. Minimalism is not....

Being minimalist does not mean eliminating everything we have, but keeping only what really gives us pleasure. A minimalist wardrobe is not based on fewer items than a normal one (even if it is), but on the 20 percent of items we wear because they really give us pleasure. By applying the Pareto principle to our wardrobe, in fact, we could in fact eliminate 80 percent of clothes because we wear them once in a while, often just because we own them, and that if we had to buy them back today, we would not spend a single dollar. This rule can be applied in every area of life, from the apps you have on your phone to the people you hang out with.

8. It costs more to keep things than to give them away

Make two accounts: every object costs you time and energy. Think about the entrance hall of your home: if there was only one photo, for example that of your wedding, or your family, every day you would be greeted by the memory of a happy moment. Instead, cramming that wall with pictures, each one of them requires some time of your attention and it ends up that none of them ever get it.

9. Evaluate spaces

We live in two spaces that are not very different from each other: one real, and one mental. In the first, the only way to generate value is to start from a careful observation of the (physical) spaces required by each object that surrounds us, as well as the empty (physical) spaces we need to move and enjoy what we have. The more space there is, the more time we have to enjoy what is in this space. Likewise, the more space we have in our mind the more clarity we can have about our thoughts and actions, and this is one of the main reasons I decided to start meditating and continue to do so.

10. Decluttering in every area

Remember with fewer items on your bedside table you sleep better. So get rid of the superfluous in any room.

11. Quality vs quantity

The best rule to follow for a truly minimalist life is only quality things. An 80 dollars pair of pants, apart from the brand, is definitely better than a 20 dollars pair. To afford them we have to give up three extra pairs of trousers, but as Pareto teaches us, even if we had them we would probably give up because of the four we would wear one more often and the others every now and then. Isn't it better then to give up those three and take the best one directly? Which, moreover, will most likely last longer over time, and therefore will allow us to save something in the long run.

Imagine if you only had five or six pairs of pants that you like a lot instead of having a dozen that you never wear many of - wouldn't that be nice? Before you spend your money on something new, ask yourself if this is the best you can get. If it's not, save your money for when you find what's worth spending it on. And when you find it, don't mind the expense!

12. Don't feel guilty

Throw away anything you don't like, even if someone you are/were romantically attached to gave it to you. Those who love you want you to live well, not overwhelmed with junk that you keep just so as not to feel guilty, so if you keep something you don't like you cause them real sorrow. Furthermore, surrounding yourself with objects, or experiences, of others - or that you have bought in case imprisons you in the life that others have imagined for you, moving away from the one you want to live!

13. The 90/90 rule

Another rule initiated by Joshua Fields Millburn and Ryan Nicodemus. If you haven't used something in the past three months, pick it up and ask yourself if you would use it in the next three. If the answer is no - net of seasonality - donate it to someone else or throw it away.

14. Be grateful for what you have

Gratitude is not only a consequence of minimalism, but also a way to get there. Keeping a gratitude journal helps us to take time each day to enjoy the pleasant times we have lived, to find something worth living for.

+1. Learn the rules so you can break them!

As in everything, to become an expert you need to learn and practice the rules. It is only when we have made them our own, however, that we can create our variants to make them suitable for our life, and why not, improve them.

CHAPTER 22 HOW TO ORGANIZE THE CLOSET

A well-organized closet is the first step in keeping a room and your life tidy. Go through your entire wardrobe to decide which items you really need, then you have to find the best way to rearrange everything, clothes and everything in between.

Part 1 Examine the Wardrobe

1

Remove all the clothes from the closet. Take them out of drawers, containers and take out the hangers. Fold them and arrange them in neat piles on the floor or bed, along with all the shoes.

Expert Advice

"Tidy up your wardrobe as often as possible. The more frequently you clean it, the less effort you will need to do it".

2

Decide which clothes you want to keep. It's not worth throwing away the clothes you use regularly, the ones you would need if they weren't already in your wardrobe. If you wore a certain dress during the last week, last month, or a few months ago, don't delete it from your wardrobe, as long as it's suitable for the current season. Create a pile of clothes to keep - the ones you wear regularly.

3

Decide which clothes you will put aside. You need to keep items that you won't be wearing for a while because they aren't suitable for the current season. If it's midsummer, keep your winter sweaters and scarves; instead, if it's winter you should put away your summer tops and dresses.

When you're done selecting your clothes, put them in a plastic container to store in the closet, under the bed, in the garage, or elsewhere in the house.

Rearrange your closet seasonally.

4

Determine which items you can donate and which ones are to be thrown away.

If a garment is extremely frayed, moth-eaten and faded, no one will likely be able to wear it again, so throw it away.

If some clothes are too tight, don't wait until the day you start the diet, but donate it.

Donate any clothes in good condition that you don't need, or give them to a relative or friend.

5

Clean the inside of the closet. You must do this before putting the clothes back in place. Vacuum, remove dust, clean the walls with a cleaner and remove any cobwebs.

If you are planning to modify the wardrobe in any way, like painting it a different color, adding or removing shelves, now is the time to do it.

Part 2 Organize Clothes in the Closet

1

Hang your clothes in the closet and organize them. Hang all the clothes you can. You don't just have to hang them, but arrange them in a particular order that allows you to find them more easily. Here's how to do it:

Organize your clothes according to the season. Organize clothes according to the type of garment; for example, it groups all the tank tops, then the shirts, trousers, skirts and dresses.

Separate your work and leisure clothes.

Arrange your clothes according to how often you wear them. Choose the organization system you prefer, but hang the clothes you wear most often in the most accessible place.

You can use different color hangers.

Arrange them by color. For example, use pink for shirts, green for work clothes, and so on.

If there is room, you could add another rod to hang more clothes.

2

Arrange the other clothes in different places in the closet. After hanging the clothes, you use most on the rod, put the rest of the clothes in order. Place the ones you use less frequently and the items that don't need to hang in the plastic containers. Here are some ideas:

Don't waste space under hanging clothes. At that point you can arrange some container or a chest of drawers.

You could add elements to the closet to organize the various spaces more efficiently.

3

Organize your shoes. Arrange them according to the model in a shoe cabinet, which you could place at the entrance to the house. Taking off your shoes as soon as you enter the house is an excellent habit to keep the house clean.

Part 3 Organize the Rest of the Closet

1

Organize all the boxes. If the closet is spacious enough, you probably have not only kept your clothes inside, but also boxes full of souvenirs, photo albums and CDs that you haven't used in years. To complete the job, you should examine the contents of the boxes and select the items to keep, throwing the rest away. Here's how to do it:

Get rid of all magazines and items stored for years even if they have sentimental value.

Arrange the boxes and group them together to save space. If the closet is already full, you may want to store a few items in different places. For example, arrange photo albums on a shelf or in the bookcase.

If you have used cardboard boxes so far, replace them with plastic containers as they are stronger and more eye-catching.

Apply labels to containers and boxes to know what they contain. They will make your work easier the next time you tidy up the closet.

2

Organize whatever is left.

If you left a box of light bulbs, comics or chocolates in the closet, it would be better to move them somewhere else, finding a location more suited to the type of object.

3

Make the closet eye-catching. You can really indulge yourself in adding a touch of style to the wardrobe, considering that you use it every day. If you embellish it in any way, in the future you will think twice before leaving everything in a mess.

Paint the doors with a nice pastel color;

Add some mirrors to make it brighter;

Hang jewelry and scarves in plain sight, as long as they are not in the way;

Hang a small poster or painting inside that will put you in a good mood when you see it.

Advice

Metal hangers aren't the best. Use plastic, wooden, or fabric-covered models as they rarely cause problems or stain clothing.

Shoe racks that attach to the doors are great for saving space compared to normal models that rest on the ground.

If there is enough floor space in the closet, you could also add a chest of drawers.

The plastic crates used for transporting milk are perfect for organizing the cupboard. You can stack them and arrange sweaters, sweatshirts, shoes and much more.

CHAPTER 23 HOW TO ORGANIZE THE DRAWERS OF THE DRESSER

When you open the dresser, do you think you see a curled-up raccoon inside? Do you feel like you have more clothes than you can keep? The solution to these problems is to rearrange your drawers: in this way, you can wear all your favorite clothes, instead of always wearing the usual two or three T-shirts.

Part 1 Select Clothes

1

Choose the items to get rid of. Start the "drawer organization" operation by removing everything you see inside. Examine each outfit and decide which ones to remove. Look for the ones that don't fit you, the old-fashioned ones, the ones that are stained or worn, and the ones you don't wear very often. You can give away clothes that are in good condition, but those that are in bad condition should just be thrown away. Even if they have long gone out of fashion, you may want to keep some, perhaps because they have sentimental value. Try to find another intended use, such as making a rug or t-shirt blanket, so they won't take up space in your drawers.

If it's a casual or everyday garment and you haven't worn it for a year, now is the time to get it out of the way. Dresses for formal occasions can last a little longer, even if they are not worn often.

2

Separate them according to the season. Once you know which ones to keep, sort your clothes according to the time of year. You can make the change of seasons by storing the less appropriate ones in a plastic container stored in the closet or basement, until they are needed again.

You can also store off-season items by placing them in boxes to put under the bed.

At the very least, try storing heavier winter clothes in the lower drawers. It will also be better for your chest of drawers.

3

Organize clothes by gender. Organize all the clothes according to their type. Normally, you can classify them into delicates, pajamas, casual and elegant shirts, casual and elegant trousers, heavy and light sweaters. Trousers should be stored separately, like sweaters, so try to set aside a drawer for these items only.

Typically, these items can be easily divided between four drawers. Delicates and pajamas in one, shirts in the second, trousers in the third and sweaters and other items in the fourth.

4

Organize clothes according to their usefulness. Within each category that you have established, it will be appropriate to arrange the garments according to how they should be stored within their section. You can divide them by utility or by color as you like.

If you want to follow the criterion of utility, separate them by looking at the similarities: light garments vs heavy garments, casual clothes vs elegant clothes, more provocative clothes vs work clothes, and so on. Keep together even those that have similar fabrics.

The color separation will give your drawers a much nicer look and help you find the right motivation to keep them organized.

5

Separate your clothes once you have established the best way to store them. Having all the clothes divided in front of you, you will have to decide which ones to store and in which drawers. In general, it is best to put the clothes you use most often on top.

Special care may be required for certain types of clothing. For example, to combat moths it is important to put a cedar tablet or mothballs in the drawers that contain the sweaters.

You may even need to hang certain clothes or arrange them in protective bags rather than drawers. Therefore, it would be better to keep silk or more expensive garments, separate them from others and especially the expensive sweaters, put in moth-proof bags.

Part 2 Divide the Clothes

1

Divide the drawers into sections. Usually, a drawer is too large to hold various types of clothing. So visually divide it into compartments. For longer drawer's three-part division will work, while for smaller ones two sections will suffice.

The compartments can be further divided according to need. For example, you could divide the longer upper drawer into three parts: in the first you can arrange the bras, overlapping them; in the second put socks and pajamas, separating them into two other compartments; the third can be divided into three other sections to be used for different types of underwear.

2

Try using containers. Use open containers, such as the wicker or fabric baskets you see in home improvement stores, to respect the divisions established in the drawers. Get containers of different sizes and put them in the drawers. You can arrange the clothes inside them.

3

Try using dividers. Get some similar to extendable curtain rods, but flatter, and adjust them to the size of the drawers. You can easily buy them at stores where household items are sold, such as baskets and ironing boards. You can make cardboard or foam dividers.

Or use those contained in packaging multiple of wine.

4

Try using bookends. Place them in drawers and you will get a simple but functional solution to divide the space inside.

However, they are perfect for sweaters, jeans and rolled-up sweaters.

Part 3 Store Clothes Functionally

1

Try rolling your clothes. You've probably heard of how practical rolled-up clothes are when packing your bags. The drawers at home make no difference. Rolled up, your garments will take up less space and avoid wrinkling if you do this correctly. Roll them slowly, with a certain symmetry and tightly, to prevent them from creasing.

2

Use a shirt-folding cardboard. When folding clothes, use a shirt-folding cardboard. It is a sheet or a piece of cardboard, similar to a clipboard, which is used during the phases of folding shirts and trousers. Place it in the center of the shirt near the collar. Place the left sleeve over the right, folding it along the side of the cardboard, and then repeat for the right sleeve. If necessary, adjust both sleeves and then fold the bottom edge of the shirt. For the pants, simply fold them in half and then wrap them around the cardboard.

It is a system that facilitates the organization of garments and their overlapping in a very similar way to that used to neatly display shirts on store shelves.

To make your shirt folder, cut a rather thick piece of cardboard measuring 38x45cm.

3

Place the items in a row, do not stack them. When storing clothes in drawers, do not stack them. This is the most common way to put clothing in a drawer, but it is very easy to crease and it is more difficult to find what you need. Instead of stacking them, "line them up". You can roll them up and place them perpendicularly or sideways, or fold them with a shirt folder and store them in a row.

4

Slip the bras into one another. For a space-saving solution, you can arrange them along a single large line or place the left cup inside the right, although this method risks deforming the central part of the bra.

Advice

Give away clothes if they are not damaged.

If you have enough space in the closet, hang larger and more voluminous items. Drawers are more functional for smaller and more numerous items.

Get rid of the clothes you don't like any more.

You can also not fold the underwear. Nobody will come to check if it's wrinkled and you will save time every time you have to fix the laundry.

CHAPTER 24 THE KONMARI METHOD

We all need more order in our lives. This is proved by the success of the KonMari method by Marie Kondo, which in a few years has conquered those who made disorder a lifestyle (or simply did not have time to tidy up).

What is usually missing is time, looking for ways to save it and doing things so that next time it is easier to tidy up the house or find kitchen utensils, is what the book focuses on: "The magical power of tidying", which now stands on the bedside tables of those who want to embrace this new method.

The philosophy behind it is to let go of all objects that do not make us happy or that do not give us positive feelings.

Basically, the rules are few and simple and are based on the concept of happiness and slowness, of relaxation and serenity. If we don't need a garment or it doesn't communicate anything to us, why keep it? And why take up more space by balling up clothes, when there is a more effective method of folding them?

In 2015 Marie Kondo was proclaimed one of the 100 most influential personalities according to Time and in 2019 Netflix dedicated a series to her. If you have been looking for a long time to put your house in order, but find it tiring, here are some ideas from the KonMari method.

Let's see these 10 rules together to become part of the magical world of tidying up:

1) Reorder for use

Proceeding by use: the order in which you store things will be the one in which you will use them, so think carefully about how you live in the spaces before proceeding with the cleaning! First throw away anything you don't use and anything that is visibly worn or deteriorated.

2) How to arrange bags

You will never believe it, but the best way to keep bags beautiful and tidy is to insert them one inside the other according to the shape according to Marie Kondo. The reason is simple: the larger ones will hold the medium ones and the medium ones will hold the small ones. Obviously, it is advisable to keep the shoulder straps in sight so as not to forget them between one season and another.

3) Keep the objects that stir up memories

If an object has an important history for you, it is right to keep it: an old cigarette lighter, a set of glasses, a vase, can arouse in us emotions, daily, as they are linked to particular moments of our life. So, keep these items for as long as you want.

4) Fold the clothes into origami

You don't need to know the fine Japanese art of origami to fold clothes to save space! In fact, Marie Kondo suggests forming a rectangle with the garment, folding it lengthwise in two and then folding it lengthwise in two or three. By storing it vertically in the closet or drawers, you will get much more space for the rest of the wardrobe.

5) A custom-made wardrobe

Not all wardrobes are the same and not all are suitable for our needs. The important thing is to visualize: make a drawing of the space you would need in the wardrobe and give it a shape; this will make it easier to choose the wardrobe that best suits you and your home. The element of personalization is important to keep the clothes you have decided to keep in order.

6) Hang the clothes in the wardrobe

There are those who hang them only by color and the result is certainly of impact, but according to the KonMari method it is better to hang the clothes and jackets also in order of fabric, or from the heaviest to the lightest. The longer, heavier and darker garments will go to the left to begin the roundup of hangers (if possible, get them all the same and thin) up to light and short clothes.

7) How to pack

Perhaps no one has ever thought of filling the suitcase vertically and not horizontally. In fact, the vertical side is longer and allows us to use more surface. Always fold the clothes so that they take up less space, the suits instead, which cannot be folded into origami, can be folded in two and arranged horizontally on the rest. Always choose to also reduce the volume of shampoos or creams by replacing the original jars with travel jars. Once the suitcase is unpacked, also clean it externally to store it until the next use.

8) Order in the home and in life

Creating order can make us tired, and if we proceed in stages the work will be longer. Instead, decide to gather everything to rearrange in a single point, proceeding one at a time to decide what you want to keep and what gives you an emotion, and what can be given away or thrown away. You will always find yourself in an impeccable home and retrace the important stages of your life at the same time.

9) Find a place for ourselves

"There is no place like home," said Judy Garland in the famous Wizard of Oz. And in fact, in which place, if not your home, is it more suitable to create a corner dedicated to us and our regeneration? A place to relax and recharge your batteries? The objects that will surround you in this space are also important, look for your favorites and furnish this little corner of paradise.

10) Proceed by categories

The most important rule, however, is never to lose focus. When we are surrounded by clutter we can be tempted to proceed by room, but in reality, the best thing is to put in place the second category: all the clothes, all the books, all the kitchen utensils and so on. In this world we will save time and group together all the similar objects that we happen to use every day.

Getting rid of useless objects helps to make space not only in your home or office but also in your life because only by setting aside what is old can we really be able to welcome the new.

The Konmari method on the whole may seem quite drastic but if we do not want to apply it in its entirety there are no problems since we can still take a cue from Marie Kondo's advice simply to have a tidier wardrobe.

Both in Japan, where she was born, and all over the world, Marie Kondo is now considered an international expert in the art of tidying up. She is now very famous because of the books she has written and the television shows she has participated in.

Of course, embracing the Japanese mentality, which is really very minimalist, is not easy, but we can still draw some useful advice from the author's books.

Over the years we accumulate many objects and some of them, with the passage of time, we no longer need, yet we continue to keep them, perhaps because they are memories or even because we think they could be useful to us in the future.

The order of the physical space in which we live is reflected in order and a feeling of calm in our mind. This explains in a nutshell why living in an orderly space makes us feel more relaxed and organized.

Konmari method, how to tidy up the kitchen

According to the Konmari method, it is certainly not the dishes and glasses that we use every day but the kitchen utensils that take up a lot of space in our kitchens. Many utensils have really been lying in kitchen drawers for a long time, even though we haven't used them for years. At this point, if we really need to make space, we should make a selection of the utensils to keep at hand every day in the kitchen and those that we could store elsewhere because they are little used and take up precious space.

Konmari method, sheets and blankets

You should never leave sheets, pillowcases and blankets trapped in their plastic bags because unfortunately they tend to retain moisture. You risk finding moldy old sheets or pillowcases that may have remained in a very humid place. Better to keep only the pillowcases, sheets and blankets that our family and guests really need. To make room in the wardrobe we can give away sheets and blankets that we no longer need. The sheets and pillowcases that you usually use to change the bed should be kept within reach in the closet.

Konmari method, towels

You never know where to put the towels? Marie Kondo gives us a very logical answer in this regard. Towels should be placed in the most useful place where they should be, i.e. in a cabinet near the bathroom so that they are always available when it is time to use them. Even old towels that you would like to use as rags should never be rolled up but you should fold them just like the others so that they take up as little space as possible. Of course, you can separate old towels from new towels and guest towels.

Konmari method, sweaters

To fold sweaters, follow the basic method already indicated for the t-shirts and in addition add these instructions useful for both sweaters and all long-sleeved shirts, following the image.

Konmari method, hooded and high-necked sweaters

For hooded and high-necked sweaters, you must follow the same procedure valid for sweaters with the difference of having to fold the hood or the high collar down after folding the sleeves so that it is inside the garment to be stored in the wardrobe.

Konmari method, stockings and tights

According to the Konmari method, stockings should not be tucked into each other and rolled up while tights should not be knotted at all because they risk getting damaged. Both stockings and tights must be treated carefully and must always be folded lengthwise, trying to form rectangles or squares as for all other garments. Even in the drawers, socks and tights should be arranged vertically and not horizontally as we are used to. In this way we will not have to dig into the drawers to find the right socks because we will immediately recognize them from above by seeing the edge.

Konmari method, change of season

The Konmari method shows us how to avoid the change of season. Noting the change of season is necessary for those who have the habit of storing summer clothes that will not be needed during the winter season in boxes to be placed in the upper part of the wardrobe and vice versa. Marie Kondo, on the other hand, suggests you can overcome this type of obstacle, and to divide the clothes according to the material from the outset by providing, for example, very specific drawers for light cotton sweaters and other drawers for heavy or woollen sweaters without ever mixing the whole. So even in summer you will have some heavy clothes on hand in case the temperatures drop from time to time.

Konmari method, don't throw away, donate!

Often the author, in her books, suggests throwing away everything that is no longer needed literally and without remorse and on this point we do not feel at all in agreement. Fortunately, there are many alternatives to throwing clothes, books, accessories, utensils and objects of various kinds in the trash. In fact, you can give to those who need it or donate to charity what is no longer needed, or barter or resell it. There are now many channels, both online and at thrift shops and bartering outlets, which facilitate gifting, exchange and sale. It would really be a shame to allocate goods to the landfill that can still have great value and maximum usefulness for other people.

CHAPTER 25 TIPS FOR ORDERING THE LIVING ROOM

Although it is a multipurpose space, in which to spend especially the time of relaxation, the risk of accumulation and disorder is always present.

Keep only a selection of books on view: the ones you like best, those of art or simply those with the most beautiful covers.

This way you won't have to dust too many shelves and keep them tidy.

The other books (and CDs) can be hidden inside some cupboards, so that they are still within reach.

In general, use the open shelves to expose a few, selected objects. If you don't know how to choose, you could periodically rotate the exhibits, so as to change the setting, as if it were a small personal exhibition!

You can do the same thing with paintings, posters and prints, by rotating the hanging works like in a museum!

Use a chest or trunk to store the blankets, spare sofa cover and extra pillow cases. If there is space left, you can store other household linens that you don't use very often.

If you have a sideboard, use the space above it too, but without cramming in too many things: maybe you can arrange a nice decorated paper box and a hanging decorative plant.

Look around and study the possibilities: often in the living room it is possible to create some niche to be transformed into a built-in wardrobe.

Organize the cables of television, stereo, video game consoles, etc. with the appropriate tubes or with clamps that help to keep them in order: if your TV cabinet does not have it, consider whether it is convenient to make a circular hole on the back wall, to pass all the cables through (modern furniture usually already comes with them).

For the sofa area, choose a coffee table that has a lower shelf, so you can arrange the magazines and perhaps the basket with your latest knitting.

Alternatively, or in addition, you can use one of those hanging pockets on the side of the sofa (where it is less visible) to store the remote control and the book you are reading.

If your apartment opens up directly onto the living room, even plan a console with some nice bowls, if necessary, hold the objects in order, but when they are empty will decorate the environment.

CHAPTER 26 HOW TO ORGANIZE A SMALL BATHROOM

Putting on make-up and taking care of our beauty routine is a treat, relaxes us and cheers us up. It can be frustrating to do it in an environment that is not functional or that we do not feel is "ours". Often on social media we see celebrities wearing make-up in huge and luxurious bathrooms, but even a small bathroom can become delightful, and perfectly suited to our needs. We then decided to collect a few ideas to transform our small bathroom into a warm and comfortable space, even spending very little.

THINKING VERTICALLY

Having little "usable surface" available, we take advantage of verticality! But given that the space is already small, this does not mean hanging a thousand shelves full of objects on the walls.

A good idea is to hang towels, strictly clear, a bit like in hotels. There is nothing like soft colors, such as white, beige or powder pink, to optically enlarge the space by creating a bright and uncluttered environment.

On the other hand, it must be said that many cosmetics are also beautiful objects to look at. So, two or three small shelves on the sides of the mirror are welcome, containing the products we use every day and that in this way will always be on hand ... even when we are rushing!

Always "thinking vertically", a space to be absolutely exploited is that, partially hidden, next to the sink. Here you can hang a container intended for a hairdryer, which will always be convenient to reach even when it comes to taming a single rebellious tuft that has sprung up or treacherously during the night.

Above the door is another great area to place a shelf with various products. It's another idea to make the space appear larger and make the overall effect cleaner and tidier.

CHAPTER 27 CONCLUSIONS

For sure you have always noticed this, but you may not have known that there is scientific evidence to confirm it: mental health and a clean and tidy home have many points in common. It's something we've been hearing a lot about lately, so much so that decluttering - the activity of throwing away everything we no longer need - has become a very popular activity. In fact, experts in the sector and everyone agrees that a crowded house is also a sign of a crowded mind, and that to live better you need to get rid of useless objects.

Not only decluttering, however, serves to keep the mind in the right conditions of balance, but all activities related to the cleaning and order of one's home. Are you curious to know why and how to make your home a place where the mind can rest and regenerate? Then you just have to keep reading!

Relieve stress with intensive cleaning.

It's a benefit that people who tend to get angry often know very well: nothing helps relieve stress more than rubbing the tiles until they are shiny like a mirror. In fact, cleaning is sometimes a tiring activity, which certainly requires a lot of energy and concentration. The extra advice? Find out which is the best steam cleaner on the market: nothing is better for relieving stress than knowing that you have killed all the germs and bacteria.

Meditate while sanitizing the house.

Household cleaning is an excellent adjunct to meditation. Don't believe it? So, think: for the house to be really clean, you have to focus on repeating a series of actions in a specific order. Now it's clearer, huh? Concentrating only on cleaning, and while you clean, focusing only on the object you are healing at the moment will eliminate any unnecessary thoughts from your mind. After cleaning, your mind will also be cleaner and you will feel more at peace.

Increase productivity by learning to optimize.

By cleaning your home, you learn how to become a better professional. How? Learning to program, optimize times, get better and better results in less time. A fully-fledged mental training, which can also become your routine at work, making you much more productive people.

Mens sana in corpore sano

A clean, neatly organized home immediately gives a feeling of both physical and mental well-being. In fact, after passing the steam cleaner over the mattress and all the textiles, you can breathe and sleep better, and this is a great help to start the day more rested.

Living in a tidy home helps you feel more at peace.

Even though lazier people seemingly feel at peace by putting off cleaning in favor of a nice nap, actually living in clutter is extremely tiring. Not only because it usually takes twice as long to find anything, but also because the disorder creates over-stimulation for the eyes and brain. Conversely, ordering helps save time, and returns a soothing image that instantly calms the nerves.

Order and cleanliness reduce domestic conflict and help sociability.

The habit of systematically leaving one or more areas of the house dirty or in disorder is, as we know, one of the first sources of domestic conflict.

And, you can't live well, in peace and without stress, in a house where you spend time arguing. Furthermore, people who have always dirty and untidy homes tend to reduce their sociability, because they are ashamed of the judgment of others.

The result is fewer friendships and moments of leisure, and more discussions and jitters. Not quite ideal for feeling good. Advice? Develop the art of delegation, empower everyone and assum the leadership of the house. It is also used to educate children to take care of their belongings, as well as to make the house a welcoming environment in which to feel good.

By adopting some simple daily habits of order and cleaning, keeping the house tidy becomes simple.

The health benefits are at least three:

Lower risk of disease. Accumulation of dust and bacteria is a common cause of allergies and other reactions.

Good mood. Who doesn't like seeing order and smelling a pleasant smell in the house?

Exercise. Cleaning involves an energy expenditure which, however moderate, is good for the body. Eventually, you will feel satisfied and relieved.

How to get into the habit of maintaining order in the house? With a few simple gestures. You will see, it is small daily efforts that make life easier.

If you set aside five minutes a day to clean the floor, you will find that keeping it clean will be easier. Do not allow dust or food spillages to accumulate: sometimes it is sufficient to pass the broom or a damp cloth. Try to do this every day after eating.

2. Make the beds to keep the house tidy

Yes, we know it's one of the most annoying jobs. Making the bed, stretching the sheets, but it gives the bedroom an immediate sense of order. Do it in the morning, before you go out. If you can, leave the windows open to ventilate. Wash the sheets weekly with hot water.

3. Fold clothes or put them on hangers

Clothes scattered everywhere are one of the elements that contribute to making the appearance of a house less pleasant.

As soon as you get back into the house, hang up your jacket. After taking a shower, put your dirty clothes in the basket. Place your clothes for the next day folded on a chair, or in their place in the closet. These are small gestures with an enormous visual impact.

4. Clean the shower and bathroom every day

It may seem tedious to clean the shower after using it, but it's a great habit. You can wipe the walls with a cloth with disinfectant liquid to prevent soap or mold residue from accumulating. Take a couple of minutes to clean the toilet and sink as well. The appearance of the bathroom will change dramatically.

5. Establish a time for collective cleaning every day

To keep the house tidy while engaging the whole family, try assigning a task to each member: washing the dishes, taking out the trash, feeding the dog, or sweeping the floors.

These are small tasks that, if left unresolved, together increase the sense of guilt and heaviness. Sharing tasks helps develop a sense of responsibility in children and improves coexistence at home.

Last, but not least: the above does not mean that you have to "live to clean". There is no need to go to extremes to maintain your well-being and balance.

Rather, it is about finding a routine that helps us to live in a healthy and pleasant environment, without obsession but with constancy.

The liveability of any home, starting from the smallest studio apartments, certainly grows with order. Knowing how to organize the interior spaces of our home can help us a lot in this, also because, you know, we are all a bit lazy when it comes to ordering. Often, however, tidying up the house from head to toe is not easy and we can think that we do not know where to start. For a sure result, here are *9 simple and achievable tips for ordering any environment and even your mother will be amazed by the order that reigns in the house (or in your bedroom).*

1. Identify the areas of the house that are most used. We could divide the zones of each environment into active, meaning those places of the house used daily, where we spend every day or where we spend part of our time. And, of course, passive, that is, those corners where you never stop, you don't pass and often don't even look. Ideally divided the house into active and passive areas, we can "fill" them by differentiating objects of daily use and objects of sporadic or no use. The former will be placed in convenient places to reach; the latter, on the other hand, can be stored in the less used areas of the house. In this case, we are also talking about the most uncomfortable drawers or shelves to reach or about unused corners in everyday life such as the basement, for example, or the space created between the wall and a wardrobe.

2. Value the so-called open solutions. These are those places where you store objects and knick-knacks that are visible, therefore shelves and

shelves, tables and display cabinets, whose fillings are always under the eye of those who live in that environment. And which therefore should be enhanced with objects or a set of objects pleasing to the eye, colored or valuable. Probably no one would ever have spare bulbs on the shelves in the living room, party games with old and worn boxes or garden tools... And there is a reason! Preferably you can use, just a classic example, books for the living room, crystal sets for the kitchen or for the display cabinets.

3. Simplicity is the golden rule. To increase the ease of finding objects, it is useful to arrange the most used ones in easy-to-reach places, so that it is also more instinctive to store them in order after their use. If I put the stationery items in the study in a box, in a cupboard, on a high shelf, they are more likely to remain on the desk than to return to their place.

4. Give priority to availability. To find everyday objects with ease, it is advisable to store them in places that are easy to reach and use. In the kitchen, for example, we can order transparent jars for utility or alternatively label them with the name of the content (or maybe a photo?). In the bedroom, however, especially in the children's room, we use open baskets, so that it is possible to know their contents at a glance.

5. Group objects by categories. When ordering your things, it is always useful to group everything you may need for a particular job in the same place, as is done, for example, with the toolbox. To do this, cabinet boxes or even usable independent boxes come to the rescue. The most classic example is that of the medicine box or office supplies. It is important to always use labels that say what the contents of the particular box are, so that it is intuitive to find what we need and also put it back in its place.

6. Create a safe passageway. That is, find a space near which you need to pass before leaving the house. A place where passing objects can be

temporarily left, such as those on loan or those that need to be repaired. But above all, where you can store the essential items when you go out, such as house keys, car keys, wallet. In order to have a place to store them once you return and where you are sure to always find them, especially when we are clearly late.

7. Learn how to use drawers. Drawers and chests of drawers are the realm of accumulation and disorder. Trying to keep them tidy and to separate various objects of the same type in different spaces will certainly help you find them again. And it will save you from having to mess up the room every time you can't find something. If possible, it is always recommended to use drawers with dividers, a bit like the cutlery drawer.

8. Sort vertically. In this case, or we do not mean like towers of Babel, or rather the boxes which contains various objects. To avoid this situation, it may be useful to use shelf extensions, in order to also increase the capacity of furniture, cabinets and cupboards.

9. Store heavy items at the bottom. This is a basic rule to avoid unnecessary risks on stairs and ladders in an attempt to lift or retrieve heavy objects from shelves or boxes located very high. Therefore, keep the heaviest objects on the ground or, even better, at waist height, it will be easier to lift them to move them.

SUSTAINABLE MINIMALISM

Zero Waste Living. Habits, Decluttering and Design for a Simpler and Authentic Life

Noelle Gill

INTRODUCTION

L ook around you and take an inventory of the objects you see. Do you have the feeling that there are many things accumulated? More than what you need? Are you one of those women who have a huge bag that you haven't seen the bottom of for some time? Do you have clothes you haven't worn for over a year now? Kitchen utensils that you have only used once?

We live in a world where it is normal to stockpile more items than you need, be it office tools, clothes, shoes, make-up, tools, etc. These objects take up physical space in our homes, they mess up wardrobes, chests of drawers, chests, shoe racks, etc. But the worst thing is that they also occupy our mental space and our time since we have to classify, order, and clean them.

Well, there is a philosophy of life that can help you see and manage this accumulation of things differently. Let's talk about minimalism. Minimalism is not about having less, but about making room for what matters.

What is minimalism?

The idea is to live with the bare minimum, which for each of us is based on our life circumstances, and differences to have fewer things, to have more physical and mental space. In the process of reflecting on why we accumulate objects that we don't use, we will realize that there are many reasons of an emotional nature, in addition to the typical "if I ever need to".

Clothes, gifts, letters that we are unable to get rid of because they remind us of moments from the past as if memories were hidden in material objects. Minimalism is an exercise that helps us separate from material objects and realize that memories live within us, not in objects. The less you need, the freer you will be.

How to put minimalism into practice

The ideal is to start a little at a time, divide the objects into categories and evaluate what you need, which objects you are not sure you need and which ones you are sure you want to discard.

In the kitchen: what are the kitchen utensils you haven't used for more than a year? Do you use all the spices you have?

In the closet: what clothes or shoes are no longer fit or have not been used for more than a year?

In the study: do you have notebooks, old diaries, notes that date back to years ago, or drawers that you practically never open?

There are a few challenges that can help you put minimalism into practice:

Project 333

Project 333 invites us to choose 33 items of clothing (it is not necessary to throw the others away, just put them aside) and spend 3 months using only those. So we will realize how little we need to get dressed and how much time we save choosing what to wear since we don't have much to choose from.

Minimalist race

Another challenge is to agree with someone who is going through the same process to embark on a kind of minimalist contest. On the first day of the month, both of you will have to get rid of something you own; the second day of two objects; the third day of three objects; and so on until the thirtieth day. Whoever manages to resist longer wins. Once you have your heap of items to get rid of, you can donate many or sell them to second-hand shops.

Benefits of minimalism

I.   It helps us keep the house tidy and get rid of "junk".

II.   There is a new way of understanding minimalism in the home.

III. It is no longer the simple aseptic design stream that looks like it just came out of a magazine.

IV.   More people are finding great benefits from the minimalist lifestyle, whose basic concept is to eliminate excesses, what annoys, what is no longer needed to make room for what you like, is useful, and makes you feel good.

V.   So this way also invests in other fields, both at home and outside, not only from an aesthetic point of view, thanks to a much broader and more complete vision.

VI.   It is a matter of reducing the numerous commitments you have during the day to the essentials, better selecting the people you frequent, eliminating harmful foods, using products that do not harm your body or the environment ... but it is not limited only to this.

VII. Minimalism pushes you to focus attention on one thing at a time and makes you fully understand the importance of time since you are the only one who decides what is the best way to spend it, since we all have 24 hours available in one. day.

VIII.   From here an inner analysis automatically arises to understand exactly how to make the most of the time left to live.

"Live every day as if it were your last and ... one day you will get it right"

-Woody Allen

When you then start living according to your priorities, you will wonder why you didn't start doing it sooner.

The house is the place where most of the time this journey of discovery began

It often comes at first the has frustration of clutter and the awareness of having too many things. Then the decision to eliminate the superfluous and to bring order. And hence the infinite happiness and satisfaction for having found peace by creating more space in the house.

Your mind sometimes resists change:

- ✓ "It might take one day."

- ✓ " I paid very much for him, it would be a shame"

- ✓ "It's a gift!"

- ✓ "I used to like it, it suited me well"

You have to answer in kind:

- ✓ "How long has it been since I last used it?"

- ✓ "Can I sell it?"

- ✓ "Do I need it or could it be useful to someone else?"

- ✓ "Now I like it, is it okay?"

- ✓ "It works? Is broken?"

This reasoning can equally apply to many aspects of life at home:

- ✓ Cohabitants

- ✓ Daily commitments

- ✓ The food you put on the table

- ✓ The clothes you wear

- ✓ The materials you surround yourself with

- ✓ Products to clean the house

- ✓ Personal hygiene products

Use these tools to find the most suitable one:

- ✓ Weekly menu

- ✓ To-do list

- ✓ Bullet journal

- ✓ Fly lady method

- ✓ Kondo method

Minimalism at home helps you organize the domestic management

A minimalist home allows you to simplify everyday organizational management as much as possible. An organized life is essential to face the days more peacefully and serenely, and you can optimize space and time.

The organization is a tool that, if used with flexibility and kindness, can improve your daily life.

There are 4 main factors which if well managed and balanced can help reduce stress:

- ✓ Space

- ✓ Weather

- ✓ Money

- ✓ Resources (physical and mental energies)

Learning to be organized is possible at any age, so it's never too late (or too early) to start.

Minimalism at home helps you to choose the suitable materials

The materials you surround yourself with contribute to your well-being, especially at home. If you use natural materials you can reduce the level of pollution inside your home.

Minimalism at home helps you reduce waste

Can you lead a life without producing waste? Once you start thinking differently, then your habits change too, and little by little, you feel involved in helping to improve the world you live in, without necessarily having to upset your days.

These are the "5 Rs" indispensable for sustainable waste management:

- ✓ Reduce

- ✓ Reuse

- ✓ Recycle

- ✓ Collect

- ✓ Recover

Minimalism at home helps you to feel sustainable

Do we know the quality (and quantity) of the food we bring indoors and to our table?

Minimalism in the kitchen could result in:

- ✓ Prepare simple dishes, not too elaborate, quick, and easy to make, (especially for everyday life or for those with small children who do not want to spend all their time cooking)

- ✓ Pay attention to waste and therefore, for example, reuse food scraps to cook new dishes.

- ✓ Reduce excesses, avoiding big binges, but also not buying more food than necessary, risking making it expire.

- ✓ Prefer quality over quantity, through the careful choice of the foods that are brought to the table

Minimalism at home helps you to make special encounters

However, it is not always possible to organize a party at home or it happens to get discouraged by the amount of work that must be faced to prepare everything, with the terror that a disaster will emerge.

Minimalism at home helps you dress consciously

STYLE is a way to communicate one's identity, manifesting it through the choice of furniture, a dress, behavior, or anything else.

ELEGANCE represents research and attention to detail, with care and full consideration for oneself.

In practice, being able to show who you are with simplicity and authenticity, to live more peacefully. When you wear the clothes that you like and that represent you, then you look good and you are happy, this also happens with the house.

How to find the style that suits you best?

Simply by getting to know you, investigating your tastes, experimenting, and training yourself to perceive your feelings and emotions. Not surprisingly, most people who approach minimalism do so after having freed and lightened the wardrobe from all those clothes that no longer represent them, they feel truly satisfied and regenerated.

To apply these principles you must:

- ✓ Organize life at home
- ✓ Living small
- ✓ Choose natural materials
- ✓ Reduce waste
- ✓ Feed yourself sustainably
- ✓ Carry out special meetings
- ✓ Dress consciously

CHAPTER 1
WHAT IS SUSTAINABLE MINIMALISM?

Minimalism is a happily polysemantic term that embraces many areas of our knowledge, which in history has come into contact with architecture, design, literature, cinema, music, and many other artistic spheres.

A brief history of minimalism

At the level of the figurative arts, it was in the 1950s that the new minimalist current took hold, based on the belief that art has its reality, which is therefore not an imitation of that reality.

First, it is an artist like Frank Stella who exhibited the Black Paintings in 1959 at the MoMA and proposes a new way of thinking and living art, against an elitist tendency to understand the work of art. Others after him, Morris, Judd, LeWitt, readjust the concept to the sphere of design, towards a deliberate absence of expression, to give due importance to focusing on the single artistic object: linear and repeated geometric shapes, single objects that were as neutral and impersonal as possible.

In 1974, on the other hand, minimalism reached the musical sphere, with pianist Michael Nyman coining the expression minimal music. Among its various artistic applications, the concept of minimalism is characterized by less is more.

Minimalism as a way of life

Here I would like to talk more precisely about minimalism as a lifestyle, that is, I would like to bring the discourse back to a level that is delicately ethical-philosophical, restricting the great container of the concept of Minimalism to the sphere of your personal daily life. So let's try to see how it is possible to assume a minimalist belief and see how it can help you reach an inner serenity that will healthily lighten your quiet life.

Although with other denominations, the convinced fight against vices, surplus, and the desire to reduce the superfluous to understand more intimate and fundamental parts of one's self is a concept that has its roots since the period of great classicism.

The desire to move away from the futile and to agree on inner serenity has been constant prerogatives of the man who starts from the dawn of civilization and then passes from the advent of the industrial revolution; with the establishment of consumerism and its new cultural paradigm that tends to commodify the individuality itself, the minimalist belief as a lifestyle has taken hold more and more, up to today on this site, with this proposal.

Minimalism as a lifestyle is a way of thinking that embraces simplicity and tries to move away from easy consumerism, it is an attitude that is not forced deprivation, but acceptance of what we are emotionally linked to. It is therefore not a simple and bland operation. Proceed by points and you will see that, armed with your willpower, you too will be able to free yourself from material and emotional surplus.

1. **Focus on one thing at a time**

   Yes, trying to embrace this lifestyle is certainly a delicate operation, but don't lose heart, the hardest part is the initial one. So where to start? The first point is to clarify yourself; take a break

13

and focus, remove all thoughts and distractions and take stock of the situation.

Are you thinking of the neighbor who asked you for the oil he was missing? Greet him momentarily and be quiet around you. Becoming minimalist involves facing one thing at a time calmly and without other thoughts, first breakfast, then working hours, then going out with friends.

Let the others be multi-tasking, allow yourself the calm and serenity, just like the minimalists of the Sixties: a single object, clear and linear. Do you want to become minimalist? it can be done, first make yourself mentally comfortable to do it.

2. **Evaluate your space and review your priorities**

Finally ready, calm, focused, and examine your space. What have you surrounded yourself with over the years? Not that you've exaggerated maniacally with anything in particular, but try to reconsider your actual priorities! What do you feel you need? Or, what are you honestly pleased to have with you?

Take a step back and look around. How many items are stacked on your desk? How many business cards from ten thousand different restaurants are hanging on your bulletin board? And all those pens and pencils, all those markers?

Maybe if you only had one, if you only had one poster, only one or two photos, and only one cup in the kitchen you might feel more fulfilled and differently for all those precise objects that are the cup I recognize.

3. **Decluttering in every area of your home**

Then start by doing a decluttering operation in all the rooms of your home. It starts right from the entrance to the apartment: what catches your eye as soon as you cross the threshold? Having ten thousand sets of keys hanging from those who know which cellar or bike lock ever existed is ultimately more deleterious than having one, the right one. Clean up! Put order! You will see that you will feel better.

Perhaps all the objects we have to give us a sense of protection. Relaxing, getting to know each other, and knowing what you want or like is a very good defense against subliminal, twisted and ambiguous messages coming from the outside.

Go to the kitchen and open the drawers, how much delirium do you find in there? How many tea filters are there in there? But then, do you really like tea? Proceeding with the order, calm, willpower, and declutter in the bathroom, bedroom, closet, living room, and kitchen. Give a new breath of air to your space.

4. Regularly reduce the number of objects

You don't have to do everything right away, give yourself weekly deadlines. Similarly, regularly reducing the objects around you by taking and throwing everything in a box without making a meaningful sorting on an emotional level will not help you.

Don't make a compulsive blank slate, really think about what gratifies you and what doesn't. Maybe the dirty sock you found next to the dumpster on a crazy night means something to you, just hold on to that sock. Don't send everything to hell, but for every old and new item, think about it. Thanks to the rapid evolution of technology, nowadays just a few objects are enough to be functional in all respects.

5. The 6-month rule

If you find that you have difficulty getting rid of something that you regularly propose or repurchase uselessly once a month without ever feeling satisfied with either the old or the new, allow yourself to make a choice here too. Take every single item, item, or other and ask yourself how long have I not used this thing? But how long have I not opened this magazine here? If you haven't seen certain things for more than six months, maybe it's because they don't have too much meaning for your life throw them away, give them away, tear them up, give them away, and get rid of them!

The same with relationships or dating, maybe going to have a certain experience once every forty-five days is fundamental for you and if that experience is a ritual for you, persist and keep it tight, because it is yours. Everyone needs their fixed points, just identify them!

6. Disassociate yourself from your material possessions

Be careful though, you don't have to coercively deprive yourself of anything. Detaching yourself from your material possessions is also regaining possession of them. To move away and look from afar is to recognize yourself again with a clearer and more lucid eye. Do not get carried away by the trend of the moment, leave the latest new technological devices to others, leave the best-selling perfumes to others if you realize that you can do without them. Less is more precisely because that less is your very personal essential which you cannot and above all do not want to do without.

7. It costs more to keep things than to give them away

Indeed, it costs more to have too much than just right! Like thoughts that distract you from what you are doing, the supernumerary of objects can also confuse you.

Accumulating is an almost instant process nowadays, but you still try with a little effort to walk away from it! And above all, how much effort does it take to live with ten thousand visual stimuli?

Pause to think about how much more tiring it is to be surrounded by many impulses, rather than one, clear and substantial. Dealing with an experience and a life in a minimalist way involves becoming aware of that given experience.

So, if those ten thousand business cards there are only two that remind you of the company and the moment and the feeling with which you lived that lunch or that dinner, leave only those two hanging on the board. Throw the others, tear them up.

Enjoy those two memories to the full and realize how much more fulfilling a single beautiful moment is, rather than confusing your head with a thousand fleeting encounters and a thousand different sensations! Emotional or material overload costs more and more.

8. The 20/20 rule

There is a nice and simple way that some minimalists have thought of to help you recognize what is a symptom of impulsiveness and what is not, if the taking of an object takes you less than twenty minutes and less than twenty euros, surely it is a thing you can do without.

The decisions that require hours of reflection are the important ones, if you only spend two minutes on a question it is easy for you to care little about that question. So, for objects or new experiences, try to apply this method to calibrate their importance.

A one euro t-shirt at the market is very easy to buy, but is it why? Imagine the total expense saved minus all those single euros invested in the market every Saturday morning. Imagine how much better you can sleep when your day has been lived according to your gratifications.

9. Quality vs quantity, look for high-quality things

Quality must be your new paradigm. How many of those t-shirts hoarded from years of stalls did you end up wearing? Not to mention all the encounters with people who aren't important to you. Remember well that relationship quality is also fundamental.

It doesn't matter to hold on to many objects and many people, it matters to hold on to the things that matter to you. Not surprisingly, it is better to invest a lot and consciously in a single thing than casually in a varied number of objects. Do you need and want a t-shirt? Identify which one you want, spend even fifty euros and all afternoon to find it, but make sure for example that it is good and lasting. Choose the people you like to spend time with.

10. Think before you make and buy new things

Always ask yourself why you are making a purchase or an experience before starting, but seriously I'm about to get other pants that, oh well, almost fit me, so I only leave five euros at the most, then I throw it away? Leave it there! At most then I give it or at most I use it in that given circumstance are excuses that you can happily do without.

But do I want to spend three hours at the table with friend X this Wednesday evening too, who complains to me about the other friend Y for hours, when maybe I have other things to do? Realize that you just want to do something else and that's okay! Don't weigh yourself down if you don't feel like it, don't feel guilty about rearranging your relationships too.

11. Dress on less

The wardrobe, for many, can be the most hellish place in this case, and fortunately, Courtney Carver has thought of Project 333 for those who are interested in approaching minimalism.

The Project 333 is a program to follow to be minimalist right from your wardrobe, choose thirty-three items to wear for the next three months and seal the rest in a box. But be careful, in those thirty-three garments are included rings, necklaces, sunglasses, but also shoes and gym suit, outfits for the evening if something breaks or deteriorates, you can replace it, nothing extreme.

Indeed, the program helps to regain possession of one's things, the intimate and important ones. Having thirty-three garments implies having chosen them with care and respect for yourself. Above all, once chosen, it also implies the lightness of no longer having to face that decision every morning before facing the day.

Free yourself from the heaviness of always having to be on top: did you choose a shirt or tank top x rather than y? That's okay, don't worry about it anymore. Donate all your one euro t-shirts, clean up everything and happily feel lighter.

12. Be grateful for what you have

When you have cleaned the apartment of various objects, when you have avoided those other three hundred t-shirts for one euro of the market, when you have also managed to re-evaluate your relationships, you will feel that wonderful sensation of unique and rare lightness that only a few things can give you.

Living well and serenely with your Less is living peacefully with yourself, it is accepting yourself. At the end of this speech, why choose minimalism then? Wanting to adopt minimalism as a lifestyle is a very intimate choice that puts you in front of many difficulties and impasses. It is not trivial, but when you have been able to reach the end of your journey, you will realize how many steps forward you have made towards self-respect.

Focus on Important Goals: most people generally have a large number of goals they want to achieve. A minimalist life has a clear purpose. To do this, you need to discover the few things that interest you most and dedicate yourself to them.

Taking care of body and mind: health is the starting point for feeling good. Therefore, it is essential to take care of yourself on two levels; the physical and the mental. Physical activity, nutrition, and sleep are the three key elements in this regard.

Cultivate Full Attention: Minimalist life requires a quiet mind and that means being free from contradictory thoughts and in tune with the present moment. Practicing mindfulness or meditation for full attention helps to recover a peaceful state of consciousness. You will be able to observe your thoughts and feelings without judging them, resisting them, feeding them, and consciously responding to situations, instead of overreacting or being exhausted by them.

CHAPTER 2

MINIMALISM: THE FIRST STEP TOWARDS A SUSTAINABLE LIFESTYLE

If you've just embarked on your journey towards a sustainable lifestyle, minimalism is a fundamental concept that will be of great help to you. Minimalism is a lifestyle that consists in eliminating the superfluous from our life, making room for the things that are important to us, surrounding ourselves only with what adds value, and improving it.

Today we live in a consumer society that bombards us with advertising, with the false promise that the latest news will improve and simplify our lives. Has it ever occurred to you that having your new cellphone, purse, or anything else would improve your life? Then, once you get it, maybe it no longer satisfies you, or you have been but for a short time, then the very latest version of the same product made you feel "backward".

Very often, we realize that we were happier when we didn't have that thing, but we wanted it, rather than when we got it. Furthermore, this mechanism leads us inexorably to find ourselves with a house full of objects that, over time, are not so useful, nor do they add value to our life. Indeed, they often end up causing us anxiety for two reasons:

1. They increase the disorder in the house

2. They make us emotionally attached to them. Sometimes for us, the loss of an object could mean losing the person or the memory

connected to it.

Minimalism teaches that we don't need objects to remind us of things. This is not always the case, it happens to everyone, to find something that brings to mind beautiful moments that we didn't even think we remembered anymore. The point is precisely this, we must not eliminate everything indiscriminately. We must ask ourselves what value a certain thing has for us, and decide based on this to keep it or let it go.

Simplify our life

This concept does not extend only to things, people, daily commitments, etc. Having a sustainable lifestyle, in practice, means living your life with respect for the environment. So make choices that always take into consideration the environmental impact of what we do.

In general, it is a question of trying to reduce waste, recycle waste and use natural and sustainable products, that is, obtained through the respectful and conscious use of the resources that nature offers us. Ask yourself questions about the product from the composition to the production process.

Sustainability and minimalism could seem disconnected the two concepts, because:

- ✓ Minimalism focuses more on quantity
- ✓ Sustainability is more about quality

In the first case, a person focuses on having fewer things, which may not even be connected. In the second case, a person can own many objects, but ecological.

These two concepts have a conception because a minimalist person surrounds himself with few things but of value. So he invests in durable objects that he knows he can reuse for a long time, without having to constantly buy them back.

A person who leads a sustainable lifestyle knows that every object has a cost and an environmental impact. Therefore, it tends to buy natural, quality, reusable and long-lasting products, precisely to reduce its impact on the environment, avoiding unnecessary or disposable things. So it is clear that in reality, the two concepts are more connected than they seem. Thanks to minimalism we learn to give the right value to things. We choose higher quality items that truly bring an improvement to our life.

So, the first thing you should ask yourself before buying something is if you need it. And if that product will add value to your life and be useful to you. Once you understand this, then you can make sure that that object is also sustainable.

A lifestyle is accompanied by a zero-waste philosophy, having been born in response to consumerism and the tendency to spend on superfluous goods, filling one's street with useless things. According to Joshua Baker, minimalism is all about owning fewer things and intentionally living only with what we need, that meets our needs.

Minimalism is a clear and intentional lifestyle choice and means:

- ✓ Eliminate the distraction of the things we own in excess so that we can focus more on the things that matter most.

- ✓ Promote the things we care about most and remove anything that distracts us from them.

By promoting a simple lifestyle, minimalism bucks the mainstream culture. In addition, minimalism frees us;

✓ From consumerism.

✓ From waste and helps us reduce our environmental impact.

Minimalism and zero waste lifestyle are closely related. Living according to a zero-waste philosophy means consuming less and consuming only what we need. When we choose to be minimalist, we go in the direction of a zero-waste lifestyle because we decide to reduce consumption.

Reducing consumption is in line with two of the fundamental principles of zero waste concerning waste prevention, refuse ("refuse what we don't need") and reduce ("reduce what we need and what we cannot refuse").

4 steps to start a minimalist life

Being minimalist does not mean having less than a few personal items, wearing only black and white, and living with little. Conversely, being minimalist means living intentionally according to your personal and individual needs.

1. **Refuse the things we don't need**

    If you want to adopt a minimalist lifestyle, you must first take a step back to reconsider what you need. For example, wondering if you need to buy that new pair of shoes. In this direction, a useful exercise is, for example, not to buy something you want for at least 30 days. After 30 days, one will be able to rationally evaluate whether we need that thing or not.

2. **Decluttering the things we don't need**

    Doing decluttering, that is, rearranging the house to eliminate clutter and help free the mind from the material things that distract us and waste time. With a view to zero waste, decluttering must be done following this guide:

i.   Do not be in a hurry

ii.   Keep items you aren't sure about for a few months in a box.

iii.   Donating items that are in good condition and that we no longer use.

iv.   Recycle what can be recycled.

v.   Throw away in the undifferentiated as little as possible.

vi.   If you need to buy something, focus on the quality and sustainability of the product

vii.   To reduce waste, it is essential to purchasing items and clothing that are sustainable and of good quality (the two usually go hand in hand). This may mean spending a little more but also buying less over the distance because quality things last longer.

viii. Give more importance to new experiences than material things.

ix.   Minimalism consists in eliminating the superfluous so that we can dedicate time to experiences that make us satisfied such as reading a book, exploring a new area of our city, planning a trip, taking a walk in the park).

CHAPTER 3
THE DIDEROT EFFECT: WHY WE BUY
OBJECTS WE DON'T NEED

Diderot 's scarlet dressing gown. Experts in the field of marketing and sales are looking for new ways to get us to buy goods. What we need to ask ourselves is whether we need it. How many times has it happened that you strongly desire a new item of clothing, an accessory, or simply something new? Here is what the Diderot effect explains; the tendency to consume too much is caused mainly by a natural need to own something new.

The Diderot effect takes its name from the well-known French Enlightenment philosopher Denis Diderot, who together with his colleague Jean - Baptiste d'Alembert published the Encyclopedie, what is considered the first modern encyclopedia. Diderot lived his life in poverty, but at the end of the eighteenth century, something happened that shook him. One day he bought a new dressing gown and was immediately fascinated by its beauty, he owned a soft and precious dressing gown. He quickly got rid of the old one and soon realized that this new dressing gown clashed with the rest of his possessions, which were not as good as the dressing gown. He then decided to replace most of the furnishings, choosing more and more new objects and filling the gaps that were created in the space. Soon a vicious circle was created that led Diderot to go into debt.

The story of Diderot's dressing gown, of which the philosopher only later understood the effect it had brought in his own life, might seem ridiculous. Today, however, we behave the same way without realizing it. For example, we change the dining room table and then we want to change the chairs too, to match them with the new material. Then we feel the need to buy a new chandelier and maybe some flower pots to fill the new bigger table. Perhaps unconsciously, we are all touched by the strange effect studied by Diderot.

Diderot effect: the term coined in the twentieth century by Grant McCracken

The term Diderot effect arose only in the twentieth century when the phenomenon was better described and studied by the sociologist Grant McCracken. According to McCracken, consumers tend to buy goods following a logic consistent with their style but also following a more compulsive impulse. It is at this moment that we enter the vortex described by the term " Diderot effect ".

This mechanism arises because all consumers are driven, often unconsciously, to attribute a symbolic value to objects. This value is then exploited by marketers, who push us to buy other items that we often don't need. The Diderot effect, therefore, seems to work precisely because we are the ones who give value to objects.

The Diderot effect shows just how despite several centuries had passed, obtaining a new possession creates a spiral of consumption that leads us to always buy something new. For this reason, in the end, we buy goods that we would never have needed before. Naturally, there will always be things that necessarily have to be bought, but it is possible to put some techniques to focus only on what matters. If the human being enters the vortex almost unconsciously, he can defend himself, however, with small measures to no longer be a victim of the Diderot effect.

The first solution to counteract the Diderot effect is to minimize exposure: the idea is to unsubscribe from all commercial sites that offer endless catalogs of products. Then, it is necessary to get used to buying objects that fit our current style. For example; when buying new clothes, a good tactic is not to change the style, but to buy clothes that can be easily matched with the ones you already own. Learning to set limits is another fundamental practice; for example, go a whole month without buying something new. Finally, make peace with the desire for new objects: there will never be a level where people stop wanting, so accept that desire is an option provided by the mind, but not an order to follow.

CHAPTER 4
BECOMING AWARE CONSUMERS

It is becoming easier and easier to access products and services; in light of this, it is more important than ever to become aware consumers.

Conscious consumers: how do you become?

We are surrounded by products, services, and information, too many and unfiltered. Many companies, and all interested in offering us the product we cannot do without. Brilliant minds that devote all their energy to understanding how to create or strengthen needs and desires. In this scenario, it is more important than ever to be aware of consumers.

Conscious consumption has to do with the purchase of products or services that take sustainability into account. It means being able to choose responsibly and consciously the impact produced on the environment. Ultimately, this means choosing with respect for others, for oneself, and the environment.

Conscious consumers breaking down the barrier of immediate satisfaction

Conscious consumption invites us not to ignore the impact caused on nature and other living beings. It also stimulates reflection on how we invest our resources.

The environment must be taken into consideration and not just the satisfaction of an immediate need. The question we should ask ourselves is, how can I make my contribution to reducing environmental degradation? It is necessary to choose less destructive alternatives that favor collective well-being.

As consumers, therefore, we should acquire a perspective of awareness and responsibility in purchases and at home. For this, we try to offer you some simple ideas to become more eco-friendly citizens. The word "responsible" could give a feeling of heaviness, duty, and fatigue. Instead, it gives me a sense of freedom, empathy, and collectivity. Being responsible consumers, or "critical consumers", is a free choice, dictated by profound values and the desire to respect and protect our planet. Don't you think it's wonderful?

Let's start with the definition of responsible consumer, which is divided into two parts;

Consumer: the one who "consumes" goods or products from the economic system (called the market).

Responsible: someone who is responsible for their actions and behavior, suffering the consequences.

The two terms used together form the concept of responsible consumer, that is the one who buys a good or service not only based on the quality and price but also based on the environmental impact of that good or service.

But how do you become a responsible consumer?

The responsible consumer is the one who has a critical mentality on the quality and ethics of what he buys. He also has a keen sensitivity to the impact that a given product or service has on someone else. Try to find the best compromise between the buyer (himself) and the seller/producer. Sounds complicated? So let's make everything clear with the Responsible Consumer Practical Guide.

A practical guide to the responsible consumer

1. Buy products at 0 km

Have you ever heard of it? The 0 km products are those that are produced and resold in the local area. They are great for several reasons.

Support territorial and local realities

Have fresher and more seasonal products (which have not spent days or weeks in the transport phase). They are usually cheaper (because they save on transport and, sometimes, also on the packaging). They often come to markets where it is possible to buy without using plastic bags. It is difficult to find 0 km products in supermarkets of international chains, but they are very common in markets and stalls or smaller and local grocery stores. Open your eyes and ask around and I'm sure you'll find you have some solutions right under your nose.

2. Seasonal products are better

The ideal responsible consumer always pays attention to buying seasonal products, because all the off-season ones are imported. That is, they come from foreign countries and very often very far away. It means that bananas all year round, or strawberries in winter, or chestnuts in spring are produced in another continent, harvested when they are still far behind in the ripening phase, spend a few weeks in the transport phase (by ship or airplane), are distributed in the various centers of the Italian territory before they reach us.

A long journey that brings with it various consequences, often the products are not very nutritious (they are harvested too early), they have a surcharge (to cover transport costs), it is not clear which substances were used for production (maybe some substance considered harmful here but who knows in Ecuador or Chile) and the lack of transparency of the producer (difficult to know the quality of life of workers, perhaps exploited or underpaid). In short, the next time you have an incredible craving for strawberries in the middle of December, think twice!

3. Sustainable and responsible tourism

For travel lovers or for those who can't wait for the next vacation, well even in this sector it is possible to make more responsible and careful choices. First of all, choose how to travel appropriately, you know, the plane is the fastest solution but it is also the one with the highest environmental impact. Are there any viable alternatives?

Furthermore, eco-sustainable and environmentally friendly structures should be chosen.

4. Make Fair Trade Choices

Fair trade products and chains are the ones that want to guarantee the respect of the worker. It is very common that they sell products from developing countries and has the aim of raising awareness of the conditions in some countries and guaranteeing the respect of their workers. They are based on direct distribution with the final consumer and go against large producers and forms of intermediation.

This is a great choice for becoming critical consumers and supporting a more ethical form of marketplace. Personally, fair trade products have often been real gems, especially as Christmas, birthday, and wedding gifts.

5. **Pay attention to energy consumption**

Paying attention to your bill benefits not only your wallet but also the environment. Avoiding waste of consumption (such as turning off the light when not necessary) is a form of sustainability and respect

6. **Reduce waste production and recycle**

Many believe that recycling is the solution to all evil but unfortunately this is not the case. What am I referring to? You can find the answer in my article

It is a journey that starts from outside the walls of the house and that influences the choice of products on the supermarket shelves. Not only that, favoring certain materials (such as glass and paper) rather than others (plastic) are characteristic elements of any responsible consumer.

7. **Charity**

Donating a portion of your profits to charity is a very noble deed.

8. **Sober lifestyle**

The responsible consumer always tries to maintain a sober

lifestyle. This does not mean living a life that is poor and absent from leisure but rather choosing to marginalize waste and avoid surpluses. It is often the awareness that there is between enjoying the pleasures of life in a balanced way without harming other people or the environment. A sober lifestyle often also benefits one's health, both physical and mental, not to mention environmental ones.

CHAPTER 5
LESS PLASTIC

It is no coincidence that plastic is the major component of the vortex of garbage (called the Great Pacific Garbage Patch) which has now invaded several points of the Pacific Ocean, becoming enormous and surpassing the plankton itself in quantity. Plastic waste has invaded rivers and seas, settled on beaches and shores, and is everywhere.

Reduce plastic waste in 14 steps

1. **Discard the straws**

   One way to get plastic out of your life is to stop using plastic straws. Just ask for a glass at the bar or restaurant and decline when they offer the children the straw. Getting your children used to do without it is easy, just don't offer it to them but give them a nice cup maybe full of fruit juice!

2. **Eliminate the shopping bags**

   Use bags or recyclable bags, clean them thoroughly as food, fruit, and vegetable residues can deposit.

3. **Give up chewing gum**

   Giving up chewing gum is a small thing but it will work wonders! The 'butt' is not good for you and contains plastic both inside and in the packaging.

4. **Purchase detergents in bulk**

Again, ELIMINATE the plastic container and bring one from home to be filled with detergent 'on tap'.

5. **Buy food in bulk**

Always prefer bulk food as well, i.e. anything you can buy without packaging. Remember that one of the expense items of the manufacturing company that recharges this cost to the buyer. YOU KNOW? Why buying in bulk is worthwhile

   ✓ Keep the glass containers and reuse them.

   ✓ Keep the glass, wash it and reuse it for food or other uses.

   ✓ Reuse bottles and cups.

It's not weird. Avoiding disposables at bars and in the office means protecting the oceans and the environment from the ever-increasing number of plastic landfills. Glass mineral water bottles are more sustainable than plastic ones. Use home water, tap water is of good quality and you can drink it!

6. **Bring your food containers**

Shall we eat out for lunch? We get into the habit of carrying our container and asking the fast-food restaurant or restaurant where we go to put the food there. Reducing plastic waste is necessary if you care about the health of the seas

7. **Reduce the use of lighters**

They are environmental 'killers', difficult to dispose of, they can remain unchanged even for hundreds of years. If you use them for smoking, they do double damage. If you really can't do without it, buy rechargeable: at least you will reduce waste as much as possible.

8. **Skip the frozen food counter**

It's true, they are comfortable: you go home in the evening and dinner is ready in 5 minutes. But beware: frozen foods are the 'kings' of plastic. By buying them, you actively contribute to polluting. By trying to remove frozen foods from your diet, you will return to a healthier cuisine with natural and seasonal ingredients, of which you know the origin, and you prefer organic food.

9. **Eliminate disposable glasses, cutlery, and plates**

Do not use disposable plates, cutlery, and glasses. They too are difficult to recycle and major polluters. Prefer the new bamboo cutlery to the classic carbon ones, they are beautiful to look at and useful.

10. **Bring the containers back to the market**

If you buy fruit and vegetables at the market, you can bring the containers back and have them refilled. Ask your greengrocer if they take back containers, bags, and boxes to reuse.

11. **Use washable nappies**

To produce the disposable nappies consumed by American babies every year, it takes 80,000 kg of plastic and the cutting down of more than 200,000 trees. By simply switching to cloth diapers, you can not only educate your child to respect the environment from an early age and save money.

12. **Say 'No' to fruit juices**

They often come in PET bottles and are as difficult to dispose of as or worse than a water bottle. To fruit juice, prefer a fresh fruit smoothie, you will get more antioxidants.

13. **Don't buy unnecessary detergents**

For marketing reasons, the manufacturers differentiate detergents (floor washing, tile cleaner, countertop detergent), but this makes us spend more without counting the clutter of bottles and drums inside the house. By using vinegar and baking soda with the numerous self-made recipes, you can save money, save space and not use those harmful plastic bottles that are bad for the environment.

14. **No plastic on food**

Avoid pre-packaged snacks and snacks, use reusable bags, plates, and containers, of the resealable type, to take the children's snacks, fruit, or lunch with you to the office. You will thus avoid packaging the food. Try just 1 of these tips, and you will have significant cash savings and also do the planet a great service.

CHAPTER 6
THE CARBON FOOTPRINT

We live in a world that is increasingly aware of climate change and the negative consequences that the carbon footprint causes to man and the environment.

The carbon footprint

The carbon footprint indicates the number of greenhouse gases generated during the production of a product or service. Accounting begins with the procurement and treatment of raw materials, then continues with the processing and production of the product, transport, use, and, finally, the disposal of the product.

Even the activities we carry out daily, such as the use of electricity from polluting energies or the use of non-electric means of transport, increase the presence of these gases and raise the average temperature of the planet leading to the catastrophic scenario of climate change. From this derive environmental disasters such as earthquakes, sea-level rise, the disappearance of species, thaw, etc.

Start reducing your carbon footprint

Currently, the carbon footprint is around 50% of the entire ecological footprint which shows how essential the reduction of this metric is to put an end to the overexploitation of resources. We must act responsibly towards our consumption.

How to calculate the Carbon Footprint

Calculating your carbon footprint is simple. It is necessary to know the number of greenhouse gases that a given activity produces and the duration in time of this activity, or the distance, in the case of transport. By multiplying the number of greenhouse gases emitted in a given time interval by the time of activity, the carbon footprint is obtained.

Let's apply the calculation to a common activity like driving a car. A diesel car produces on average 2.65 kg of CO_2 for every liter of fuel burned. In the case of a petrol car, approximately 2.37 kg of CO_2 can be produced per liter of fuel. Let's say the two cars travel 100 km. The average diesel car consumes around 7.5 liters of fuel per 100 km, while the petrol car consumes around 8.3 liters. Over a 100km journey, the diesel car produces 19.87kg of CO_2. On the same journey, the petrol car produces 19.61 kg of CO_2.

Considering these two cases, the difference is minimal. However, if we include electric cars in our calculation, the picture changes. Indeed, electric cars consume an average of 5 kWh of electricity per 100 km. This equates to 5.8 kg of CO_2 over a 100 km journey, almost a quarter of the emissions from diesel or petrol cars. Even with these activities, we generate carbon daily footprint;

- The home: the more energy we use inside our homes, the greater the carbon footprint will be.

- Air travel: the class of flight, the number of stopovers, and the number of trips are three factors that affect CO_2 emissions.

- Traveling by motorbike

Purchases, also known as secondary Footprint, include all the expense amounts incurred for a series of product categories. Expenses include TV fees, hotel and restaurant reservations, recreational and sports activities, and insurance. To the carbon footprint generated by individuals, we must also add the calculation of the carbon footprint created by the product and by an organization. Let's see them below!

Calculation of the carbon footprint generated by the product. The calculation of the product's carbon footprint includes all greenhouse gas emissions over the entire life cycle of the product. The starting point is therefore the extraction of raw materials up to final disposal. The calculation of the carbon footprint can be done by including all phases of the product life cycle, or by considering only some of them.

Product life cycle phases

Carbon footprint is calculated in compliance with the requirements contained in the technical specification known as PAS 2050. The unique international standard reference is also the ISO / TS 14067 technical specification.

Thanks to these two nomenclatures it is possible to quantify the CO_2 emissions of a product or service. The carbon footprint of a product, also known as the carbon footprint of products (CFP), is defined as the sum of the total CO_2 emissions and removals of the system that generates an asset.

Calculation of the carbon footprint generated by an organization

The organization's carbon footprint (CFO) is the quantification of greenhouse gases associated with a company. Emissions can be direct or indirect:

- ✓ Direct emissions are those coming from the company's sources or those controlled by the company itself.

- ✓ Indirect emissions are a consequence of the organization's activities, but the source of which is controlled by other companies.

The international standards for calculating this carbon footprint are the GHG Protocol and UNI EN ISO 14064-1. Both regulations provide for the obligation to consider direct and indirect emissions generated by the production of electricity and heat. We can all reduce our carbon footprint by managing and changing our consumption habits, such as;

- ✓ Use renewable energy sources: solar energy, for example, is clean and renewable energy. Furthermore, the pollution generated by the manufacturing process of solar panels is minimal and is also compensated for by the high recycling rate of these devices.

- ✓ Choose electric means of transport: As we saw in our example, an electric or hybrid car pollutes much less than a diesel or petrol car. Currently, charging stations for electric cars are very easily found in large cities, usually in parking lots or under photovoltaic shelters, which allow cars to be easily recharged. Furthermore, making sustainable mobility choices, such as using public transport instead of private ones or renting electric scooters, helps to protect the environment.

- ✓ Contribute to reforestation: A tree can absorb 40 kg of CO_2 per year.

- ✓ Use low-energy light bulbs to save on your electricity bill too.

- ✓ Do not leave your electronic devices connected to the power for a long time.

- ✓ Be aware of the appliances that consume the most energy (e.g. hair dryer, conditioner, etc.) and buy them of the latest generation.

- ✓ Reduce your consumption of meat: Animal farms are very polluting because they consume a lot of water and increase CO_2 emissions.

- ✓ Reducing CO_2 emissions is an individual choice of environmental responsibility. We must choose sustainability in every action we take every day, such as, for example, the production of clean energy for our homes.

- ✓ Use cloth bags for grocery shopping.

- ✓ When shopping, bring your cloth bag. Plastic and its production increase the carbon footprint

- ✓ Choose class A ++: Be aware of the household appliances that consume the most energy (e.g. hair dryer, conditioner, etc.) and buy them of the latest generation.

- ✓ Do the separate collection: separating and recycling waste is important! In this way, he can receive a second life.

- ✓ Develop your creativity: give new life to old objects, indulge in modernizing them, and give them new uses.

CHAPTER 7

DIFFERENCE BETWEEN

SUSTAINABILITY AND MINIMALISM

Similar in appearance but with different values, despite everything great friends. It is good to know the basics to appreciate its character and to understand its complementarity minimalism and sustainability have a lot in common but they are not the same thing.

- ✓ Both are against consumerism for different reasons.

- ✓ Both seek a "superior well-being", one more focused on the person and the other on the environment.

- ✓ Both value quality, but only one focuses more on quantity.

- ✓ Yet you can be both, one does not exclude the other. You can be minimalist, sustainable, or minimalist-sustainable.

But let's start with the basics;

Minimalism means living with the minimum. Disclaimer: I did not say "live with less" but, rather, live with the minimum. We must dispel the myth that living in a minimalist way means having a lower quality of life. Nothing more wrong! Minimalism aims for something else such as; higher quality of life, based on a key concept that we all know but few have internalized. I'm talking about the concept that "to live well it takes very little".

You don't need a thousand shoes or bags, or the most expensive car, or the most distant vacation. It doesn't take much to be happy, as long as it is intentional.

Here, the notion of "living intentionally" is one of the foundations of minimalism. I find it very fascinating. Living with "intention" means living "actively". In contrast to the passive life, where decisions, actions, and life, in general, are subjected to. The intention is the awareness of one's decisions and the commitment to achieve one's goals.

That's why being minimalist often "doesn't happen" but is instead a clear and defined intention. I like to think that minimalism only focuses on the essential, leaving everything else out. The antagonist of social pressures, he listens to only one thing: himself.

He surrounds himself with only two things:

- ✓ What is needed (food, a bed ....)

- ✓ What brings value and, therefore, a little happiness (a souvenir photo, a symbolic object ...)

Minimalism is pure simplicity. It is made up of space, air, neutrality, and silence.

What is sustainability?

Sustainability is similar but different. In common minimalism and sustainability they have an aversion to consumerism (especially unsustainable ones, such as fast-fashion) but with more scope for customization. Sustainability is also simple, but it can be colorful and confusing. You can be sustainable if you buy a lot of eco-friendly things, but you are not a minimalist. Sustainability favors a humble lifestyle, yes, but without stakes.

In the end, what matters is only one thing, is to love and respect the environment. Finding a balance with the Whole. I am aware that sustainability also means reducing one's environmental impact, and that to do this it is necessary to buy and have less. Unlike minimalism, however, sustainability leaves room for choice: buy less if you want, otherwise buy better (for example, buy used or fair trade).

A responsible consumer takes responsibility for the consequences of his actions, trying to reduce the negative effects to a minimum. A sustainable life takes responsibility for the well-being of the environment and the community, near and far. Unlike minimalism, which has no responsibility towards others, except that of living according to its principles. Ultimately, the core of a sustainable lifestyle is based on a few simple concepts, live responsibly or live without harming anyone or anything live in a balanced way with the environment and with other people live in a conscious way of one's actions and consumption.

Minimalism: it focuses on a few things but without necessarily taking care of the origin

Sustainability: allows you to own many (but not too many) things of sustainable origin (which does not harm other people or the environment)

Sustainable Minimalism: it values the quality and origin of the few things it surrounds itself with

Responsible Consumer: the one who buys also considering the environmental and social impact of this good or service

Consumerism: an attitude of indiscriminate purchase of consumer goods, especially non-primary and unnecessary goods.

CHAPTER 8
THE DECLUTTERING

Have you ever felt suffocated in the house due to all the objects in every room that create disorder? Do not worry, it is a sensation common to many homes that are often excessively full of objects that risk-taking over and creates chaos that can generate a feeling of discomfort and throw you into despair.

What to do?

The secret is to eliminate, in a conscious and reasoned way, all that we have accumulated over time and which is useless or does not represent something necessary or important for us. The way you organize your space can therefore affect, both positively and negatively, your state of mind and your mood. A tidy and organized home makes us feel better, at peace with ourselves, and decluttering can help.

What is decluttering?

It is therefore the ability to make room and get rid of the superfluous.

It is a very powerful weapon to improve your life, to make you master your space and time again: by learning to get rid of the superfluous, you will immediately feel better and in a good mood. Here are 5 simple steps to eliminate the superfluous from your home

   1.   **Things to know before you begin**

Decluttering requires a good dose of decision and the ability to live with small moments of melancholy and nostalgia. While you make room and get rid of the superfluous, you dive into the past. So decluttering becomes a way to also do inner cleansing.

Don't be in a hurry to do everything right away, but proceed step by step so that you can choose whether to dedicate half an hour a day to decluttering or to do everything over the weekend.

Don't move deleted things to the attic or basement for decluttering to make sense, the things you don't need must be eliminated. The decluttering process should not be seen as deprivation but as a fun and creative journey towards a regained simplicity.

2. How to recognize a superfluous object?

This is the focal point of the whole process. The first few times it may seem difficult, but slowly you will be able to recognize superfluous objects on the fly. Look at each item in the room you are tidying up, and ask yourself:

I.   If you still like it.

II.   If it is useful.

III. If it has sentimental value.

Any item that does not meet one of these three criteria must be put aside. Do not keep an object just because your mother gave it to you and you think she would be upset if she didn't see it anymore or because "one day" it might come in handy; if you haven't used it so far, it means that you can make use of it, unless forever.

Decluttering means just getting rid of the superfluous and tidying up. The idea of living a simpler life with fewer material things interests many, but they often find themselves not knowing where to start and asking themselves many questions, such as:

"What if I still need this object?" As we said before, if you haven't used it until now, you can do without it. "Isn't it bad to throw away things that still work?". You don't have to throw them away, you can give them away, sell them or donate them to charity, but more on that later.

The wardrobe is the perfect example; how many useless clothes do we tend to accumulate without realizing it? How many clothes do we wear? Take it all out, choose and then decide what to donate and what to throw away.

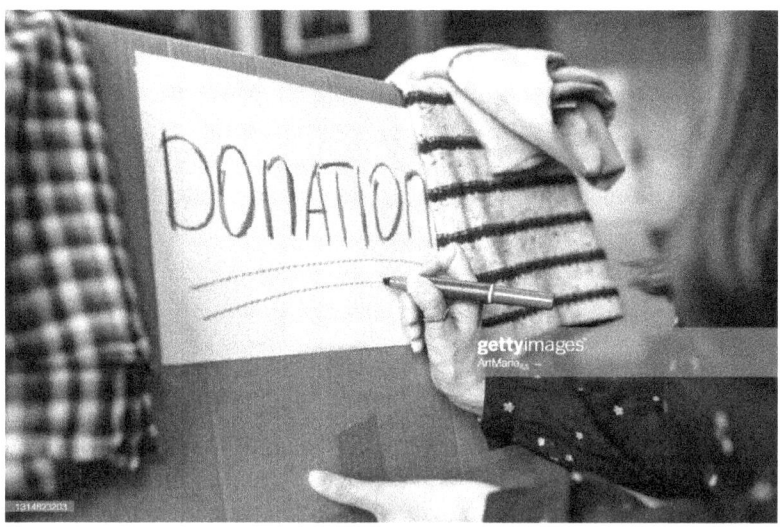

Some shops take old clothes back in exchange for shopping vouchers.

Here are some examples of items to delete;

- ✓ Dry cleaners hangers
- ✓ Sports gadgets

- ✓ Tablecloths too large or small

- ✓ Mismatched socks

- ✓ Unnecessary business cards

- ✓ Souvenirs you don't like

- ✓ Stained, torn, or frayed towels

- ✓ Outdated video games

- ✓ Notebooks that are no longer needed

- ✓ Store catalogs available online

- ✓ Ruined clothes

- ✓ Broken electronic appliances

- ✓ Cookbooks you've never used

- ✓ Shoes that hurt, old, or worn out

- ✓ Broken toys or board games with missing pieces

- ✓ Dishes you never use

- ✓ Greeting cards, wedding invitations, etc.

- ✓ Old calendars

- ✓ Empty shoeboxes

- ✓ Boxes of electronic devices whose warranty has expired

- ✓ chargers and old cables of various types

- ✓ Unused or damaged backpacks and bags

- ✓ Decorative elements (favors) that you no longer like

- ✓ Cosmetics that are out of date or you don't like and nail polishes that have congealed

✓ Damaged or unworn jewelry (e.g. mismatched earrings, broken necklaces)

✓ And here's why you won't miss these things:

✓ They are old: you will never wonder why you have thrown away all those unused cables or those uncomfortable shoes.

✓ They're broken if you wanted to fix those things, you would have already done so.

✓ You and your family no longer need them; don't forget, if you needed them you would use them.

3. How to organize the decluttering

There are two paths you can take, depending on how you are best at the organizational level:

1st method: go to rooms.

2nd method: go for types of products.

Go for rooms

It is the simplest system to follow because it allows you to work on something targeted: just choose the room to arrange and work on it until you have obtained the desired result.

How to organize the work?

Take out everything you want to analyze (for example all the clothes in the closet) and place it on a free surface. Divide all the items by choosing whether to keep them, throw them away, or give them away.

Make a thorough cleaning of the spaces, and store the objects to keep organizing them as you think best suited to your needs.

It is essential to put away everything that is used regularly and instead put in the most uncomfortable places what is used occasionally. Using suitable quality boxes and baskets will help to keep things clean and tidy more easily and to put things away quickly once used. Finally, it is very useful to use labels when storing something that is rarely used.

To simplify the process, you can divide it into two stages. Sure you'll be sure you want to delete some items, but you may have some doubts about others. Then put all the objects in "maybe" in a box or bag; after the first elimination you will have a clearer idea about the usefulness of keeping something of what you have temporarily placed in the box and you will be able to act accordingly. Proceed in this way room by room, until you have completed the whole house.

A little trick: to keep your clothes tidy, buy some fabric boxes (you can buy them from Ikea or online) and put away the clothes. If you roll them up, when you take them out to put them on they won't have creases!

Go for types of products

It is the most complicated system since not all clothing is in the bedroom wardrobes in the house, electronic equipment is not all in the same room as well as ornaments, books, magazines, etc.

Going for products means examining the whole house by focusing on a certain product (example: electronic equipment) and acting on it. The work is certainly more complex, but in many cases, it offers better results.

Look for all the objects of a certain category and store them, if you can, all together so that you always know where they are. You can put all your phone accessories and chargers in small bins - these bins are also used to organize drawers.

Decluttering: keeping the "memories" yes or no?

Most of the objects we have at home do not serve a specific task, but are part of the "memory" of the life of one's family; I'm talking about letters, photo albums, objects dear to our ancestors, and much more. In this case, the choice is personal and must be made after careful reflection on the importance that certain memories can have in family life.

4. **What to do with the objects to be eliminated?**

    Donating to Associations: I always recommend donating as much as possible to local charities and organizations. Donating what you don't need is twice as good: you'll have fewer things taking up space in your home, and other people get items they need.

    Give to someone you know: maybe relatives or friends need something that you own and no longer use but it is in good condition, give it to them: from clothes put on once and never again to equipment for children (seats, cots, etc.), anything that can help them will be seen as a very welcome gift.

    Resell: if you have any valuables you don't use (jewelry, appliances, silverware, etc.) you can always resell them online or in thrift markets. In case you want to get rid of antique furniture, call an antique dealer for an appraisal so you know their exact price.

Throw away: Finally, don't feel guilty if a lot of things, especially if broken, end up in the trash. Always remember: your home is not a warehouse. Some things must be thrown away, adopting the most appropriate system from time to time; undifferentiated or differentiated garbage for small and medium-sized objects, while landfill for larger objects and household appliances. Remember to respect the environment!

Special Mention: The Decluttering of Books

A necessary premise: books should never be thrown away, for any reason in the world. So, if you need to make room in the library or your house is too crowded with books, the keyword is given as a gift.

If you have accumulated too many books, you could try donating them or you can simply give them away to your friends and family. Among the possible recipients of the books, you have discarded are neighborhood libraries, schools, hospitals, retirement homes, prisons, and other types of communities.

5. **The trick of the bag**

To keep the house tidy after fixing it or before, to make an initial roughing;

✓ Get a bag.

✓ Decide what to focus on (Paper? Plastic? Other?).

✓ Take a tour of the whole house.

Throw everything that is too much into the bag, without thinking about it so much. Fill the bag as fast as you can. When it is full, do not put it on hold get out of the house immediately and throw everything away. How do you feel?

Do you feel a feeling of relief and lightness? The secret of the success of this system is zero organization.

✓ It's so simple it can't fail.

✓ It is perfect for giving a first "blow" to an overcrowded house.

✓ It gives a feeling of relief and success instantly and with little effort.

✓ It is very effective as a maintenance technique.

✓ It can be applied in the vast majority of situations.

The technique has its limits, it cannot take you alone to "solve" an entire house but to do skimming and to start a decluttering that seems stuck to the starting grids, the bag trick is ideal. What do you think about it? Try to make sure you go by material: use a plastic bag for all plastic objects, a paper bag for sheets and documents, and so on, to simplify the recycling of materials.

Finally a tidy and livable house

When the job is done you will have the surprise of discovering a more spacious house, where everything has its place and there are no piles of unused objects.

How to keep the results over time?

Make purchases aware that they are not going to fill your home with superfluous items again. To adopt this little rule for everything that enters one must go out. Use the bag trick frequently to avoid the new accumulation of items.

I'm sure that once this hard work is done, you will have no desire to go back to your old messy and stuffy house, the satisfaction of being surrounded only by beautiful objects that represent us will be stronger than any form of laziness. A roundup of ideas for ordering your home after throwing away the superfluous elements.

Bathroom idea

Idea 1: if you have a drawer, organize it with small boxes to divide the various products in this way everything will have its place and you will not waste time looking for things.

Idea 2: if you have doors instead of drawers, no problem. Store the products in baskets, better if made specifically for the organization then divided internally.

Wardrobe idea

Idea 1: for the drawers use dividers to find everything on the fly.

Idea 2: instead of folding sweaters and T-shirts, roll them up on themselves so as not to create creases and to optimize space.

Closet idea

Idea: To organize the closet, you can use boxes. This will facilitate not only the organization but also the change of season just swap the boxes with the clothes of the past season with the boxes of the current one.

Kitchen idea

Idea 1: to make more space, use shelves.

Idea 2: make the most of the space under the sink by using containers for bulkier products and a basket to hang on the door for smaller products.

Idea 3: even in the refrigerator, use containers to separate the various products and keep everything in order.

As we have seen, it is good to get rid of what we do not need to have more space for what makes us happy.

10 tips for tidying up

Any advice to get started?

1. If nothing is upside down in the house, everything will be fine. Yes, even on Monday morning.

2. Get rid of what you don't need so that you can have more space for what makes you happy.

3. Give a second life to what you don't use. So, you are good for the planet.

4. Labels are your best friends.

5. Do not leave anything to chaos, not even the wardrobe.

6. Remember, if order reigns supreme, live like a king.

7. Keep everything you care about in plain sight. Not everything, everything.

8. Plan your way, perhaps by color.

9. Say goodnight to clutter: you will have better dreams.

10. Order everything and then reward yourself with a box. Yes, but biscuits.

CHAPTER 9
MARIE KONDO 'S RULES FOR HOME DECLUTTERING

The KonMari method, invented by cleaning guru Marie Kondo has conquered the world. It all began with the publication of the best-seller "The Life-Changing Magic of Tidying Up; The Japanese Art of Decluttering and Organizing ", published in Italy with the title "The magical power of tidying up: The Japanese method that transforms your spaces and your life ".

A bestseller that has only anticipated a real revolution in the world of tidying, or rather the Netflix series "Let's tidy up with Marie Kondo ", boom! A method that promises to restore order, light, and joy in the home (and perhaps in life), through many small tricks, however, applied with particular rigor. All very interesting, but in practice where do you start?

According to the KonMari method, it is not necessary to proceed by room, but by category of objects, strictly in this order: clothes, books, papers, and Komono (or ... miscellany). Everything, therefore, belongs to a macro or sub-category and it is strongly recommended to collect all the objects belonging to the same category, arrange them on the floor, or in any case on a flat surface, which can be a bed or a table and analyze them one by one to choosing to know their fate. Before deciding what to keep and what to throw away, and before letting yourself go to the memories, ask yourself "Does it make me happy?"

This is a key point of the KonMari method you have to surround yourself with beautiful things, which remind us of happy moments and which, looking at them, make you feel joy and well-being.

So let's throw away that pair of jeans that we have been promising ourselves to wear for two years when we have lost 5 kg (making us feel inadequate in the meantime), away with those books that collect dust and we haven't opened for ten years, away with that box full of papers, ribbons, pens and objects of various kinds that have been closed for months.

Not everything should be thrown in the garbage, indeed, when possible we strongly recommend donating, giving away, or reselling what you no longer use, but in some cases, the only possible answer, unfortunately, is the garbage nerd.

Everything at once

KonMari's method is unforgiving is best to apply it all at once, even if this means taking a whole day in the intent. Postponing or dividing the method into too many phases would seem the best way to fail. If Madame Marie Kondo says so, who are we to contradict her?

Clothes

How many clothes have been sitting in the closet for months, if not years? In addition to the clothes, even those socks that have been unmatched for months, the underwear with the now gone elastics, scarves that we last put on back in 2005 everything has been put away.

Only clothes that are worn regularly in the Spring/Summer and Autumn/Winter seasons should remain in the wardrobe, while everything else must disappear. How clothes are folded and hung is also important, here are some demonstration images of the KonMari method for bringing zen joy to the closet.

Books

Even if we like full bookcases and houses overflowing with books, in fact over the years we risk accumulating a good amount of titles that we will never read again, and that only take away space, accumulating dust.

The used book market, for example, is very active, but associations, literary clubs, bookcrossing, and libraries can also be good choices to "free" the books that we no longer need.

Sheets, slips, and scattered papers

The great enemies of clutter, pop up in all corners of the house, from the desk to the bookcases from the fridge to the drawers. Old receipts, photocopies, flying notes, printed lists are all things we haven't looked at for months, but which continue to make the house and our life more messy and crowded.

In this case, no mercy, the important thing is to save the important documents, the rest must be thrown away. The miscellany is perhaps the most complicated part to fix because it encompasses everything. Everyone knows what brings disorder into their home, the important thing is to keep in mind another tip that is part of the KonMari method opines that before putting everything back in order, immediately throw away all the discarded things, avoiding accumulating them in the garage or a box.

The KonMari method recommends proceeding by rearranging the objects by category following this ladder; first the clothes then the documents followed by various objects to concentrate only at the end on the objects of emotional value or the memories, considered the most difficult to let go of.

Marie Kondo argues that we should only keep objects capable of arousing us joy and positive feelings. This will make it easier for everyone else to fit into the pile of objects to separate us from. The golden rule shouldn't be choosing what to throw away, but selecting what you want to keep.

The tidying up exercise should be constant over time. It might be useful to apply the golden rules of the decluttering guru.

These are:

- To put in order.

- Imagine and commit to pursuing the ideal lifestyle.

- Sort by category and never by location or one room at a time.

- Follow the order indicated and ask yourself for each article if it arouses joy.

- The state of mind of the people will also benefit. In this way, we will eliminate the superfluous, even objects and clothes that can arouse bad memories in us.

- A useful tip, in case of indecision, is to put objects in a box that we are not convinced we want to throw away. Taking back its contents three months later to understand that it was not necessary to keep those objects, so we can permanently eliminate them in a convinced and conscious way.

- Among the tips that come from the Kondo tidying method, we remember the grouping of objects by categories: fabrics, paper, and electrical material.

- Other labels will be liquids, such as hygiene, cleaning and beauty products, food, and tableware.

Tidying up the cupboard

Each space containing the aforementioned objects, such as wardrobes, doors, boxes, and drawers, must be filled to 90% to make the most of the space. As for the arrangement of the wardrobe, Marie Kondo's method suggests perfectly folding clothes, including dresses, as well as t-shirts, shirts, and trousers. Only heavy fabrics, jackets, suits, and coats should be hung. We proceed with the arrangement by completely emptying the wardrobe and then start selecting, choosing what to keep and what to get rid of.

Closet decluttering

Arranging things vertically is the most effective solution for Kondo to visualize everything well. Even the accessories must be rearranged following rules: the bags placed one inside the other, the folded canvas bags and the same goes for underwear and socks.

Even for the arrangement of documents, as happened for the wardrobes, the method of emptying everything and throwing away as much as possible applies. The documents must be divided by types such as guarantees, bills, contracts, and each placed in a special container.

Furthermore, we also want to suggest the rules of another exponent of decluttering Geraline Thomas

Geraline Thomas decluttering rules

Geraline Thomas, an expert in home organization, also teaches us methodically how to organize the house, eliminate the superfluous and make room only for the necessary. For her, all the things you don't use, you don't like anymore, you don't know what to do with them and you don't want to clutter, that is, to be eliminated.

Not doing this is just an excuse

Always starting from the wardrobe, it is important to remember that each garment should spend 80% of its life on us and not hanging. If it doesn't, because it no longer fits, we have changed size or tastes. We proceed by donating it to friends or charity.

It is starting from the entrance to the house, everything we do not use at least once a week must be eliminated, it is not needed and clutters the area that should be our business card. As for Marie Kondo, also in this system, the likes must be put together with the like this is true in the bathroom, in the pantry, and the wardrobe. This way you will find everything easily.

Reorganize spaces and tidy up the house

Avoid creating spaces where articles of different kinds converge: in the mixed drawer we will never really know what to look for or find. Using better means using less and in the same way, buying fewer means using more we keep this mantra in mind every time we are about to make a purchase.

We proceed by eliminating gadgets, giveaways, and other items we have at home for no real reason. Finally, we pay attention to products to clean the house: we often accumulate bottles, we buy them in quantity in case of offers but not everything is needed and above all, it takes up space.

CHAPTER 10

HOW TO ORGANIZE YOUR CLOSET WITH THE SSO METHOD (EMPTY, SELECT AND THEN ORGANIZE)

Are you renovating your bedroom and would like to buy a new wardrobe? Would you like to size and organize your wardrobe with a precise and functional method? The wardrobes we see on the various sites are very beautiful, right? But then when we find ourselves replicating that situation in our home, we don't even see the shadow of the wardrobe we were inspired by. We want to show you all the necessary considerations to make before buying a wardrobe and all its magnificent interior accessories.

First, you need to do some decluttering, get rid of the superfluous, or identify what you need and eliminate what you no longer use. This initial skimming will help you get a more complete view of what you need and how to organize it. Only later, when it has been decided what to keep, can we move on to the organization, that is, to assign a well-defined location to each item of clothing.

Apparently, it may seem a boring and complicated operation (in fact I am honest, well done decluttering takes time and effort), but if applied with the right method and with a bit of willpower, you can get great results and enormous benefits, both physically and mentally. How cool is it to immediately find a thing when looking for it? How nice is it to know what to wear in the morning, without spending hours in front of the wardrobe?

To be honest, your closet contains a lot of things that you never put on, that no longer fit you, or that have worn out over time. What do you do with these things if you don't need them? They only take up space for nothing, space necessary to keep the garments less pressed to each other and to see them better. Thanks to this method you will understand how pleasant it will be every morning to find what you are looking for immediately, moreover, your garments will have much fewer creases than now, because they will no longer be compressed inside the wardrobe.

The SSO method: clear select and then organize

This reordering method brings together the decluttering phase with that of the organization. A method that can be applied throughout the home and for every category of objects, but in this chapter, we dedicate ourselves to the wardrobe: let's start. An easy-to-apply method that allows you to organize and make your wardrobe functional.

Empty

Empty the wardrobe and place all the clothes on the bed, I recommend not leaving anything out. This exercise is used to become aware of how many things you have and above all how many things are unused. Who knows, maybe you can also find something you thought you lost.

Select

For each item, ask yourself these questions;

- ✓ Do I use it frequently (during its season of course)?

- ✓ Do I have nothing else like it that performs its function?

- ✓ Is it in good condition and not damaged or worn?

- ✓ Is it the right size and does it enhance me?

- ✓ Does it excite me when I hold it in my hand?

If you answered yes to at least 3 out of 5 of these questions, that item is to be kept. Everything else must be eliminated (give, sell, exchange, recycle or throw away). Focus on what is to be kept and not what is to be discarded.

Do you have doubts about some items and wonder if you will still use them? Generally, if you never wore it the previous season, you probably won't wear it. If you still have doubts, put those garments in a closed box, which you will take to the basement or attic, or garage. If in the following months you do not come to look for them, then you will have the confirmation that those clothes were no longer needed and then proceed with the elimination, without any remorse. All those garments related to memories, the wedding dress or the dress of your graduation party, which for obvious reasons you will no longer wear, are put in a closed container.

Organize

After deciding what to keep, you need to arrange and organize all the clothing items in their location. Everything must be in its place. Using the bed as a support surface, divide all the items into categories:

- ✓ Clothes

- ✓ Tops and blouses

- ✓ T-shirt

- ✓ Jeans

- ✓ Trousers

- ✓ Skirts

- ✓ Sweaters

- ✓ Cardigan

- ✓ Sweatshirts

- ✓ Shirts

- ✓ Jackets

- ✓ Coats

- ✓ Blazer

- ✓ Pajamas

- ✓ Intimate

- ✓ Socks

- ✓ Shorts

- ✓ Swimwear

- ✓ Sportswear

- ✓ Shoes

- ✓ Bags

- ✓ Accessories

- ✓ Jewelry and watches

After dividing these categories, you will better understand the volumes and quantities to be organized. The next step is to understand what to hang and what to store in specific drawers or containers.

Based on what to put where you should be able to roughly identify how many drawers you need, how much hanging space, and how many other interior accessories. Grab a pen and paper and try to draw the prospect of your ideal wardrobe. Alternatively, you can also help you with the Ikea Planner, very useful for composing the wardrobe and previewing the final result.

One last tip

To further organize the hanging area of your closet keep the categories divided and keep them separated simply by a play of colors. I'll give you an example if you have to organize blouses, shirts, and blazers in a hanging module, place the darker blouses from left to right up to the lighter ones, then move on to the darker shirts up to the light ones and proceed to the same way with everything else. Now you can organize your closet and that of your children efficiently and functionally.

CHAPTER 11

20 MINIMALIST HABITS FOR A SIMPLER LIFE

L ife, if you prefer, is made up of routine, of small daily gestures that follow one another. Acquiring minimalist and healthy habits improves your life considerably because it simplifies the way we live. Without realizing it, we often tend to complicate life when it is much simpler and more beautiful than what we believe. So let's see how to improve our life.

The minimalist habits that change your life

1. Do not depend on the opinion of others

Simply put, you have to give a damn about what others think. How can this habit make life easier? Because doing what you want while ignoring the common thought or of other people who may not even know each other, makes you happy and satisfied with yourself without unnecessary stress. This habit changes life because as soon as you learn not to think about the opinion of others it will be possible to live an authentic life and make choices dictated by personal preferences.

2. Having few clothes

How many times have you found yourself in front of the open wardrobe wondering what to put on? In reality, this is a real waste of time as well as energy. Thinking less about clothes, about buying them and how to find the best combination makes life easier. Having too many clothes means occupying not only a physical space but also a mental space. At this point, the best thing would be to acquire minimalist habits and have fewer clothes to ensure that you don't waste time and stress every day about choosing what to wear.

3. Remain silent

It may seem strange to say but saving on words is important. Making too many speeches to fill the void leads nowhere. Being silent from time to time and listening is instead a profitable and pleasant habit. If you adopt this habit with the simplicity you will find that people enjoy spending time with you and you can gain in mental health and relaxation.

4. Ask yourself questions

Often we find ourselves taking actions without thinking about what we are doing or the reasons why they are being done. It can happen, for example, when you eat out of habit and not out of true hunger, or when you are buying a dress without needing it and we like it. Stopping to ask every now and then why we perform certain gestures can significantly improve our attitude towards life. This attitude allows you to get out of habits that you do not like or that are unhealthy by simplifying your life.

5. Choose a dress code

To further simplify your life by acquiring minimalist habits regarding the choice of clothes to wear every day, my advice is to choose a sort of uniform and have a minimal dress code that you can interchange and therefore spend less time choosing the right clothes. to every day. The important thing is to choose clothes that are comfortable and suitable for multiple occasions, thus creating a functional wardrobe or capsule wardrobe. A capsule wardrobe means having a (limited) number of easily combinable and interchangeable clothes belonging to a color palette with which you can create a certain number of outfits.

6. **Make the to-do list**

This habit is a must to increase your productivity and clear your mind. Drawing up a to-do list the night before for the next day, or organizing a list for the coming week helps you stay organized, don't waste time and always know what to expect. The to-do list also helps you understand how many activities you can bring.

7. **Stop doing multiple things at once**

Multitasking is a skill that is always required in the workplace but is not healthy. Dedicating your mind and body to one task at a time makes it possible to pay more direct attention and focus well on one goal and accomplish one at a time. It is never really possible to focus on multiple things at once and for this reason, it is best to learn to be more selective.

8. **Start saying no**

Simplifying life and feeling good is also synonymous with having to give up something. Say no to meetings or appointments in which you have no interest, say no to collaborations or job requests, even if it means missing out on some opportunities. We must learn to prioritize the things that make us waste time.

9. Take deep breaths

Focusing on your breath allows you to relax, establish contact, and have a firm point with the present. Remembering to breathe means putting your feet back on the ground and being more aware. You should start taking this as a minimalist habit to do in the morning, perhaps taking three good deep breaths before starting the day.

10. Step by step

Routine is something sacrosanct, it serves to understand which moments of the day to dedicate to a certain type of activity and establishes an order of things. Minimalist habits are acquired, with time and organization, and proceed step by step, without wanting everything immediately. To get started, just prioritize and focus on one thing at a time. Not only that, there we will simplify life but we will have more time for ourselves.

11. Do not pollute the visual environment

Having a tidy and clean room, with the cables of the electronic devices well hidden and objects arranged in an orderly manner, allows you to live in a more relaxed way and to have an orderly, light, and peaceful mind.

12. Decluttering thoughts

Every day we are exposed to a flood of constant thoughts. What minimalist habits allow us to do is to avoid harmful and futile thoughts, leaving room for what matters. It must also be done decluttering of thoughts and throwing away what is thrown away. Maybe instead of postponing a commitment, it is better to do it, and implement the theory of the famous saying "easier said than done".

13. Always carry a bottle with you

Drinking enough water means feeling good and thinking about your health. One of the minimalist habits that make life easier is always carrying a water bottle.

14. Practice half-yearly decluttering

A couple of times a year are enough to take stock of the situation. Letting go of useless things and objects means simplifying your way of life and knowing which things matter and which ones you can start doing without. I recommend watching the video: Decluttering wardrobe after 3 years of minimalism

15. Eliminate distractions

Between computers, smartphones, social networks, and various things, it is always easier to be prey to unnecessary distractions. A few simple gestures are enough to avoid getting distracted:

✓ Turn off notifications on your smartphone

✓ Unsubscribe from unnecessary newsletter subscriptions

✓ Delete intrusive applications

✓ Mute WhatsApp groups

✓ Set a timer for time to spend on social media

16. Clean rest

You have to choose to have a quality rest, perhaps without background noise, such as radio, TV, and music. Peace of mind can be achieved simply by silence.

17. Stroll

No one could have imagined this activity among the minimalist habits to be acquired to live in a simpler and better way, yet walking helps to clear the mind. It relaxes the mood and mitigates ailments. You should take a daily walk to stay active and healthy.

18. Minimalist furniture

The best moments in life are those spent with people who love each other without too many worries. Essentially furnishing your home helps you not to waste too much time on cleaning and therefore to have more time to spend as you prefer. In short, a simple house is also a panacea for daily chores.

19. No make up

In the morning, when you wake up and get ready, you waste a lot of time in the make-up phase because there are so many women who can't help but put on make-up before going out. For many people, make-up has become an addiction and not a pleasure or a will. For this reason, it is advisable to ask yourself why you wear makeup and rediscover the pleasure of not wearing makeup.

20. Don't try to fill all your time

Many tend to obsessively fill their days with activities and often can't find time for the simpler things. But now and then you also have to indulge in sweet idleness.

CHAPTER 12
HOW TO SAVE WITH MINIMALISM

Let's talk about budget and minimalism. Minimalism isn't just about cutting down on all the things you buy and letting go of the objects. You can also incorporate it into your finances. The idea is simple. We need to understand what are the superfluous things we can do without. But how does a minimalist budget work? Let's dig in and find out exactly how to incorporate a minimalist budget and minimalism into your finances.

What is a minimalist budget?

Minimalism means identifying and understanding what you value most in not just your physical assets, but your life as well. According to Joshua Becker, an author, and advocate of minimalism, minimalism is all about intentionally removing things that distract us from what matters most to us.

Anyone can have a minimalist budget. It's good for people who want to cut down on their expenses or set up a new budgeting system. If you're looking to cut back on expenses but find yourself shopping a lot, then a minimalist budget might be worth considering.

The secret to financial well-being exists. What does it mean to feel good? In general, it means having enough money to live and not having large debts on your shoulders, rather having even the little that remains to be set aside for the future or any eventuality. Saving with minimalism is a completely different approach to money and life than usual.

The minimalist lifestyle incorporates the idea that you can live with less to live better. It is a lifestyle that is not only practical and material but also a mental one. A simple and authentic life cannot be exchanged for any other false and wasteful life. Minimalism is practiced by many people, even without others noticing. It is often associated with austerity, but the intent here is precise to make it clear that minimalism is not renunciation, but rather it is a considered choice.

The basic idea to incorporate is that money makes us free to do everything, and it is important not to trade our freedom for useless objects and empty experiences. You do not have to give up a good coffee at the bar with friends, because the mere giving up as an end in itself does not lead to anything, but it worsens the situation and does not allow you to save. A bit like what happens when you fast as a punishment and then eat more than the previous day. What the minimalist attitude helps to do is improve one's relationship with money, and this results in actual savings.

The rules for saving with minimalism

There are several ways to approach the minimalist lifestyle to save;

1. **Don't buy what you can't afford**

   It sounds easy but not everyone follows this simple rule. Sometimes, being able to buy things in installments gives the impression of being able to afford many things, but buying things that you cannot afford puts you in the position of debtors, and therefore a disadvantageous position. Consequently, you will depend on your job and therefore you will make life choices dictated by money rather than by desire or interest. Buying things that cannot be afforded limits freedom and oppresses, limits the personality, and involves life choices that do not belong to us. Can I afford what I'm buying? Could the purchase I am making affect my freedom? Asking these questions can truly change your life and save you from situations that may cause difficulties in the future.

2. Do declutter (letting go of the superfluous)

Essentially, not wasting also means saving. Getting rid of unnecessary things is liberating, things that you have and that you don't need to tend to occupy not only space but also the mind. Having too many things also means worrying about your belongings and living in constant stress.

3. Don't spend to impress

If you are not rich it is useless to spend as if you were rich. Don't spend money on others, to impress them, or to get social approval. Living below your means is the only real way to save, but you need to free yourself from the social pressures that may arise.

4. Saving money with minimalism

When it comes to saving with minimalism, we are talking about a lifestyle, an approach to money, and a life that is completely different from the usual. It is not to be seen as renunciation or sacrifice. It is about welcoming a new philosophy that makes you fully enjoy what you have and what you can afford.

5. Eliminate impulse buying

It is enough simply to assume a different mental form and ask yourself; Do I need it? Do I need to drink coffee at the bar or can

I do it at home? If drinking coffee out with my friend makes me feel better, then it's okay. However, there are many purchases made on the spot that does not have a positive effect on our life. Avoiding impulse purchases is a symptom of wisdom and allows, in addition to saving, to have a low impact on the environment and make a gift to future generations.

6. Don't confuse needs with desires

Often the objects you see in advertisements, on billboards, and on social media, clothes worn by influencers or things they own, do nothing but fuel the public's need to own those products. The desire to be like them becomes a primary necessity. Advertising must create a need where it did not exist before. Unfortunately, more people are fascinated by false lifestyles, created specifically to confuse us and push us to buy. The advice that is always valid in these cases, given that in one way or another we are all victims of advertising, is to remain true to yourself. Knowing exactly what you want, what you need is the first step towards a more conscious life and guaranteed savings.

7. Enjoy what you have

Perhaps not many people know that in reality we only use 20%8, of what we own, the rest is confusion, wasted time, and money. There are more times that one passes by desiring things that one does not have than those spent appreciating what one has instead. Now it would be enough to stop and consider this aspect of life, the one that sees us as privileged people compared to others who do not have everything, and suddenly we will be happier.

8. Inquire about

This step towards awareness cannot always be done independently. Sometimes it is necessary to inquire and find support in books that can give advice, and open the mind. For this reason, reading is a valuable aid towards change and there are some interesting books regarding personal finance that can make a difference.

If I think about how much money I have wasted in vain in recent years, I'm scared. I've been decluttering this weekend and I'm still in disbelief at the amount of stuff I have. I have so many summer dresses that I could wear a different piece every day all summer long. Of all those items, I'm sure, I will always wear the same dozen or so things.

9. I certainly learned my lesson

Shopping consciously and in the right proportions helps us to set aside money that can be invested in experiences that improve our lives, or that simply make us grow, make us happy and make us feel good without having to have something material to flaunt

10. Have more budget for experiences

Since I stopped filling gaps by buying random things that I didn't even take out of the bag once I got home, I realized that I had a lot more budget for travel, for courses, for cinema, exhibitions, and theater, for everything that at the end of the month it would make me feel happy with a life well spent.

11. Work less for more

What if I told you that if you want less you can also afford to work less? When I bought my first home, I compromised. I would not have had it in the chicest neighborhood, I would not have had a terrace and I would have been in an apartment building. The house I chose was in an area that I knew well, with many services, and that allowed me to get to the center and to work on foot if I wanted. And while it doesn't have amazing views, it has two balconies, is exposed on both sides, and is much larger than what I could have afforded downtown.

Being essential leads to downsizing the things you need, the minimalist mindset helps you do just that. In not complicating your life.

Having material assets to manage is exhausting. Having a car means taking care of it, investing in insurance, expenses, costs of various kinds that are practically constant. I have a car, I bought it used after they stole the first one I had received as a graduation gift from my parents, a Yaris, and even used I always chose one of the same models. Ditto for a large house that has more space than what we need. One step at a time but you can make a lot of difference.

12. I want to save money!

These are simple tricks with which you will be able to easily save hundreds or thousands of euros every year, according to your economic possibilities. The challenge itself is very simple, for each week of the year (52 in fact) you will set aside its monetary consideration.

Example: week 1 = 1 €

It is very simple, you start with small amounts to create a habit of saving and then gradually continue until you reach the required amount without having to force yourself too much.

13. 30 days

Simple, before buying something, let 30 days pass. If after 30 days you still want to buy that item then buy it, otherwise no. I can guarantee you that with this method you will not buy 90% of the things that go through your head.

14. Why does it work?

Because in this way you will avoid impulse purchases which are ultimately the ones that steal your wallet. By doing this you will only buy items/experiences you are truly interested in and avoid getting caught up in the consumer syndrome.

15. Extra savings

This third method of saving money consists in becoming "engineers" of one's assets, that is, how to manage money and purchases in full lean and Kaizen style.

16. What's it about?

Easy, make a list of all the regular purchases you have to deal with monthly and understand what you can save on

For example, you can change the telephone rate, electricity supplier, limit the consumption of meat and fish within the shopping cart, declutter your things and sell them to get some extras, the possibilities are endless

17. Why does it work?

Well, it works because we often don't realize how much money we spend, especially when we take out subscriptions. Doing a check now and then can only be good for our wallet.

Caffeine - Detox

OK, if you're caffeine-addicted too, this is more of a challenge than a money-saving method.

What's it about?

Well, the title speaks for itself; stop drinking coffee outside the home. Do people spend at least € 5 a week on coffee at the machine? To which you can add just as many for the coffee at the bar if you usually go there (look for useful data).

Why does it work?

As I said above, the figures speak for themselves! Coffee alone saves € 400 a year. If you can't or don't want to give up the coffee you can do as I do prepare a thermos of coffee and take it to the office. Alternatively, you can try to convince your colleagues to buy a pod machine: it will reduce the cost of coffee and will undoubtedly be of better quality. Another alternative is to cut back on your daily coffee if you drink a lot.

Disclaimer: You can use this strategy for any daily habit you have that makes you spend money. From breakfast at the bar to the purchase of paper newspapers, smoking, etc.

Save cent

This is a saving method that my dad taught me when I was little.

He called it the holiday piggy bank.

What's it about?

Whenever you have loose change in your wallet, set it aside. Which and how many depends on you. For example, you could only use the leftovers from the grocery store or the bar, and so on, in the piggy bank. My dad, for example, only uses 1 or 2 euro coins and diligently shoves them into a piggy bank when he has them. The collection for him begins strictly on January 1st and lasts until the day before departure. Based on the content we used to choose the extras of the holiday (such as boat trips, restaurants, etc.)

CHAPTER 13
TEACHING SUSTAINABLE MINIMALISM TO CHILDREN

Why teach children about minimalism?

T
hink of today's children. Think about society today. This juxtaposition always makes me think a lot because today's children will be the men and women of tomorrow. Today the society we live in is very stressful. Just think of how the job search has become more frenetic, precarious, unstable. Suffice it to say that today, at a fashion level and therefore at a commercial level, there are no longer only 4 seasons but more than 50. What if we look at the backpacks, school supplies, and clothing of our children? We see a great social divide and a lot of competition for the climb to success.

Today we give our kids expensive cell phones and then tablets, consoles, PCs, electronic devices of all kinds. Alt a deep breath. Given that the term minimalism has been coined, or at least spread, quite recently, many people still aren't quite sure what lifestyle it is. Everyone thinks that " minimal " stands for "less" or "renunciation".

In reality, the minimalist philosophy was already known in the past only under a different name. Being minimalist, in the most common sense and not in some extreme form of deprivation, means living WELL with the necessary things to be WELL.

Being a minimalist means detaching oneself from material things, that is, not becoming a slave to them. I'll give a practical example: " oh that skirt is beautiful, I have to buy it!" or " no I can't throw away the notes from middle school, sooner or later I will need them or my children will need them!" Serious? Do you think that in 20 years your children will pick up those notes? Even in elementary school (primary school) everything has now changed. It would make no sense to re-propose outdated notes or methods.

A minimalist means feeling free to move forward without carrying the burden of the hundreds of accumulated things. I tried it on my skin. Being minimal means having priorities and not an agenda that is overflowing with commitments, sometimes even those we don't care about or we know we won't participate in, and they are there to make us anxious every time we turn the pages.

Minimal means letting go, breathing, being grateful for what you have, and buying only what is useful or makes us joyful, which makes us feel good. For me, the transition was also to have fewer material objects but to invest more in experiences. And from here I would engage with the combination of minimalism and children.

Why should you teach children about minimalism?

1) Because replacing material objects with concrete experiences improves relationships within the family and adds quality to life. Even simple but meaningful experiences are enough. Going for a walk instead of staying at home, one in one room and one in another, going out for sports together, parents and children in the fresh air, taking trips, going to the pool or an exhibition, or attending a children's workshop. Do these things cost?

I am the first one who could not pull at the end of the month but the dress was there, the dinner, the drink, the ballad, the breakfast outside the house were there, creams and scrubs were there, objects just for the sake of having them there, the exit to the shopping center "no, I don't buy anything" and then mysteriously there was bags and small bags. In short, there were many things but then I lacked the money to do something I liked yoga training was too expensive, the vacation was too expensive, attending an event was expensive, taking a cooking class was expensive. But in the end, what added value to my life? The clothes? Creams? Expensive dinners? or maybe I would have given meaning to my life perhaps with that distant destination, that cooking class, the diploma to become a yoga instructor, the show at the theater, or the conference on nutrition? Sure, everyone has their priorities but what information would you prefer to pass on to your children? Who will be successful people with that designer dress or with the right skills given by a training course? Would you like to teach them that hoarding things makes "rich" because they will have so many things or would you like to teach them to invest their money in something that can improve their quality of life? They are choices, hence, establish your priorities.

I assure you that, since I stopped buying junk and useless things, not only have I had the necessary sum to do all the experiences that I had always put off, in addition, I have also advanced. Mind you that 50 euros here, 20 there, 100 and then another 30 slowly make a sum that you would not imagine if you spent them all together.

2) Teaching children about minimalism promotes concentration.

Children are continually distracted by the nonsense that does not allow them to concentrate. Upstream is the technological discourse. Children should not study with mobile phones, youtube, TV on, and other sources of distraction. This would already be a step forward. Doing it together is not functional unless they are learning English for example through a cartoon, a funny video, etc. We understood each other!

Furthermore, the study plan should also be free of things that can distract our children and teenagers. A free, clean, and spacious surface leave no room for distractions. Try studying with a desk full of stuff! You will get distracted without complicating anything. (Mettere foto scrivania disordinata) The surface must be clean and shiny after use. We, therefore, teach children and teenagers to put things back where they came from.

3) "One in and one out" rule. How many times are children's rooms full of games, books, trinkets, junk, changes and spare parts, stuffed animals, collectibles? If we removed everything from the cupboards, over the shelves, and from the desk, there would be no more room for us. What are we teaching the children? To have, to have, to have!

We buy a new stuffed animal and we keep all the old ones, we buy a new toy and we never throw one away, we constantly buy clothes but then we keep the old ones "just in case .. ". Here we start from the "case never .." that applies to adults but also children. The "case never" almost always translates to "never". Since adults choose what to keep and what to sell for clothes, let's make a good selection considering which things your children wear the most and which ones they haven't worn for months if not years. Donate, give away, give away, sell those you don't use. You are not only doing good to others but also yourself. You are freeing up space, don't think about replacing that space right away.

Ditto with the games, ask your children (don't surprise them, it could be a bad surprise for them) which are the 10 games they love the most among the ones they have in the room. Tell them a good story about a journey and a choice of only 10 games. I assure you that after the first moment of difficulty because they would like to keep them all, they will begin to choose those "of the heart". You can also involve them in the donation. Maybe you could physically take the games to places where your gifts are welcome and show them that they are doing a beautiful action! Do a flea market. It will be funny!

Suggest that they find a place for each game or each book so that they know immediately where it is without turning over the house every time they search for something. Teach them to tidy up! However, having space to store them is already a bonus for tidying up. It will all work out in minutes!

4) Having fewer things, consuming less, throwing, or donating with awareness helps both the environment and those who need it. The toy that one child does not use can make another child happy instead of gathering dust. Fewer games and less material to dispose of is a gift for the environment. The people who follow this philosophy of life are also more attentive and respectful of the environment that surrounds them. For example, children can be taught to use water bottles at school instead of continually using

plastic bottles. You can make workshops and games by recycling. You can brush up on the old games of the past where a piece of paper, a pen, and a bit of memory were enough or games of movement games Teach them to have fun with a few things.

5) Thanks to minimalism, children already learn the value of things from an early age. Gifts must be made at the right time. Today, hearing from my students, some parents give out prizes all the time, sometimes even small ones but still prizes and gifts. Reward if you have been good, reward if you got a good grade, reward if you scored a goal, reward if you helped mum or dad to clear the table. While they are small, the rewards may be cheap but as they grow, they certainly won't be.

They must be taught that some things are good to do without necessarily having material feedback instantly and it is equally important to teach them that a relationship is not based on things. Parents do not love their children only when they give gifts and children are not loved. more only when they receive awards. Children especially need you to dedicate time to them. Ask him maybe your children would prefer to do an activity with you, than not have a new toy.

In summary: why teach children about minimalism?

1. To add quality to life: + experiences and - material objects.

2. To ensure order on the surfaces to be used and therefore mental order.

3. To have fewer distractions and thus promote concentration.

4. To learn how to get rid of one thing before taking another home.

5. To establish a precise location for everything.

6. To respect the environment.

7. To transmit the value of sharing, giving, and generosity

8. To find that you can play and have fun even without expensive toys

If we think about it, children are by nature minimalists. They love to play outdoors, draw, dance, ride a bike, play with the ball; instead, they hate cleaning, tidying up, tidying up.

When my daughter was born, I embraced motherhood with the best of intentions. I invested all my energy to give her everything and more. Love, opportunity, safety, fun, entertainment, dialogue, growth, education, healthy food, quality time, and more.

Also, feelings of guilt and inadequacy, because it seems that you can never do enough. In reality, I don't know where mothers' feelings of guilt come from, no one has ever openly told me "you must always play with your daughter and offer her the most incredible things". Then slowly I learned to get rid of so many thoughts, so many useless purchases, and too many commitments.

I happily embraced a simpler approach

I understood that family happiness lies in shared experiences but that everyone, even children, needs moments of solitude, silence, calm, rest, and empty spaces. We spend too much time protecting our children. We would always like to avoid their pain, disappointment, tension, and problems. But unfortunately, our children too must learn that life is also made up of negative things.

We have to manage our fears, let our children live without undermining their trust and autonomy with our fears. We must try to foster their sense of responsibility and enhance their natural curiosity for the world.

Let them play alone without anxiety

We don't have to entertain our children all the time (we don't even have to do the opposite, abandoning them in front of a screen). Working at home, I have often told my daughter that I cannot play with her. After huge feelings of guilt, I noticed how these moments become an opportunity to create and explore new ideas on my own.

When she says to me "I'm bored", I reply that it is excellent news because boredom brings innovation and creativity. She gets a little annoyed, but then she immerses herself in something wonderful.

Let them create

A space full of useless games leaves no room for creativity and free play. An empty, clean and tidy space is a fertile field for invention and imagination.

Let them rest

Every year in September we would like to enroll our children in all extra-curricular courses, in language and artistic workshops. To these are added birthday parties, family commitments, and many other appointments. After a few weeks, we are already tired and stressed. In reality, we just need rest and empty time. Both us and the children.

Rest must become a priority, not a luxury.

We need to learn to plan a lot less and accept fewer invitations (for the good of all). During the weekend at least one of the two days must be completely free of commitments. Reduce the number of sports afternoons (between 3 to 2), compensating for the need to move with an hour of walking a day (30 minutes to go and 30 to return from school).

Let them solve

Children need a lot of practice to learn how to do things and solve problems. We must give them the opportunity and the time to do it, calmly and with serenity. These rules will help us be happier with our children

Remember:

1. Explain to your children that material possessions won't make them happy, as illustrated by the intact toys in their bedroom closet. Talk about living by one's means and not pursuing a life of debt just to maintain a lifestyle. Helping children think about the purchases they make, ask them, "Is this something you need and will use, or do you just want to spend your check?" Let go of the belief that possessing objects is important. Be generous to others so the children can follow your example.

2. Emphasize the benefits of a minimalist life to your children. Say, "Did you notice that it only took a few minutes to clean your

room? Now you have more time playing outside!" Encourage your children to live with fewer items, but spend your time focusing on what's important like relaxing together, going to the park, or volunteering as a family. Let them experience the positive benefits of minimalist living without the pressure of giving up everything at once.

3. Avoid filling your schedule with appointments and activities. Predict downtime to get creative, relax, or try something new.

4. Start the battle against the stuff by eliminating what your kids no longer use. Slowly remove other unnecessary items with your child, asking, "Are you planning to use this again?" or, "Do you want to donate this to another child who wants to play with him?" Make piles of items throw, recycle and donate with your child's input. Give sturdy, best-quality gifts to your children in the future that will be lasting. Scan your kids' school and art projects to save them without adding clutter piles to your closets.

5. Set the example of a minimalist lifestyle for your children by getting rid of your excess personal possessions first and shopping for unnecessary items.

Suggestions

Do not force children to dispose of toys and personal items before they are ready. Give them time to see the benefit of a minimalist lifestyle.

6. Keeping a thing as a reminder is fine, but keeping everything as a reminder involves reordering, reorganizing, and wasting time that we can avoid. Space also has a cost whether you have bought your

home or are renting it, you should know this well.

7. Do frequent cleaning of what is broken, useless, or that no longer attracts the attention of children (and realize the time spent throwing away things you bought with money earned working).

8. Limit the space where toys can stand. For example, when I notice a toy, a crayon, or a pendant in the same dusty corner of the kitchen or bathroom for more than two days, I throw it away without regret. Nobody ever claims it.

CHAPTER 14
CREATING A MINIMAL WARDROBE
FOR CHILDREN

As children grow up, their clothes can pile up and clutter your home. Superfluous things must be eliminated. To keep the room clean, try to organize the remaining clothing by creating a tidy and accessible space for it. Once you've organized their clothes, you'll need to enforce this minimalist lifestyle by taking care of the clothes you currently own without buying any more.

Steps

Method 1: Organize their old clothes

1. Make a list of how many clothes they need: try to identify the types of clothing your child needs and how many of each one

needs. Calculate how often you do your laundry to decide how many items of clothing you need.

You may decide that they need seven casual shirts, three pairs of pants, one dress suit, two hoodies, one coat, one pair of trainers, and two pairs of pajamas.

Your child's age can also influence this decision. A child may only need three or four different onesie, while a teenager may want a few more outfits.

Don't forget to consider both winter and summer outfits. You may need seven different shirts for summer than for winter. If you live in a rainy area, you need a raincoat and boots. If your child plays sports, consider the equipment, uniforms, etc.

2. Tidy up all their clothes: go through their entire existing wardrobe to see what you currently own. Make piles of clothes to keep, clothes you want to donate, and clothes you are throwing away. Donate any clothes that no longer fit your child. Places like Goodwill and Salvation Army accept donations of clothes. Local churches, thrift shops, or children's shelters may want them to. If clothing is torn or stained, throw it away. This includes the old underwear. Make the pile of "maybe" clothes

3. Keep plenty of underwear and socks: underwear and socks cannot be reused like other items of clothing. Create a stock of just over a week for each. A value between ten and fourteen days may be sufficient.

4. Let your child choose which clothes he likes: your child must have a say in what they will keep and what they won't keep. Don't throw

out clothing items your child likes to wear or wears repeatedly. Have him choose one or two clothes to keep. If your child has trouble expressing an opinion, ask him how each piece of clothing feels. Do they like how it looks? It is comfortable?

5. Choose items to mix and match: since your child's wardrobe will be much smaller, be sure to choose items that can be combined and matched with as many different outfits as possible. This means keeping at least some neutral garments, such as blue jeans, khakis, and white shirts. Although you may still have colorful or patterned items, this choice will help to match them better.

    If your child has a yellow and red striped shirt, he can wear it with khakis or jeans, with a sweater or no sweater, with a long-sleeved shirt under it, or a pullover sweater. If you have a hard time choosing multifunctional clothing, you may choose three or four different colors for your entire wardrobe and miss out on anything that doesn't work with these colors. Older children, especially teenagers, may want to buy more clothes as they start developing their unique style.

Method 2 of 3: Create a tidy space for clothes

1. Choose a space that is easily accessible to children. To help keep things tidy, you should teach your parents how to put their clothes away. While a young child may not understand this right away, you can help by placing their clothes in a place that is easy for your child to reach and handle. Some ways to keep the space accessible include:

    ✓ Installing a low bar for hanging clothes

✓ Place on child-height shelves

✓ Using soft-sided bins

✓ Hang clothes on child-friendly hangers

2. Install shelves in the closet. Create shelves and drawers in the closet. When the door is closed, clothing is hidden from view. You can do this by adding cubbies or shelves in the closet.

   Cubbies with removable containers are easy for children to handle. You can store folded garments inside these. You can even purchase modular cubbies. Modular cubbies are the ones you put together yourself. You just have to buy exactly how many cubes you need or have space for.

3. Hang the warehouse behind the door. The back of the cabinet door can be used for hanging storage. This keeps the room tidy when closed, but provides a great way to individually store things like socks, underwear, scarves, belts, jewelry, and shoes. You can hang a string on the back of the door as a DIY clothesline. Hammer two nails directly across from each other on the back of the door, leaving an inch of space between the nail head and the door. Tie the string to your nails. You can thread scarves and belts over the twine. Command hooks can be attached to the back of a door for jewelry, scarves, belts, or bags. Soft hanging boxes can be used for shoes, underwear, socks, or accessories.

4. Place a laundry basket in their room. To avoid clutter in their bedroom, make sure your child knows where to put their clothes when they are dirty. It can be in a corner, near the bed, or in the closet. Teach them to always put dirty clothing in the bin when

changing. This will prevent the clothes from ruining their room.

Teach your kids by showing them where the basket is. If they are young, give them their dirty clothes and say, "Put them in the trash can." Let them do it themselves to learn the habit. Ask him how each piece of clothing feels. If your child has trouble expressing an opinion, ask him how each piece of clothing feels.

Method 3 of 3: Manage with a smaller wardrobe

1. Maintain a strict laundry schedule. Since your child will have fewer items of clothing, you will make more washing machines. Choose one or two days a week to do laundry and apply this schedule so you never run out of clothes.

2. Buy superior quality clothes that last over time. While cheap or used clothing can be affordable and cheap, they may not last very long, forcing you to have to buy even more clothes for your child. Instead, invest in some solid pieces that will last for a while. Sturdy trousers, such as jeans or khakis, are important. If you live in a cool area, buy a good quality winter coat and boots.

3. Reduce the number of clothes you buy. Try to resist buying more clothes for your kids unless they need them. You only buy new clothes when the old ones no longer fit.

   If your child needs new clothes and a holiday or birthday is approaching, you can ask for clothes as a gift. Send your friends and family a list of clothes your kids need along with their sizes.

4. Teach your child to put away their clothes. Even with a small closet, children's clothes can still clutter a room if they are dumped on the floor or tossed around. Teach your child that their clothes

have a "home" to encourage them to store them in the right place. If the clothes are dirty, they go into the laundry basket. If the clothes are clean, they go "home" to the closet or drawers. Teach him: "Dirty clothes go to the bin; clean clothes go to the shelf."

Reinforce this lesson when your child cleans his room by asking questions. You can say, "What's the place for clean clothes?" and wait for them to respond.

5. Teach children to accessorize instead of buying clothes. Older children, especially teenagers, may want to buy more clothes as they start developing their unique style. Instead, encourage them to use accessories to make any outfit unique. As children can go through many stages of fashion, this will prevent unwanted clothing from forming. Some good accessories include:

✓ Straps

✓ Scarves

✓ Hair

✓ Jewelry store

✓ Gloves

✓ Socks

Enforce this minimalist lifestyle by taking care of the clothes you currently own. Once you've organized their clothes, you'll need to enforce this minimalist lifestyle by taking care of the clothes you currently own without buying any more.

Suggestions

Talking to your child about why you are organizing his clothes can help him understand what it means to live minimally.

Some people require more types of clothing than others. Remember that you should judge the wardrobe based on what your child needs. Involve your child, let them decide what to keep, and teach them to take care of their belongings. Make sure any heavy furniture for small children, such as a chest of drawers or freestanding cabinets, is fixed to the wall to prevent it from falling on the child.

CHAPTER 15

CAPSULE WARDROBE: A NEW
APPROACH TO WARDROBE

T alking about sustainable fashion means opening Pandora's box. It is based on the selection of a few essential items that follow a chromatic logic and are divided by seasonality. This choice facilitates combinations and allows you to make the most of every single piece, without giving the impression of a boring and monotonous wardrobe.

Does the idea of owning a few clothes upset you? Breathe, let's try to reason. Let's think about how many clothes are in our closet and how many we use. Impulsive purchases, crazy and fanciful items are the ones we use the least

The capsule wardrobe is mostly composed of basic garments, well made and therefore durable over time, in natural materials such as the timeless white cotton shirt to be combined with denim with simple lines or a black knee-length skirt. A wardrobe in which each garment can be combined with at least 5 other combinations without clashing. A container of clothes, elegance, and serenity. Thinking about this, it's not that hard to imagine saying goodbye to frills, sequins, lace, and neon colors.

5 TIPS

Quality: few but good items. The change of season is an excellent time to identify the pieces we already have that adapt to our needs and on which to rotate future purchases as well.

Natural fabrics: pleasant to the touch and allowing the skin to transpire, such as cotton, linen, jute, hemp if we prefer vegetable fibers, while silk, wool, cashmere, and leather are of animal origin.

Sober colors: easy to combine

Fit and sensations: choosing pieces that enhance the body according to our characteristics and that make us feel good when we wear them is the key to choosing with awareness and joy how to present ourselves to the world. Because yes, sometimes, the dress makes the monk.

No taxation and a lot of common sense: some capsule wardrobe experts have drawn up lists of "mandatory" items, others have set a maximum number of dresses. Virtue, in our opinion, lies in the middle, so we abandon the schemes and try to live our minimalist being with serenity without trapping ourselves in generalizations and restrictions that could become counterproductive. There are useful alternatives to avoid throwing away clothes that we no longer feel are ours, but still in good condition.

Charities: The simplest option is to donate them to a charity, such as

Humana, or local Facebook exchange groups.

Physical/online sale: if instead you want to try to sell them, you can turn to second-hand shops - in Italy the Mercatino chain - or to web platforms such as Shedd app or Depop.

Exchange: an excellent opportunity to do business is the alternative of the swap party, we organize ourselves among friends and acquaintances to exchange clothes and accessories, renewing the wardrobe at no cost and without waste.

CHAPTER 16
BE MINIMALIST EVERY DAY

✥✥◗◖◗✥✥

here are 7 main areas in which I apply it (and I'm sure that over time I could increase them, even more, to do better and better!) But for the moment they are:

✓ Clothing, shoes, and accessories

✓ Food

✓ Equipment

✓ Furniture, and accessories for the home

✓ Apps and programs for the pc

✓ Leisure and recreational activities

✓ Social media

Clothing, shoes, and accessories

This is perhaps the area in which I can best express my concept of minimalism. About two and a half years ago I decided that I would make a clear change to my way of dressing and to the criteria by which to buy clothing, shoes, and accessories. To tell the truth, I've never been much of a consumer when it comes to clothing. I read some articles that talked about how some of the richest and most influential men in modern history had very simple and minimal wardrobes. Entrepreneurs of the caliber of Steve Jobs, Bill Gates and Mark Zuckerberg, Jack Ma Yun, for example, are among them.

These gentlemen could afford the most expensive clothing on the market, but instead, decide to dress in simple and cheap clothes. Steve Jobs for example, who out of "laziness", if we want to call it that, did not want to occupy his thoughts in the morning in finding the right clothing item for the day and therefore decided that he would buy a sufficient number of the same garment to cover all days of the week and would always wear that.

So he could take the first thing that happened to him, without having to pay attention to the right color combinations or other "rules" imposed by the fashion of the moment.

So I decided to buy a bunch of clothes;

- ✓ 1 pair of shoes
- ✓ 3 pairs of jeans
- ✓ 9 short sleeve shirts
- ✓ 4 long sleeve shirts
- ✓ 3 sweaters

For a total of 19 items. From then on, that was going to be my wardrobe. I did not purchase clothing until the following month of May when I replaced the 9 short-sleeved shirts (black) with as many but in pastel colors, more suitable for fighting the heat of the upcoming summer days.

This allowed me not to spend my time looking for new clothing items to wear, neither online nor around the shops. In addition to saving a lot of money. In the following years, it was enough for me to replace the garments that have worn out over time with as many of the same type \ model.

Food

I like food, I like good food and I like to try new dishes and pairings. I like to share cooking too. What I don't like is wasting food and having the fridge and pantry full of things that I can't consume within a certain time. It has happened to me in the past (who has never?) to buy more food than I could consume before it became unusable (fruit and vegetables for example) and throw them in the trash.

It is a speech that is also worth making for water, but maybe I will make a separate speech about this later on. I try to do is the plan as much as possible what the menu will be for the whole week (with a slight margin of deviation and modification "on the run") so that I can only buy the food that I am sure to consume.

To save money, you don't have to buy junk food but by the right amount. How many times do we buy products on offer which then expire?

Work equipment

It's a moment to find yourself submerged by components that in some cases we will never use. I too had my semi-compulsive buying period in which I was constantly looking for the new. I apply the Pareto principle or the 80 \ 20 law according to which in most cases 80% of an effect is due to 20% of possible causes.

I think this principle is adaptable to any profession that involves owning the equipment. Let's say a blacksmith who owns three welding machines but who then always uses the same one, for example, or who owns five angle grinders but then always finds himself using the same two, let's take a carpenter who owns four circular saws "just in case" but then always use the same cutting table because it is the most functional one. The examples could be many others and on more or less every working area. Apps for mobile phones and tablets and computer programs in the "equipment" category, then the speech could be adapted to practically every profession. "Just in case" are those objects that we keep because they could come in handy in a distant, hypothetical, sometimes non-existent future as TheMinimalists suggest. We don't need these items.

Furniture, furnishings, and accessories for the home

The question is, how do I furnish the house? I feel that I am a little bit favored, perhaps compared to the average, because I don't particularly like furnishing objects, furnishings, and everything that orbits the world of "furniture". I like beautiful, linear, and simple objects and I especially like that they are few, that everyone has their own space and their location within the furniture. This allows me not to accumulate too many and rather try to have as little as possible to maintain linearity and cleanliness in the rooms that belong to me.

Mobile app

Cell phones once didn't have apps. Then came the apps so many apps, more and more apps for everything. They were beautiful, they were colorful, you could finally do with the phone all those things that until then you had been forced to do on the computer, such as managing spreadsheets and pivot tables with Excel, taking freehand notes, writing complex documents with Word, cropping images with photoshop, and many beautiful and very fun other activities, until you realized that doing it on the phone was inconvenient, slow and inaccurate and you went back to doing it as usual on the PC.

Anyway, my dashboard started filling up with apps (like I think anyone over 12's). The apps that I have never, ever, ever used are the ones for making music. I installed them all.

Apps and programs for the pc

Analogous but much more complicated speech for apps and programs for the PC. For these I admit, I still have a lot of work to do and I can improve. I have a lot of software installed, most of which I use for work but I have to admit that I have a lot that I hardly ever use.

If the battery is a tool of virtually infinite size, plugins take this concept, amplify it to the nth power + 1 and shoot it full force like a huge laser beam in the infinite cosmos. Only the sky is the limit (and the space on your hard drives)

Leisure and playful activities

In this section, I enclose all the activities such as cinema, theater, concerts, museums, and other various events. Let's say a little about everything that can be enclosed in the category "cultural activities".

I like to attend in general all the events that I think can convey emotions to me and increase my soul in one way or another. Ok, but how do I know if a business will give me something back if I don't start it first? I don't know.

My being "minimalist" here too lies in the fact that I always choose very carefully which event to attend based on what I believe I will draw from it on an emotional level but without being influenced by fashions or simply by the fact that: "It's Saturday night and therefore we go dancing "or" everyone goes to the So-and-so concert, so I have to go too ",

What I try to do more generally is to let myself be advised more by my instincts than by external inputs, especially if they come from social media.

Social media

Facebook, Twitter, Instagram, Foursquare, Snapchat, Clubhouse, TikTok, etc. although I have an account on each of them, I try to keep away from them as much as possible and not get sucked into the black hole of infinite scrolling. I dedicate a small part of my daily time to "update" on what happens through social networks, but:

I take any news coming from these media as "to be verified"; never come across infinite flames to assert my opinion, I find it a useless waste of time; publish very little, I only do it when I have something to say and I don't expect any likes. This allows me to always remain quite detached from any mood the network wants to pass me at that moment and to close the social network instantly to move on to other things.

Another thing I often do is to rotate the use of social networks, so if I have used Facebook today, tomorrow I will probably not open it but instead, I will use Instagram, Twitter, or maybe neither. There are whole days in which I happen not to open any social network. The only media I really can't live without is YouTube, which though:

- it cannot be defined as a social network
- I use it basically to learn new things

However, digital minimalism is a much more complex topic than that and I think I'll write more about it in a future article. Have you ever eaten on a table cluttered with other things? Not to resist during the sales and to buy things that you don't need? Has it ever happened to you to buy that shirt or leggings that the influencer had sponsored, but then it didn't look so good on you and you got frustrated? How did it go? Have you found yourself in any of these questions? Minimalism for me means, adding rather than removing, that is, having fewer things around, fewer clothes in the wardrobe, less mess in the head, to have more energy, more creativity, and more clarity. LESS IS MORE or LESS is MORE

Principle Of Improvement By Subtraction Applied To Life

The expression used by a great master of architecture Ludwig Mies Van Der Rohe in the context of a minimalist style to be reached through A WORK OF SUBTRACTION in a CREATIVE PROCESS of continuous SEARCH FOR SIMPLICITY to ADD QUALITY " Less is more "is that more than comes from less.

Now we transpose it from architecture to mind and body and also to lifestyle. Yes, I like to think of minimalism with a holistic approach. Let's see in practice how to apply it and you will also find my approach

Wardrobe: fewer clothes, more decisions, more creativity in creating outfits If you buy consciously, that is, you buy what you need and take interchangeable and combinable garments, you will actually have fewer clothes in the closet, but more creativity and also less energy expenditure. For example, I buy things that make me feel at ease, without letting myself be influenced by the dictates of fashion.

By doing this, I also reduce stress, yes, I don't waste time choosing what to wear or trying on clothes that I have in the closet, but that half of the dress which I no longer used, but I keep them there in the hope of putting them back on. Body changes and also our tastes, I prefer to immediately select everything and what I did not wear the previous year or give it to a

124

friend or give it or sell it at every wardrobe change.

You minimize the decision fatigue, and this mode is useful not only for clothing but applies to all other sectors, such as the refrigerator for example or the pantry or the office

Desk: If you work from home or in the office, the less you see on the table, the greater your concentration (put photos of the messy desk) When I started to approach this system, I started looking at images of desks on Pinterest and I came across those cool photos of desks with only a pc, a notebook and a pen, at most a map, there I was dazzled, it was what I needed. I discovered then that the lean desk, free and clean, would become my mood and so it is, today I don't dream of starting to work or write in the casino, the chaos outside reflects the chaos inside

But sometimes, in moments of creativity, when I have to design courses or lessons, then I scatter everything around, but it's only because that way I find the ideas, but immediately after everything returns to its place and my rule is this: " one-touch "that is, I touch and put it back.

As I do?

I no longer buy a thousand notebooks and then not use them, today I choose my notebooks with care, because they are both my fundamental work tools, but also "clear heads", and I buy them when I no longer have anything to write on. It applies to pens, I buy them all the time, but I buy the ones I know I will use, and even in this case I choose them consciously In this way, there is an incredible saving and you buy things of higher quality!

Minimalism and Mind

Now let's talk about two processes that cause stress and how a more minimalist approach can help improve the situation and reduce anxiety.

1. **Over-thinking:** having redundant thoughts, brooding, being indecisive, causes psycho-physical stress and energy consumption and often leads nowhere, undecided between thinking and doing. When you feel your mind so cluttered and the thoughts that run speak to yourself saying "Stop".

   Take a deep, diaphragmatic breath, that is, place a hand on your abdomen, listen to the breath grow in your belly, then return to your body. Stay with your mind in the here and now and take back control.

   As I do?

   I write a list of all the things I have in mind (the famous "empty head" notebook I mentioned earlier) "If you can't do it right away, WRITE IT" Then I evaluate the thoughts that I have written, projects, fears, things that I am putting off and I put myself in action mode, instead of thinking I do. So you clear your mind and also become incredibly more productive. Constantly thinking about something we want to do, and then we don't do, makes us waste days and hours. Fewer thoughts, more action

2. **Multitasking:** doing many things together you waste energy and time. Yes, so at SINGLE TASKING fewer things, but done well!

Minimalism and Body

Having a MINDFUL approach, that is aware, being present in what you do, inhabiting the body. LITTLE AND OFTEN Even strictly physical work for me uses the same principle, little by little is better than time and time again, I prefer to create my training plans starting from the easy, little

126

by little, 15 minutes of physical activity daily, rather than 2 hours twice a week.

These are also the principles of Laizen, the Japanese mechanism of progressive improvement, I accustom the body to train and move gradually and pleasantly.

What do I do?

While I walk, I just walk, while I train, I train and I stay in my body, if the thoughts arrive, and they do arrive, then I move them for a moment in a corner of the mind. With practice it becomes inevitable, you never go back because the benefit is tangible

Purchases To Improve, Compensate, Cover Minimalism, and Acceptance

We buy new clothes especially when we don't feel good about ourselves;

1. **Unintentional Purchases**

   The non-acceptance of the body leads to seeking elements of compensation and, remaining on the subject of material things, it will be clothes, accessories, shoes, an accumulation of things that compensate you at that moment, but then, the situation returns.

   Then there is the strong media stimulus, which invites you to buy clothes and make-up, dissociating yourself more and more from your body and inviting you, indirectly, to want to resemble those aesthetic models proposed. This generates frustration, insecurity and feeds the continual search for other things to try to compare you

   Thus, it happens that the attention is completely outside of you, it is shifted to material resources, to build a reality on the surface and each offer is not limited only to the object itself, but to the construction of your being, of an identity. They take advantage of your desire to change.

What do I do?

I stop to recognize my primary resources and when I want to buy I ask myself two questions

- "Do I need this purchase? "

- "What value does it add to me?"

You have to learn to choose what you want.

2. Unintentional Physical Activity

Over-training! Overtraining to get to a result, to get perfection, to get to a very specific aesthetic canon, to no longer love the body. You should train intentionally, to progressively improve, to feel flexible, strong, and healthy. Minimalism here is understood as love for the body, respect, and care, dosing fatigue, effort, returning to inhabit the body, and recognizing that the body does wonderful things that we realize when we miss them.

Do not look for a thousand Christian-smashing workouts, accumulating saved videos, other people's files, work on yourself by dosing your energies with a view to progressive improvement for a healthy body and not to have everything immediately, the body is like nature, it has his times. We have to listen to our bodies.

All these actions of subtraction will lead to a greater benefit in your body;

- To energy and economic saving.

- Less stress.

- Less anxiety and more energy.

- Start by becoming aware of this less phrase is more - less is more and start evaluating the waste in your life

- Start with a specific area.

- Start by buying a notebook, or see if you already have one at home, and write down everything you would like to change/modify/replace.

- I have a "wish list" where I mark the things I like / need/want and as I assign them to me, that is often when I set myself a goal, I give myself a gift.

- As for your body, write down the things you want to change and work on, overthinking we have seen how expensive it is and leads nowhere, don't tell you all the time I should lose weight or exercise, write it down now and plan it.

CHAPTER 17

MINIMALISM SKINCARE

The minimalist approach finally comes to skincare. The Skin is born Minimalism, or Skinimalism, to take care of your skin in a few targeted steps. How many times have we found ourselves making room in our wardrobes, getting rid of clothes that we don't wear, or that "don't give us joy" as Marie Kondo teaches?

What happens when this attitude applies to skincare?

Lately, in the beauty community, we are starting to talk about skins minimalism, or minimalism, a term that describes an essential approach to the skincare routine. What exactly does it consist of?

Skin minimalism, as the word itself suggests, is based on minimalism; the skin has few needs that can be largely satisfied with the use of a few effective products, included in a fast and minimal routine.

What makes this approach successful is undoubtedly the ease with which it adapts to the demanding lifestyle of many of us, finally offering us an alternative to the complicated and time-consuming routines that involve the use of many products, often similar to each other. they. But skin minimalism or minimalism is much more than this; it means a more edited and intelligent routine, made up of a few essential products and above all aimed at achieving a result.

But the skin does minimalism work? Can a minimalist

routine work on the skin?

Here is our answer: absolutely yes, as long as you choose the right products. Minimalist skincare does not simply mean using a few products randomly chosen from the shelves of a perfumery. It means taking the time to listen to your skin, understand what it needs, and then turn to targeted products, capable of enhancing its natural beauty.

Choosing beauty minimalism above all means giving up layering and complex passages. An advantage also for the skin: the wrong combination of ingredients could trigger irritation and allergic reactions, making the beauty routine very ineffective. The wrong combination of exfoliating acids, for example, could make the skin hypersensitive, and excessive layering weighs it down, making skincare much less pleasant. The less approach is more to skincare, then, is perfect for giving the skin everything it needs, observing which ingredients are beneficial. Give up some cosmetics or choose 2-in-1 formulations.

The Real Needs Of The Skin

Cleansing, exfoliation, hydration, and protection. The skin doesn't need anything else to be healthy. And, precisely for this reason, minimalist skincare can only be based on four fundamental steps. A very important step is cleansing, to be performed morning and evening, to eliminate excess sebum, pollution, and dirt from the skin, allowing subsequent treatments to penetrate more deeply.

Equally essential, hydration allows the skin to remain young and vital, luminous. In both cases, customization cannot be missing: every skin type needs specific ingredients and textures.

The skin also needs to be renewed through exfoliation. Eliminating dead cells through a scrub, a peeling, or, simply, an exfoliating tonic has, in fact, an illuminating effect and allows better oxygenation of the tissues. The last step of minimalist skincare can only be protection; the SPF is the best anti-aging in existence and allows you to keep the skin healthy.

The Must-Have Products In Skincare

The minimalist approach to skincare manifests itself in the form of different beauty trends, above all Skinimalism. A vision of skincare that is based on reducing the number of cosmetics in the beauty routine. In the center? The multitasking formulations.

A very different approach from that of Skincare, which re-evaluates what the skin needs by literally skipping a few steps. A trend that comes from Korea and that immediately involved millennials, eager to reduce waste generated by the cosmetics industry. Minimalist skincare by definition, whose cornerstones are cleansing and hydration. At the heart of Skincare, there is the health of the hydrolipidic film, capable of regulating skin hydration and defending the skin from free radicals. The key, in both cases, is the ingredients. The skin can never lack Vitamin A, E, and C, as well as a series of antioxidant substances.

CHAPTER 18
MAKE-UP DECLUTTERING

What is decluttering make-up for? How to choose what to keep and what to throw?

Decluttering make-up is nothing more than the reordering of our make-up and the workstation dedicated to them. The usefulness of decluttering make-up is easy to say: we get rid of products that we no longer use or have expired, and make room for new tricks!

In general, having a well-organized make-up station is essential because it allows us to achieve many different looks, using products that we thought we no longer had or that remained hidden "under the heap". There are some criteria of choice, such as reading the cosmetic PAO or observing them understand if they are still usable or could give us adverse reactions to the skin.

There comes a time when decluttering make-up becomes a necessity. If the make-up is overflowing and we realize that we don't use everything we have, well, it's time to tidy up! The philosophy of decluttering tricks is very useful, girls because by getting rid of unused objects we will also make order in our mind, freeing up space for our creativity and why not some new product that we are sure we will use. To reorganize the make-up and make-up station we have to ask ourselves some very useful questions, such as "is it expired?", Or "do I use it?".

Why do decluttering make-up? What is it for reorganizing the tricks?

Girls, as we said, reorganizing make-up with decluttering is a necessary operation, to be done 2/3 times a year. First of all, it helps us to identify, and therefore throw away, all the expired make-up that could be non-performing or even harmful to our skin.

To understand if a product is to be thrown away, our advice is to attach special labels on the bottles bearing the opening date: in this way, then reading the PAO on the back, to immediately understand if that given product is "safe" or must Leave. The PAO reports the life of the product from its opening: indicating that,

Otherwise, another way to understand whether to keep or let go of a product is to observe it, smell it, and spread it; regardless of the PAO, if a cosmetic has been stored poorly it may have expired prematurely.

The usefulness of make-up decluttering is therefore linked to the exclusive use of "good" products, which have not gone bad and with good performance.

Furthermore, organizing the tricks with decluttering allows us to understand if we have actually "exaggerated" with the make-up shopping, buying too many cosmetics that we will not even have time to use before their expiration.

How To Set The Decluttering Make-Up: What To Have Available To Start The Make-Up Make-Up

To begin with, we advise you to use a room or an area of the house for tidying up cosmetics: better to avoid staying in the bathroom, which normally has smaller spaces and could make us a little too messy!

The ideal is to get an old blanket to place on the ground, on which to subsequently spread all the "content" of our make-up station, dividing the products according to the category they belong to (for example eye shadows, mascara, blush, lipsticks and so on).

Better to have on hand also:

- A garbage bag, for expired and irrecoverable cosmetics

- Some transparent plastic boxes, for the tricks we decide to give away

- Beauty case for the ones we choose to keep.

In addition to products that have expired or gone bad, how do you decide who goes and who stays?

In the meantime, let's make a list of the indispensable products. An example? For the make-up base we might need:

- ✓ One - two foundations (based on texture, for example, a liquid and a compact powder)

- ✓ A concealer for dark circles and one for pimples
- ✓ A couple of blushes
- ✓ Earth or bronzer
- ✓ Face powder
- ✓ Illuminating

For the eyes always useful:

- ✓ A mascara
- ✓ An eyeliner
- ✓ Some colored and black kajal pencil
- ✓ Two-three eye shadow palettes in shades that we use: nude or more vibrant colors

Don't forget the lips: here the list would be useless because everyone likes playing with colors! So to do the decluttering lipsticks we think about what suits us best (if you want to learn more we have a blog post that talks about how to choose the red lipstick based on the color scheme) and the finishes that we need most. For example, if we spend a lot of time at home we might adore creamy ones, if we often wear the mask we will tend to prefer lip colors or very long-lasting and opaque colors.

In Addition To The Essentials, We Also Keep Extraordinary Products For More Particular Looks

Once you have identified the must-have products from our makeup collection, it's time to decide what to throw away and what to give; in the latter case, be careful because not all cosmetics are suitable for donation.

For example, absolutely no mascara or eyeliner. The rest can be disinfected with pure alcohol.

Conclude The Decluttering: In Order Not To Create Disorder, We Use Organizer And We Have Everything With Criteria

At the end of the make-up decluttering moment to buy less and better our cosmetics, girls! The world of makeup is wonderful, but waste is always a shame, from many points of view. So let's try to buy only what we are safe to use. Returning to the topic, how to make the decluttering of our cheat collection effective? The answer is to try to organize them better so that we have at hand what we use on a daily or at least weekly basis.

The make-up organizers are very useful, to be placed on our make-up station or in the bathroom on the various shelves. An idea could also be to prepare a box containing our TOP of the period (for example foundation, concealer, and mascara) to have everything at hand in the same place.

CHAPTER 19
APPLY MINIMALISM TO THE KITCHEN

⊱✦⊰

Many know about minimalism applied to art and furniture, but there is also a culinary one that also helps not to waste. Food is not entertainment. Food is fuel, pure and simple. This doesn't mean I don't like the food I enjoy it immensely.

There is a frequent image that describes minimalism, it is an empty room with white walls and a chair. "I have a bed, a chair, and a radio. I'm the one who decides if something adds value to my life", he says Joshua Fields Millburn from inside his large American house, now half-empty. With Ryan Nicodemus, he created The Minimalists, released two documentaries on Netflix, a long series of podcasts, a blog, and several books. In their bio, the two claim to have helped "more than 20 million people live a more meaningful life" with fewer things.

Minimalism is not born with them but instead develops in art, more specifically in the 60s, in America which reacts to Pop-Art and proposes a new style in which simple and essential lines, elementary designs, and geometric modules predominate. Hence the minimalist approach could broaden the gaze to also invest in music and literature and bounce back to our 20s in the form of existential minimalism. No longer just art but a lifestyle that adapts and reacts to the drifts of the 2000s consumerism, in particular, the compulsive possession of goods, the obsession with money and career, waste.

The aim is not to waste

Cooking is one of my greatest loves. Not always, I wasn't one of those genius little girls who could cook a Wellington fillet at eight. Well, let's say that before getting engaged I never touched a pan, but from then on light came on and something inside me glimpsed the immense and spectacular world of cooking. Without boring you with my culinary journey, taking the path of minimalism meant putting my concept of cooking and my style in the kitchen back in place.

Cooking is in itself a minimalist art

Avoid buying ready-made, processed, and processed products, avoid drowning among the packages and parcels in the pantry, work the raw material from its essence (flour, butter, sugar, eggs), it has a very strong minimalist component. The home cooking, that of the grandmother, frugal, made of recovery, of "nothing is thrown away" is a real philosophy of life and those who embrace it are already embracing minimalism.

1. Avoid processed food, go back to basics and cook real food with

141

your own hands right from the basic preparations. Learning to cook basic preparations, for example, has produced in me an extra awareness of how often you buy completely useless stuff, which does not help either in time or even less in health. I have often found that a basic dough takes a few minutes and simple steps, so in the end I find myself not having to buy ready-made food anymore, I don't have to stock up just because I might need it and I enjoy real, healthy food, made with ingredients I know and that I can also keep in right quantities for future occurrences when I don't have time

2. You have to buy what is necessary. Transforming and storing your food is a healthy habit that serves not to waste abundance, not to waste scraps, and to have supplies of real food in exchange for prepackaged equivalents. However, this must keep us far, indeed very far from accumulation. The handouts for "shopping crazies" are the anti-minimalism par excellence, the result of the compulsive accumulation of large-scale retail objects that often do not even serve us.

3. Minimalism in the kitchen is to transform and work your food to preserve it without wasting it. As above, transforming extra food, scraps, or leftovers and carefully storing a little stock is practically an art (for example, I'm not as good as my grandmother at making jars, but that's it). Knowing exactly what has been set aside, knowing that nothing has been wasted of what has been hard-earned, knowing that if necessary we will have something to draw on, is relaxing for the mind, it is order and security in one's means.

4. Minimalism in the kitchen is aiming for zero waste or, more

generally, not wasting.

5. Minimalism in the kitchen means abandoning large-scale distribution as much as possible and returning to consciously choosing one's food.

    I still set foot at the discount store, sometimes, to buy raw materials that I have no way to get, otherwise, I buy everything elsewhere, in theory, it should be bought; meat from the butcher, fish from fisherman, fruit, and vegetables from the farmer. It is not a snobbish choice, on the contrary, I know what to buy and how it is produced.

6. Follow the cycle of nature, eat in season and preferably local food. The mental order of minimalism also benefits from following the cycle of nature. Indeed, often the detachment of our ego that causes anxiety and frustration and drags us into the abyss is caused precisely by the fact that according to modern society it always seems that we live at the same time.

    Air conditioning all year round, all food always available all year round, work cycles with the same peaks all year round, prevent us from "Being", from perceiving our presence here and now and calming our mind. The confusion of not feeling present brings anxiety, stress, the desire to fill our gaps with purchases, that perennial feeling of dissatisfaction that minimalism has always tried to extinguish.

    Feeling the season through food serves to feel more present and more serene. Then I also consume food that comes from abroad but I don't make it my main source of livelihood; let's say that I don't live on avocado (as fashion dictates) and I don't eat red peppers in December (except the ones that I have saved on purpose to enrich the winter cuisine from time to time). So here too nothing snobbish, we just try to be more aware of where we live and what season it is, moreover, always speaking in terms of minimal, I already go out knowing which fruit or vegetables I want to buy or having a limited choice, and it is infinitely relaxing for the mind not having to choose one among ten thousand vegetables but only one among those offered by the season.

7. Take care with food so as not to get messed up afterward between medicines, doctors, and pharmacies. A true, healthy cuisine, rich in variety, which follows the seasons and which thrives on the commitment of cooking food for oneself and the pantry with one's own hands, leads to an incredible return to health. Whenever I have a problem with those banalotti, let's say for which one would use over-the-counter drugs and at most the google consultation, I study the way to better balance my kitchen and my minimal home pharmacy always thanks.

8. Surround yourself with what you need, only use tools and accessories in which to invest your money well.

I am a huge fan of technological tools, I admit. However, I strongly believe in surrounding ourselves only with useful things that truly improve our lives. When I went to live together officially, in my first home, I found myself with packs and packs of kitchen items of very little use until the time came for the decluttering of drawers and cabinets, and there I found you; mashers, cut them, cook eggs, one hundred pans one hundred other pans so huge they don't even get the heat on the fire, pans that were not suitable for induction (which I had), milk pans (which I do not drink), two herbal teas, three coffee machines (including this 1 and 12), a yoghurt machine, an electric crepe maker and twenty ceramic cheese knives.

Now, you will understand the discomfort of discovering that, for example, I didn't even have a can opener. That said, the decision was unanimous:

away (usually at the flea market) everything that has no real use or that can be replaced sensibly. So things like the yoghurt machine replaced with a multi-purpose container and a warm place in the house, the bread machine replaced with my hands and the traditional oven, the garlic press replaced with nothing ... nobody needs one. On the other hand, having made a lot of space, and left only one pan for each type and size that is used at home, here is the place to put a lot of really useful things that we didn't buy because we already had the crammed cabinets: planetary mixer, multifunction robot, programmable pressure cooker, slow cooker, vacuum machine, meat, and sausage grinder, etc. I have a lot of kitchen items, really, but all are used constantly, kept well, and the fantastic dishes that allow me to cook pay off every single euro spent.

Study, search, learn, experiment without losing your mind

Open your mind, never stop studying new foods, cultures, processing and conservation methods, techniques. Try recipes, create your style, and most of all, make room in your head and in your home for all the amazing things to come.

CHAPTER 20
THE THOUGHT OF FUMIO SASAKI

Who is Fumio Sasaki ?

Fumio Sasaki is the author of the book "Make Room in Your Life." Fumio Sasaki is Japanese, as the name suggests. Fumio is a young man under 40 who works in the publishing world. Today we are talking about him and above all about his choice to live in the most absolute minimalism. Her lifestyle was documented and described in the book *Make Room for Your Life*. In this book, he explains his motivation and the advantages that came from this extreme choice in a hyper-consumerist world.

In his small studio of just 35 square meters, we find very few objects. In all, she can satisfy her needs with just 20 items, as you'll find out in the book. All objects that Fumio needs, are counter-current choice, minimalist choice, and courageous choice.

For Asian culture, living in simplicity is good and right. For example, for the Japanese, freeing themselves from uselessness leads to rediscovering the meaning of things.

If we then add the Zen Buddhist influence and their teachings we can reap incredible benefits in this regard. In this case, we invite you to delve into Zen Buddhism and the benefits it will bring to your wallet.

We want to give a little introduction. The first teaching of Zen Buddhism leads us to simplify and remove useless objects. Removing objects means reducing our emotional attachment to those objects. And emotional attachment leads us to suffer in the event of a lack of that good. Reducing attachment leads to liberation and takes us away from suffering. Owning fewer items will lead to a reduction in suffering. Just wellness? No, a minimal life improves the lives of those who want it. A minimal life brings big advantages:

- Organization: You will have a better-organized home.

- Well-being: by living in an orderly house you will acquire a feeling of well-being.

- Savings: the minimal style imposes a strict choice on purchases, so you will save a lot.

Because this book is for you

In this case, we are talking about ten euros well invested. The expense is definitely worth the game. In this world made only of objects, where we find pleasure only in material things, a book like this is a panacea for our well-being and to drastically improve the quality of our life.

We associate pleasure with the value of the object possessed. We want more and more and our lives pile up with useless objects and loaded with sentimental value. Learning to eliminate, to cancel, and above all not to buy, can make a huge difference. If you are still undecided, take it now and learn to rediscover the value of small things and their benefits.

I too was a compulsive hoarder. In my native home, I found the whiskers of my first cat preserved. I kept everything for fear of forgetting. I kept everything in order not to detach myself from the affections. To not have to say goodbye. Thanks to Fumio Sasaki I learned that "in a house where there are few things, there can be happy".

Most of the items we have are not important to us. And to be able to take possession of those unnecessary items we employ a great deal of work and money. This same reasoning is present in Andrea Bizzocchi 's book "Vivere senza lavoro".

When you have too many things, you can't keep up with each of them; then with all that clutter it becomes difficult to clean and the space in which you live is always a little dirty and unkempt: this helps to undermine self-confidence and the desire to do.

The book lists 55 rules for getting rid of things, plus another 15 for eliminating even more things. "What is important, however, remains with us". Some say that if you eliminate things you also give up your past, but I don't believe in such an exaggeration. The key memories of our life naturally remain etched in us.

I'd rather spend my money on an experience than on objects. Experiences raise the quality of life and cannot be compared with other people's experiences because they are unique. Read it if you want to lighten your life.

CHAPTER 21

CONCLUSIONS

❧❧✦❀✦❧❧

I t is enough to open a newspaper or watch a news program to see that the world is collapsing, waste is submerging us and the relocation of companies creates numerous abuses and victims. When I heard the word "minimalism" I was reminded of marble, white color, an empty house, and a deep green indoor plant. A stock image of some service that sells photos on the internet.

We are led to associate several concepts with this word:

The minimalism of rich white men (Americans): six-zero bank balance, house finished in marble, Macbook, iPhone, and refined furniture.

Nomadic and wildlife: unlike the first case, here we are reminded of the 50-liter backpack that contains everything you own, vans, trips to the Pacific. If you are not a rich American or a nomad you are screwed. But this is not the case. There are no established rules and anyone can start this path rich, poor, white, black, static, and dynamic. It can be applied to everyday life, to adventurous life, to any type of existence. So forget everything and start over with the fundamental questions.

What is minimalism?

A current, a lifestyle. Those who follow him at first eliminate everything they own and believe is in excess and a second moment avoids falling back into the error of possessing things in excess.

Is the aim to have as few items as possible?

The aim is to have only really useful items or what you want to have.

Are we only talking about material things?

No! Objects represent one of the first steps. What we decide to buy, however, speaks volumes about the people we are, and starting with eliminating what we possess of material triggers a large number of more intimate and abstract reflections that will affect the rest of life as well.

What are the areas in which minimalism can be applied?

Whole life and Anything.

Does being minimalist means having to think a lot?

Yes, think and reflect. Not only that, but it also implies learning to know each other thoroughly and changing one's vision. Why should I follow him?

The fewer the worries, the better life gets. The fewer things you have to do, the more time you can use for what you love. The benefits it brings are undeniable and experienced by all those who voluntarily decide to start this path (the same cannot be said for those who are forced and consequently do not have the right mental predisposition). It is a way to grow, to question oneself, and to get to know each other deeply. To make room to fill with what truly makes life worth living.

How to become a minimalist?

As I said earlier, there is no magic formula or handbook to be meticulously followed. There can only be advised to get started and to continue. Mind you, however, they are just tips that are suggestions that you can customize, increase or modify to your liking.

- Start by writing a list of the things you feel are yours.

- Do a first declutter of the house and everything you own.

- Starting with objects is certainly the wisest choice.

Make a first complete declutter of your home. Dividing it by categories and not by rooms is more convenient because it allows you not to eliminate the same things placed in different environments but to do everything at once, so you don't have to think about it again.

You can proceed like this, starting from things you love least to go gradually towards objects that are usually more symbolic and full of meaning:

- Utensils and kitchen materials (sets of dishes, tablecloths, and so on)

- Small appliances and technology + accessories (e.g. phone covers, cables you don't know what they connect to)

- Household linen (sheets, towels, blankets, etc)

- Personal hygiene products, toiletries, and makeup

- Medicines

- Stationery and the like

- Paperwork (bills, payments, notices)

- Various things (drawers where everything ends, closets)

- Ornaments and souvenirs

- Clothes, shoes, and accessories

- Collectables (DVDs, CDs, video games, and the like) and books

- Do not rush

- Use what you have until its end comes

Consume what you love to the fullest. Do not surround yourself with useless things, and if you have them, give them up by throwing them away or giving them away / selling them (if they are in good condition).

Use the things you love. If you can fix what is not working properly

My PC, about a year ago, looked dead. It did not turn on and when, miraculously, it did, the keys did not work properly. I could have replaced it but I decided to fix it. It has been fixed and the keyboard has been changed. After a year I am writing again thanks to him. Until they tell me there is nothing more to do, I will continue to keep it.

- Create a welcoming environment

- Make your home as comfortable as possible

- Throw away the superfluous and take advantage of the spaces. Keep it tidy

- Clean up inside your car

Think about whether you can also do without a car using public services. Think about how many problems and hassles you would save yourself. If you can't give up the machine, it eliminates all the dirt that accumulates inside it. Finished water bottles (maybe use a water bottle), handkerchiefs, bubble gum packets, and more. Even the car is an environment that must convey serenity.

Cut out unnecessary and harmful activities

Social

When I think of malicious activities, social media immediately comes to mind. I am referring in particular to unnecessary comments, discussions, and articles. Time spent reading free spite and hate. This is the first activity that I would advise you to cut and reduce.

The rubbish tv

The same rule applies to social networks. TV has reached an awkward level when it comes to content. Enjoyable programs can be counted on the fingers of one hand. The same goes for streaming platforms, not everything is to be thrown away but it would at least be reduced. Consuming content one after another, betting on episodes, does not enrich us in any way. Don't look so much to do.

Unwanted communications

Newsletters, hammer advertising, App notifications, Whatsapp groups where 150 useless messages are equivalent to useful information. Trash everything, unsubscribe and leave.

The vices

Smoke, scratch cards, machines, compulsive eating. These activities take a lot of time and money away from us, never leading to anything good. When they become a real problem we have to turn to a specialist and, with a little effort, we will see our lives improve.

Events you don't want to attend

Don't you feel like having an aperitif with Tizio because you planned to read that beautiful book waiting for you on the table? Decline the offer without guilt. We don't always want to do what others propose. Better not to go than to do it reluctantly,

Use the time for what you enjoy doing

- Avoid doing things that don't bring any value

- Try to think about what could happen if you spent most of your free time chasing that dream you have in your drawer, or studying to improve in a discipline you like. Not with eagerness and anxiety, but with pleasure and profit.

- Think of your efforts all went in a certain direction how many improvements and milestones you could achieve. You can do it, just eliminate all those activities that lead nowhere. Calmly, however, do not get caught up in the frenzy otherwise you get exhausted. It also takes moments of pure relaxation.

Manage personal relationships

Sore spot Personal relationships are very complicated. The primary advice is to spend your time with positive people who help us grow, inspire us and treat us well. Toxic relationships, as we all know, lead nowhere.

Being a minimalist means cultivating the right level of self-love. You don't eliminate anyone from your life just because they have flaws. Only people who prove harmful on many fronts are eliminated. It means choosing people to cultivate the positive ones that we like and enrich us and make us spend quality time and eliminate the harmful ones that suck our time and energy, without giving anything in return,

Relationship management is something very personal, everyone experiences them differently because they think differently, have different types of emotionality, and have various levels of tolerance. Don't hang out with people just to do, to fill in the time gaps. It would not be respectful for each other and not even for you. Learn to be alone. Your own company is better than randomly chosen companies.

Choose carefully who to dedicate yourself to

We must try to work on the less pleasant aspects of our minds and character. Smooth the sharp corners, eliminate the automatisms that make us always react in the same way.

Changing what surrounds us and our activities is already a way to free the mind from a great deal of uselessness. Throwing away items and reducing the stress brought on by social media, TV, and whatnot is a small step forward. We cannot limit ourselves to the material side of minimalism. I can combat anxious and obsessive thoughts by writing. Pursuing a goal and trying to realize your projects improve life at 360°, instills security, and makes us feel the best version of ourselves.

When you relax, you relax

For many, the "relaxing moment" is on the sofa, shaking the home of social media. Do you think it's relaxing? No, it's a constant bombardment of the brain. Information left and right. To relax, try to detach yourself from everything, do a single activity that is truly rejuvenating for your poor neuronal connections. Detach from the bombing, turn off everything, forget about the existence of the phone, notifications, and continuous updates.

Improve sleep

In quantity and quality, sleeping well is essential to function properly throughout the day. There are some tricks you can use like:

✓ Avoid screens before bed

✓ Don't set your alarm as the last thing of the day

✓ Making the bedroom environment as relaxing as possible

✓ Use breathing and relaxation techniques

✓ Be regular in the hours

Improve nutrition

We can reduce what we eat, eat only quality food, eliminate most of the meat and prefer seasonal fruit and vegetables. It is also better to cook simple dishes, slightly spicy, light to digest. Drink lots of water, avoid what is industrial, high-calorie, rich in dyes and preservatives. Bring a large amount of fiber, reduce lactose and carbohydrates.

Exercise (or something similar)

Even just 10 minutes a day. A walk with the dog, some exercise, whatever. Physical activity stimulates the production of hormones, in particular, endorphins and hirsin; the former is considered the hormone of happiness, the latter useful for preventing dementia, burning fat, and strengthening bones.

What happens once we have done all of this?

Here comes the best. This long list of things to improve and eliminate is just the means to an end. Many believe that this is minimalism: throwing away, reducing, erasing, making room. But minimalism, the real one, is what comes next.

Having things that we like, being with people who satisfy us, no longer having the feeling of wasting time, but feeling that we like the things we do, enrich and satisfy us, make us better. In short, minimalism is about giving a better quality to one's life.

Minimalism, for me, is a life worth living, tailor-made for us, without external conditioning. It is spending the time we have truly understood who we are, and not as strangers to ourselves. It is letting go of what others want.

The key idea of minimalism is to get rid of those that don't add value to our life, to make room for what does. For example, eliminate clutter, distractions, and unhealthy relationships, and leave more room for things that are essential to our well-being, such as creativity, love, and play.

Minimalism or minimalist living leads you to intentionally focus on what's important and put the rest aside. In other words, it's about enjoying life more, having less.

Put aside everything that doesn't make you feel good: get rid of everything that gets in your way, everything that distracts you, that makes you lose focus. Get rid of everything that takes away your calm and clarity. Instead, stick to what contributes to your well-being.

- Don't buy things you don't need: don't be fooled by advertising, fashions, and the opinion of others. Having more things will not make you happier. The truth is that when we have enough to meet our basic needs, material possessions cannot improve our well-being in any way. They can only grant us a momentary gratification that disappears very soon, leading us into a worse psychological state.

- Appreciate what you have: Focus on what you have rather than what you lack. Otherwise, you will always feel incomplete, dissatisfied, and a prisoner of your desire.

- Minimize digital distractions: e-mail, instant messaging, social networks, recreational browsing... All this distracts you and makes you lose focus, attention on the present moment. Use digital means consciously and monitor interactions with other people.

- Improving interpersonal relationships: in the age of the internet, which facilitates interconnection, we are increasingly disconnected. We lack real human relationships, real ones.

- Doing one thing at a time: a minimalist life means living focused. In other words, enjoy every moment to the fullest. If we are always distracted and/or linked to multitasking, it will not be possible.

- Focus on Important Goals: Most people generally have a large number of goals they want to achieve. A minimalist life has a clear purpose. To do this, you need to discover the few things that interest you most and dedicate yourself to them.

- Taking care of body and mind: health is the starting point for feeling good. Therefore, it is essential to take care of yourself on two levels: the physical and the mental. Physical activity, nutrition, and sleep are the three key elements in this regard.

- Cultivate Full Attention: Minimalist life requires a quiet mind and that means being free from contradictory thoughts and in tune with the present moment. Practicing mindfulness or meditation for full attention helps to recover a peaceful state of consciousness. You will be able to observe your thoughts and feelings without judging them, resisting them, feeding them, and consciously responding to situations, instead of overreacting or being exhausted by them.

WABI-SABI HOME

The complete guide to finding Beauty in Imperfection and learn all about the japanese art of imperfection

Noelle Gill

Legal & Disclaimer

The information contained in this book and its contents is not designed to replace or take the place of any form of medical or professional advice; and is not meant to replace the need for independent medical, financial, legal or other professional advice or services, as may be required. The content and information in this book have been provided for educational and entertainment purposes only.

The content and information contained in this book has been compiled from sources deemed reliable, and it is accurate to the best of the Author's knowledge, information and belief. However, the Author cannot guarantee its accuracy and validity and cannot be held liable for any errors and/or omissions. Further, changes are periodically made to this book as and when needed. Where appropriate and/or necessary, you must consult a professional (including but not limited to your doctor, attorney, financial advisor or such other professional advisor) before using any of the suggested remedies, techniques, or information in this book.

Upon using the contents and information contained in this book, you agree to hold harmless the Author from and against any damages, costs, and expenses, including any legal fees potentially resulting from the application of any of the information provided by this book. This disclaimer applies to any loss, damages or injury caused by the use and application, whether directly or indirectly, of any advice or information presented, whether for breach of contract, tort, negligence, personal injury, criminal intent, or under any other cause of action.

You agree to accept all risks of using the information presented inside this book.

You agree that by continuing to read this book, where appropriate and/or necessary, you shall consult a professional (including but not limited to your doctor, attorney, or financial advisor or such other advisor as needed) before using any of the suggested remedies, techniques, or information in this book.

INTRODUCTION

Wabi-sabi is a Japanese worldview that finds beauty in imperfection and transience. Hence a simple, meditative, and authentic lifestyle.

The gaze is turned inwards, beyond the external appearance, beyond the appearance. A profound aesthetic awareness enhances feelings such as melancholy and loneliness, accompanied by the serenity of liberation from the material world.

Wabi-sabi arrives in our homes because it is a philosophy of life that Westerners have begun to imitate for 20 years. Realizing that the world of consumerism was collapsing on them, they took a step back to return to the essence of life.

A life lived in search of perfection; control over nature; attachment to stability and materiality; absoluteness and clarity of concept; durability, and at times the progressive development to immortality.

It becomes a life that loves the imperfection that leads to authenticity; who loves acceptance and harmony with nature; adaptation to change and detachment from material things; relativity and concept ambiguity; the changeability and cyclical development of everything.

In this way, life becomes simpler and more peaceful without inner struggles, without racing against time, but in full awareness of what it is.

This concept was also taken up in the conception of the house.

And here is what happens to the Wabi-sabi house: nothing is perfectly defined, and everything expresses its most authentic nature, leaving time to act.

The materials are natural and never subjected to excessive processing. Lime, raw earth, exposed bricks, worn woods, rough stones, raw linen, torn jute, soft wool, worn ceramic, and faded clay.

The colors and finishes are just as natural to everything. There are no fluorescent or industrial colors. No more shiny, smooth, and shiny surfaces, but rough, veined, dark, and tactile.

The shapes do the same. The naturalness of the curved and indefinite lines is far from any idea of symmetry and artificial composition.

Natural light becomes the touch of King Midas. This is considered in the organization of the spaces and the positioning of the furnishings.

Recycled materials and objects enter because time becomes a space to live.

Attention, we are far from a frikkettona, vernacular aesthetic, or a style of ethical recycling. The Wabi-sabi in the house is expressed with maniacal elegance. It adds the patina of the raw and the authentic to 21st-century minimalism. The elements are reduced to a minimum, indispensable, and positioned in a refined and non-trivial way. Spaces shrink and become darker and more private.

After changes, anxieties, and panic attacks, without knowing it, I embraced the Wabi-sabi philosophy, returning to the private and simple life that I had abandoned for a more public and furious one. I wish this change to everyone, perhaps starting right from the house.

This book will give you ideas and suggestions to adapt your home to this philosophy to improve your life both on an outward and spiritual level.

CHAPTER 1
WHAT IS WABI-SABI

Wabi: the absence of pathos, the refusal of luxury, "conscious primitivism." Sabi can be translated as "serenity," "sadness of loneliness," and "muffled colors and sounds." In the combined - and more extensive - the concept of wabi-sabi lies the lack of brilliance, naive simplicity, and the beauty of things touched by time and that carry the warmth of the multitude. Human hands- and therefore even more attractive. This concept has many shades of meaning, but none are precise and definite.

You can grasp the essence of wabi-sabi if you learn to understand life through feelings, discarding extraneous thoughts. The idea is that observing natural, changing and unique objects around us helps us connect to the real world and avoid potentially stressful distractions.

We learn to notice beauty in the most ordinary, natural way: for example, by contemplating the withering autumn leaves. Wabi-sabi gives the object a meditative value and, in this sense, becomes the practical embodiment of the philosophy of Zen Buddhism with its desire for isolation, self-control, and at the same time, inner strength and concentration.

Aesthetics of modesty

It is no coincidence that the tea master and follower of wabi-sabi Murata Juko (1422–1502) was a Zen monk. At that time, tea was a luxury item, as were ceremony accessories brought from China, ranging from exquisite to pretentious. In contrast to this fashion, Juko served tea in locally made utensils, considered coarse.

A century later, the son of the merchant Sen no Rikyu (1522–1591), who became master of the tea ceremony, continued this tradition: he made the tea house look like a peasant hut and integrated it with a garden and a stone path that leads through the park to the house. He ordered bowls from the famous master ceramist: they were shaped by hand, without a potter's wheel. Intentionally unsophisticated and imperfect, they eventually became covered with cracks, plaque, and chips.

Rikyu paid with his life for his commitment to simplicity: the overlord, whom he served, preferred magnificent receptions and precious utensils and ordered the master to commit suicide ritually. However, the tea ceremony school, founded by Rikyu, became the first in Japan and beyond its borders.

Relationships in the spirit of wabi-sabi teach you to accept another person with all his flaws but don't forget to get yours.

The essence of wabi-sabi can be summed up in three statements, says art theorist Leonard Coren, who has devoted many years to studying this principle: "Truth comes from observing nature. Greatness lives in secret and forgotten details. Beauty can come from imperfection. "

This philosophy extends to relationships, both with oneself and with other people. A relationship in the spirit of wabi-sabi teaches you to accept each other with all their flaws, but don't forget to get yours. After all, perfection can be tedious. And if we moderate our expectations and focus on the other person's perception: what he says and hears, how does he relate to the world? If we don't try to fix it, we will have more time and energy to enjoy the communication.

You can apply the same approach to yourself: I already have everything inside of me that I need to feel valued and be happy. It is enough for me to pay attention to the essentials. By avoiding the hustle and bustle and dictatorship of fashion, I can accept myself for who I am. Standard perfection and ostentatious luxury are contrasted by the uniqueness, imperfection, and modesty of wabi-sabi.

One of Leonard Coren's advice is: "Simplify everything to the point but leave the poem. Keep everything clean and uncluttered, but don't deprive it of meaning. "We, the modern world people, often need this kind of advice. The rejection of captivating beauty and excessive abundance is an ideal condition for understanding wabi-sabi, which has no clear boundaries and illuminated signs. Still, it can give an enlightened sensation of the rigorous simplicity of the world around us. The three exercises we propose will help you get into the spirit of this philosophy.

Three exercises for reveal the hidden beauty

The prevailing aesthetic principles shape our gaze. But suppose we want to rediscover the freedom and freshness of feelings. In that case, we need a different approach to business: more delicate and attentive, less radical about operational changes "for the better." In the context of wabi-sabi, beauty exists beyond artificiality. As evidence of the superiority of nature over man, the consequences of random changes should not be smoothed out or canceled but, on the contrary, they should be carefully preserved.

Such as? Pay attention to the imperfections of things and people. The faded folds of old fabric, the beauty of dry leaves or a falling flower, the charm of an older man's smile and the pattern of wrinkles on his face, the dance of dust in a ray of light - all this is beautiful., and therefore worthy of a lot of attention.

Distinguish the shades of emotions and enjoy them. When we enter a problematic situation, stressed or simply not very well, it is helpful to contact some object imbued with the spirit of wabi-sabi, which, according to the definition, can "excite a feeling of slight sadness and spiritual thirst in us." It helps remind us of the illusory nature of permanence and perfection, the ephemeral nature of problems and worries, and that no one can conquer time.

Such as? Wandering around the house, touching your favorite clothes, opening an old book, picking up a glass of water, stopping at some wabi-sabi object, feeling its weight, shape, and texture. What attracts you to this topic, and why is it pleasant? What memories and feelings does it evoke? Nostalgia, slight sadness, joy? By understanding this, you will feel more confident and be able to discern a whole range of different shades in your emotions.

Choose what makes us happiest. Recognize Primary Needs The best way to know yourself and get closer to your uniqueness. Wabi-sabi does not involve self-denial and forced minimalism but only a conscious choice according to one's inner essence.

Such as? For example, make a list of activities that bring you joy. Think about what exactly they are pleasant for you and what deep characteristics of your personality they correspond to. Assign these activities serial numbers 1 to 6, and ask yourself: do you spend enough time on them - and during each day?

CHAPTER 2
THE CHARACTERISTICS OF ZEN
AESTHETICS

The modern study of a Japanese aesthetic in the Western sense began only a little over two centuries ago. Japanese aesthetics now embrace various ideals, some of which are traditional while others are modern and sometimes influenced by other cultures.

Shinto is considered to be the source of Japanese culture. Its emphasis on the concern for nature and the character of ethics and its celebration of the landscape sets the tone for Japanese aesthetics. Nonetheless, Japanese aesthetic ideals are predominantly influenced by Japanese Buddhism. 5) In the Buddhist tradition, all things evolve and dissolve into nothingness. This "nothing" is not a space. Instead, it is a space of potentiality. 6) If we take the seas as representatives of potential, then everything is like a wave that comes from it and returns to it. There are no continuous waves. There are no ideal waves. Even at its peak, a wave is never complete. Nature is viewed as a living entity that must be admired and appreciated. This love of nature has been at the heart of many Japanese aesthetic ideals, "arts," and cultural elements. In this regard, the concept of "art" (or its conceptual equivalent) differs significantly from Western traditions (see Japanese art).

Wabi and Sabi refer to a careful approach to daily life. Over time their meanings have overlapped and are converted to unify in Wabi-sabi, the traditional aesthetic, the beauty of "imperfect, impermanent and incomplete" things. 6) Things in bud or things in decay are more evocative of the wabi-sabi of things in full bloom because they suggest the transience of things. As things come and go, they present signs of their coming and going, and these signs are considered beautiful. Beauty is an altered state of awareness and can be seen in the mundane and the simple. Nature's signatures can be so subtle that only a quiet mind and a cultivated eye can discern them. 7) In Zen philosophy, there are seven aesthetic principles for attaining Wabi-Sabi. 8

Shin'ichi Hisamatsu (1889-1980, Zen master and distinguished professor of religion at the University of Tokyo, decided to write down the characteristics that distinguish the actual Zen aesthetic from all other things inspired by this philosophy. He defined seven attributes with which to describe what Zen is, based on the ways of expressing itself of the formless self, which, precisely because they represent this undivided entity, coexist without being able in any way to be in contrast with each other; we will be amazed at how each time, when the object or the phenomenon we are examining is truly Zen, identifying even just one of them also brings with it the discovery of all the others: it can therefore be said that these seven characteristics are interdependent, that is, they are like many faces of a prism.

The first is fukinsei, which in Japanese means asperity and asymmetry and is an aesthetic concept, opposite to our ideal of classical beauty, which we find in all Far Eastern art, where the principle controls the harmony of a composition is not nonexistent but simply not regular. Discovering how a work of art manages to be perfectly balanced without having to resort to geometric parameters and being able to see beauty in what is crooked, incomplete, odd, broken, and inexact are experiences that approach spontaneity and randomness of nature, provoke a much more quiet enjoyment than that aroused by recognizing in the world around us those abstract forms that our rationality has studied how to measure.

The second characteristic is kanso, or sobriety, which, as we have seen before about the term Wabi, is one of the qualities that arouse greater appreciation in the Japanese soul since this is extremely simple and solid. Natural beauty, everyone succeeds, identifying himself in what he sees, withdrawing into himself and on the one hand feeling a great sense of harmony and union with the whole universe, on the other perceive the vitality, the incredible tension within apparently still and composed things. Furthermore, with sobriety, we also mean that simplification leaves room for imagination, the synthesis of an item or a concept, achieved using the least possible number of elements; this poetics of absence is also a characteristic of the Far Eastern soul in general.

In third place, we find Koko, a concept that we translate as "austere dignity," which indicates the elegant beauty of decadence, which we can see in things that are old, cracked, cracked, broken, eaten by worms, with patches, scars, wrinkles. Austere dignity is achieved only when the work is dried to its essence if clarity comes from spontaneous purity. This grave beauty brings out the rough charm and consistency of maturity. As Antoine de Saint - Exupéry (perhaps) said, "perfection is not achieved when there is nothing more to add, but nothing more to take away."

Shizen, which means naturalness, is one of the fundamental characteristics of Zen aesthetics since it is the reflection of the creative process: the creation of a work of art whose content is the enlightened vision of existence must take place without purpose, in the total absence of a will, of the self and any kind of deception; everything that is produced being in this state of grace will consequently be similar to the spontaneity of nature, wonderfully harmonious, fresh, free, fluid. However, it must be emphasized that this naturalness is not identical to Western concepts of innate, naive, or instinctive. Still, it is instead a very particular way, that is spiritual, of using a technique that we have learned by studying with commitment and effort: to achieve something that can be defined shizen, after having achieved absolute mastery of the method, we must learn to concentrate all our physical and psychic forces, to relax, forget ourselves and let creation happen spontaneously, since our ego no longer exists as such, but it has merged with the thing we are making and with everything around us. The naturalness of a work lies in showing its intentional character and purpose without being artificial or insincere. Hisamatsu writes: "Naturalness emerges when the artist penetrates deeply into what he is creating that he cancels all conscious effort." To achieve this value, constant practice, profound knowledge of the technique, and extraordinary concentration are required.

Eugen's fifth characteristic is the impenetrable depth and withheld secrecy of things, which we have already described in the previous paragraph. Yugen could be translated as reverberation. The echo principle highlights how often suggestion is much more potent than full manifestation. The work must be deep and subtle. It must stimulate the imagination, the question, the reflection, rather than immediately run out and stagnate. User curiosity is a powerful push to action, as the designer can exploit such.

The sixth is daisuzoku, freedom from any attachment, the abandonment of any form, the bonds that force us to the conventional world, ideas, feelings, and overcome any dualism. "If you see a Buddha, kill him!" is one of the many irreverent maxims of Zen that, in search of a total coherence that admits no exceptions, when he says that we must overcome all attachment, he also means that towards the idea of Buddha.

When the routine is broken, creativity and innovation emerge. This principle describes the feeling of awe and energy that arises when one goes beyond the commonly accepted conventions and rules. It is necessary to adopt what in the Zen doctrine is called "beginner's mind": the attitude to take nothing for granted, to face every problem with a fresh mind, to ask the most basic questions to overcome the usual ways of acting, and reasoning.

Zen aesthetics' seventh and final characteristic is seijaku, which means silence, stillness, and serene composure. These qualities serve to calm and relax the observer's soul and come from the state of deep concentration and the meditation of the creator. However, we must not imagine that this feeling of tranquility is due to contingent factors such as an absolute silence or immobility of things; on the contrary, the effect of seijaku is much more evident and powerful where we will be able to perceive the stillness in the movement and the silence in the noise since it means that we are in a state of mind where nothing can disturb our inner peace.

This principle presents the artist who becomes one with the surrounding reality, imperturbable. The true essence of creative energy can only be found in a similar state of active calm, solitary tranquility gained through meditative practice. And it is precisely in the most chaotic and frantic moments, that this value manages to show itself with more significant impact, as the Zen saying suggests: "With the cry of the bird, the mountain becomes even quieter."

"The others are also contained in each of these seven unitary traits. Of course, it is possible that - according to the current situation - a certain section stands out on the others and that the others pass in the background,» writes Hisamatsu. "But these essential traits do not exist in isolation each for himself; instead, they are perfectly fused and form a unitary whole.»

Here is the crucial point: if assimilated and employed as a cohesive set of design principles, these concepts can put us on the right path and guide our efforts towards that ideal of minimalism that resides in the surprising impact of simplicity.

Remaining faithful in everything to Zen philosophy, Shin'ichi Hisamatsu expresses these seven characteristics positively and negatively.

Fukinsei is also mu-ho, no rule, absence of any ordered organization.

Kanso is Mutsu, which is not complex, without too many directions or interpretations, and tension towards overcoming dualism.

At the same time, Koko is mu-i, which means indefinite, since what has extinguished in itself every link with the senses has finally come to be pure essence without form, precisely indefinable.

Shizen finds its negative form in mushin, no heart or mind (the word shin in Japanese has both of these meanings, which further demonstrates the enormous underlying diversity between this culture and the European one), i.e., not forced by thoughts and emotions but unconditional, without purpose, without will.

Yugen is also mutei, bottomless, infinite.

Daisuzoku is mu- ge, without hindrance, not conditioned by the distinction between me and not-me, devoid of oppositions, internal

22

contradictions, and obstacles.

Finally, the other side of seijaku is mu-do, which means numbness, being devoid of any emotion, be it discomfort or happiness, since any form of involvement implies anxiety, which disturbs the absolute stillness of formlessness.

These, therefore, according to Zen, are the seven characteristics of the formless self, of Buddha-nature, of the real essence of Truth. For this reason, they define the contours of the aesthetics relating to this philosophy, which is not limited to being an artistic criterion. But it involves the entire existence of every human being.

To live in line with this religion or philosophy, one should not limit oneself to using these directives to create a painting, a garden, ikebana, a haiku, work in ceramics, or a theater piece. No: following the Zen aesthetic even in actions such as the tea ceremony and the art of the sword should serve as a starting point to apply it to every gesture of daily life, to be sure to do everything correctly (a fundamental idea for Japanese culture, which also has a word on purpose to define this concept, that is kata and in harmony with the flow of the universe.

CHAPTER 3
"MONO NO AWARE"

When the cherry trees begin to bloom in Japan, the event is celebrated by a customer with a thousand-year history. The Hanami, which in Japanese means "admire the flowers," consists precisely in observing and enjoying the beauty of sakura (cherry blossoms) by organizing picnics and outdoor walks. This ancient tradition is closely linked to Buddhism and Zen philosophy: the cherry blossom is, in fact, the symbol of the transience of human life and the impermanence of reality. The incredible show offered by the cherry trees in bloom lasts only a few days, it is fleeting like everything that surrounds us, but it is precisely this that makes it so fascinating and unique. The Hanami best expresses the Japanese aesthetic concept of "mono no aware. "

If we wanted to translate it into words, "mono no aware" can be defined as the pathos of things, a feeling of emotional participation in existence. It indicates the sense of nostalgia that seizes us after having admired something beautiful but fleeting, which we know will not last long. The term is the union of two words: "mono," which means "things," and "aware," which initially indicated the 'exclamation of amazement towards a natural subject. Subsequently, "aware" took on the meaning of "compassion," "pity," and "sadness." Therefore, the "mono is no aware" is that feeling of melancholy that derives from the appreciation of incredible beauty and the vast awareness of its transience. It is the observation that becomes feeling. The poignant loneliness of beauty, what in one moment is, and the next moment is no more.

Impermanence: beauty is in change

However, beyond the resulting sadness, there is also essential teaching of oriental wisdom behind this concept: the impermanence and transience of things make them unique and enhance their beauty. If the cherry trees were always in bloom, they would certainly lose much of their charm. Furthermore, the awareness of impermanence in the Buddhist vision is fundamental to adapting to the unpredictability of events and the ephemeral nature of things. Much human suffering comes from the inability to accept detachment, change, and end. But life is an implacable flow of events, of beginnings and endings. Taking it allows us to understand that there is no need to resist and that if everything is temporary and fleeting, worrying about it becomes useless. Because this moment is brief, we must learn to enjoy it fully.

The mono no aware finds its maximum literary expression in one of the main works of Japanese literature, the Genji Monogatari. The novel revolves around the story of the emperor's son, and the speech he delivers when he is close to death is perhaps the most representative of the "pathos of things" of which the work is the symbol:

"I don't complain about a destiny that I share with flowers, insects, and stars. In a universe where everything passes like a dream, we would not forgive ourselves for lasting forever. It does not pain me that things, beings, and hearts are perishable since part of their beauty is made up of this calamity. What bothers me is that we are unique... Other women will be in bloom, smiling like the ones I loved, but their smiles will differ. Other hearts will break under the weight of unbearable love, but their tears will not be our tears. Hands moist with desire will continue to intertwine under the almond trees in bloom, but the same shower of petals never falls twice on human happiness."

We introduce this concept because, as we will see later in the Wabi-sabi design, a fundamental role is given by the presence of plants.

CHAPTER 4

FUKINSEI, REALISTIC BEAUTY: WHEN HARMONY IS WELCOMING IMPERFECTIONS

Fukinsei comes from Japan and indicates a real philosophical concept rather than a single untranslatable term. The word Fukinsei refers, in fact, to Japanese aesthetics and to that type of harmonic beauty that comes exclusively from asymmetry, imperfection, and diversity. A concept is distant from the ideal of classical beauty based on proportions falling within idealized canons. The term Fukinsei means asperity, asymmetry, a principle found in all oriental art where harmony is essentially irregularity. Geometric parameters, measurements, and proportions are banned; the natural beauty in Japanese culture is to grasp the pleasantness in what is not optimal. Seeing beauty in an out-of-proportion, the crooked, inaccurate figure is precisely the purpose of the Fukinsei philosophy.

This awareness helps men to approach spontaneity, chance, and nature in all its forms; beauty is realism in nature, and what the natural order of things offers is not governed by mathematical models, but by pure chance, by the creative power that assembles itself and is perfect in all its most minor inaccuracies. The deception, calculation, and measure is packaged perfection; what is beautiful will be beautiful despite and above all, thanks to its inaccuracies.

Art as a possibility

The concept of perfection, as well as that of immortality and infinity, is logically beyond the reach of any human being. Precisely for this reason, the philosophy of Fukinsei (不均斉) wants to convey a type of art in which everyone can reflect and recognize themselves. Asymmetry generates change, movement, and dynamism instead of symmetrical balance synonymous with stasis and immobility, as it is chained to non- transformation. We all transform in our lives, and we need to keep this in mind. Irregularity is valued when the work is not entangled in the obsessive search for perfection and goes beyond symmetrical exactness. This characteristic is peculiar to the incomplete and, translated into our field, can consist of a dynamic balance of asymmetrical shapes or in the choice of a design process that encourages active participation (co-design) by users.

CHAPTER 5
JAPANESE AESTHETICS IN DESIGN

We could sum up Japanese interior design in the word Zen

Whether you live in an apartment, country cottage, or 1970s building, everyone can benefit from these Japanese style tips.

1) A Japanese style room is Multifunctional and flexible

One reason people love Japanese interior design is its vast space improvement. And who doesn't love making their home feel bigger and airier? This is because many traditional Japanese homes embrace open-plan living areas.

This popular space-enhancing style is an excellent option if you're a city dweller who understands the desirability of ground space! Combining your kitchen, dining area, and living room into one ample space will give you more space to play and create a great, friendly space where you can host and share your time with others.

2) Japanese interior design is in tune with nature and natural light

The rise of famous and incredible cultures, such as the cottage come trend, brings the outdoors inside and makes us feel less claustrophobic in our homes. However, cottagecore is maximalist and not popular with those who like a clean, minimalist look. Japanese design responds to this need.

shizen" philosophy is a principle that recognizes harmony between people and nature and underpins many Japanese furniture design methods that often use bamboo and light woods. Thanks to this philosophy, many designers also use nature to honor the world they live in.

Large windows for smooth, natural light

First, large windows and sliding doors are crucial to allowing natural light to flood the room.

Choose large sheet metal windows to maximize light and connect with natural fiber carpets and furniture outdoors.

One of the main reasons many Japanese opt for paper blinds is because they place a lot of importance on privacy. These paper screens or "Shoji" let in light but keep prying eyes out.

You could add a sliding glass door, perhaps with a glass panel in a wooden frame.

Natural and sustainable fibers

All Japanese homes reflect their surroundings and frequently use sustainable materials mixed with natural fibers.

Wood, bamboo, and rattan are common materials used for various interior characteristics. The inserts, walls, frames, mezzanines, and screen grilles are usually made of natural wood such as cypress and red pine. Wood adds texture, serenity, and sophistication to your space.

The flooring is either wood or gray stone tiles, and most of the walls are replaced by screens covered with matte paper. This design ends up in a very neutral natural color palette.

Water features and plants

Plants are one of the most common ways to incorporate the outside into the home. However, if you want to look Japanese, stick to plants with an oriental feel.

Plants are another excellent way to bring nature into your Japanese-style interior. In a Japanese-inspired interior, a bonsai tree is a standard feature. A variety of green plants rooted indoors can also be considered. Dumbcanes, aloe vera, palm trees, and orchids are plants that you can use. The plants can also be potted or hung, which adds elegance.

Bringing water features indoors is always a good idea to get a zen-like space in your home. In addition to physical water features, an oriental water-themed mural is another way to add a water element to the house.

3) Minimalism is fundamental

Because of its emphasis on "Shibui": simple beauty, detail, and a love of natural materials, contemporary Japanese design is one of the great versions of today's minimalism.

The Japanese consider the most basic form of simplicity to be a form of luxury. Contemporary, simple, clean-lined furniture from this world often has incredibly intricate engineering with intricate joinery.

Decluttering goes hand in hand with a modern Japanese home. Just follow the famous Japanese organization consultant Marie Kondo to find out!

Austerity, minimalism, and an appreciation of memorabilia and traditions survive in a unique amalgam that adapts technology and modernism to fit into an already established aesthetic and not the other way around.

Japanese minimalism is aesthetic but, above all, functional.

4) Choose neutral colors

In close connection with nature, the most common color schemes found in Japanese interior design are heavily influenced by the outside.

CHAPTER 6
THE SEVEN PRINCIPLES OF WABI-SABI

As we have seen, the Wabi-sabi is a philosophy of life that sees beauty in imperfections. Pursuing perfection generates unnecessary stress and anxiety as we should be satisfied with the importance of being unique, with our defects, which are also a virtue.

According to the Zen monks, this philosophy consists of 7 practices:

- Finding the beauty in the underrated. Known as Shibumi.

- Enhance the subtle details. Yugen.

- To be free. Datsuzoku.

- Live with simplicity. Kanso.

- Act naturally, without pretensions. Shizen.

- Appreciate the asymmetry and irregularity. Fukinsei.

- Make tranquility your lifestyle. Seijaku.

How is Wabi-Sabi applied to decoration?

This way of life has similar principles to minimalism, as it values everything we have and reminds us that we don't need to want more and more. It is about knowing how to differentiate between what you want and what is necessary.

It is the antonym of the consumer society where duration loses value and importance is given to impulse purchases. For example, an excellent example of a Wabi-Sabi would be an old plate that was broken but was repaired by joining its pieces together.

Appreciate the beauty of what surrounds us, its history, the sentimental value of each object, and the authenticity that lies in the modest and imperfect. Nothing is permanent, and the old should be appreciated rather than rejected.

Wabi-Sabi so much?

Because it is a sustainable lifestyle that enhances natural materials, furniture, and decorations that are handed down from generation to generation and clarifies how important it is to find objects that last and are functional.

This is where traditional craftsmanship and techniques, solid wood, and natural fibers come into play, allowing the creation of unique and unrepeatable pieces with a value that goes far beyond the object itself.

Wabi-Sabi means touching the ground with your feet, remembering who you are, and forgetting what society asks of you. Breathe, think about what's essential and evaluate your imperfections and those of others.

CHAPTER 7
WABI-SABI IN FURNITURE

U ntil a few years ago, everyone was focused on hygge style, that is, on the furnishing of a Scandinavian-style house, a design characterized by creating simple interior spaces without neglecting every comfort. Recently, however, the spotlight has been on the aesthetics of Wabi-sabi, the new frontier of interior design that comes directly from Japan.

Enough with the obsession with order; true beauty lies in imperfection. It is the philosophy of wabi-sabi, which has very ancient origins but can still be applied everywhere, in life and the home.

The wabi-sabi philosophy, or the beauty of imperfection

Ancient Japanese art is to mend broken cups or plates with gold. That is proof of how much the Asian people love highlighting the imperfection of things.

Well, this is also reflected in wabi-sabi.

The wabi-sabi constitutes a vision of the Japanese world, or aesthetic, founded on accepting the transience of things. A simple translation of wabi-sabi could be sad beauty, but the word does not have a proper translation. If anything, it is the association of two terms, Wabi, and Sabi, which indicate living in harmony with nature, making the most of what little you have, and the cold, poverty, or being "withered." Towards the fourteenth century, Wabi began to identify rustic simplicity, freshness, or silence, applied to both natural and artificial objects, or even elegance without ostentation. Furthermore, the term can also refer to oddities or defects generated in the construction process, adding uniqueness and elegance to the object. Sabi is now connoted as the beauty or serenity that accompanies the advancement of age, the acceptance of the slow and inevitable passage of time, and the moment in which the life of objects and its impermanence are highlighted by patina and wear. Or any visible repairs.

Today, imperfect beauty is applied, for example, to the house's design, where chaos, at least apparent, has taken the place of clean and tidy environments.

They can be created that make you feel good, authentic pieces because they are imperfect. The wabi-sabi imperfection is not the "artificial" one of shabby chic: here, every scratch and burn to sign the inevitable passage of time.

The house becomes authentic and fully lived, and you are no longer ashamed not to make the bedroom as soon as you get up or order books and newspapers. The tables and cutting boards become lived-in objects, with marks and veins, unfinished ceramics, and raw fabrics that have not always passed under the care of the iron; the best pieces of furniture are handcrafted, and the table is weathered.

Those who have always hated using unmatched glasses and plates for their guests can permanently free themselves from the terror of judgment, and those who hastened to hide crumpled clothes in the room can instead leave them on display on the sofa. Does that seem too much? Start gradually, preferring natural fabrics to silk and country herbs in vases instead of tulips.

To honor the passage of time, durable furniture and materials to be exposed to the elements of the passing years are fundamental, such as wood, wool, clay, bamboo, linen, and stone. Even the colors recall nature, such as the gray of the rock, the blue of the sea, and the green of the sequoia.

In reality, the wabi-sabi style is not an absolute search for simplicity but a way to combine this with beauty, which should not be sacrificed, but only interpreted differently. Not necessarily as perfection and order. Philosophy invites us to rethink our concept of "essential," to be also applied to the home, which must be filled not (only) with beautiful but functional objects and which, above all else, make you feel good.

Are you ready to live without the obsession with order, or do you prefer a slow approach to philosophy not to be traumatized by the beautiful chaos of wabi-sabi?

CHAPTER 8
SOME BASIC RULES TO FOLLOW

Japanese furniture is a must these days; it can make spaces seem more significant and help create elegant and sober housing solutions, obtaining beautiful and designed environments but also convenient and functional. Bringing a breath of Japan into your home is not difficult. However, there are rules to follow. Let's see what they are.

When dealing with open or confined spaces, this type of furniture expands the areas and organizes them thanks to its simplicity and essentiality.

The characteristics of this style are exact and include clean and regular lines, a minimal design, the use of natural materials, and sober colors. The watchwords are modern minimalism, an approach seasoned with natural touches given by wood and greenery, enriched by elements typical of Asian culture. The simplicity of this furniture is also a functional and practical solution.

We could sum up Japanese interior design in the word Zen

Use furniture and accessories with clean and essential lines.

Choose low furniture solutions, almost adherent to the floor.

I prefer sober color ranges, preferably neutral colors.

Insert natural materials using them in furniture, furnishings, and carpets.

Arrange the furnishings orderly and rigorous without bringing them too close.

Enrich the rooms with elements typical of Asian cultures, such as particular paintings, tea sets, bonsai, statues, paper lamps, and other furnishings.

Avoid knick-knacks and excessive knick-knacks, eliminating the superfluous such as paintings and carpets.

I prefer windows through which natural light can penetrate.

If necessary, divide the space without closing it, but simply use shoji panels in rice paper or dividers, for example, with typical Japanese decorations (such as orchids or cherry branches).

Create small Zen corners with rocks, fountains, and plants.

To furnish the house with a Japanese design, it is essential to take care of each environment in a specific way, ensuring that the distinctive elements of the Japanese style are present in all the house rooms. We summarize them; then, we will deepen them in various chapters.

Japanese furniture for the living area

The living room is where guests are welcomed and where most of the time is spent. The Japanese furnishings will essentially be the

TV cabinet, the sofa, and a coffee table. Therefore, the room should appear almost empty, devoid of all those decorations and objects that are not useful.

The various pieces of furniture should have simple lines, preferably geometric and square, resulting in a structure that is almost touching the ground. A typical feature of the oriental world is, in fact, that of sitting on the floor, on cushions or mats. Instead of the usual carpet, it is better to choose mats in natural material or tatami mats. On the other hand, the sofa should be large and straightforward, low, and almost adherent to the floor.

Japanese style bedroom

The modern style is very close to Japanese essentiality, so the choice on the market is extensive. This is also evident in the bedroom, for example. The futon is now very easily found in various colors and patterns with a shape very similar to the traditional Japanese style bed.

The shades should be natural wood or opt for white as much as possible. The rules are the same as those followed for the stay: therefore, those elements that are too many must be eliminated.

Japanese style kitchen decor

To set up a Japanese-style kitchen, the principles to be respected are the same that is essentiality, minimalism, and functionality, favoring natural light and chromatic harmonization. An optimal solution is kitchen furniture with sliding doors to replicate traditional Japanese furniture design.

We can decorate the walls with Japanese-style wallpaper with references to oriental culture, or for a less invasive option, you can prefer stencils. A touch of real Japan is the Japanese lanterns used as skylights, or you can use bamboo chandeliers and the inevitable bonsai.

How to Apply 8 Wabisabi Styles to Your Life

The wabi-sabi style, when used at work and in life, can seem complicated at first glance. For example, when creating an interior in the style of wabi-sabi, the main thing is to meet the following requirements:

Get rid of unnecessary things in the house. Anything you haven't used for a year is considered excessive. They steal your time and energy to take care of them, but, in reality, you don't need such items. We will see in a separate chapter how to practice decluttering.

Don't buy or bring anything extra into the house. This means not purchasing goods under the influence of emotions or because everyone has "this item" now.

Don't expose too many things. Let it be just one or two things you care about.

Do not try to fill the whole room with things, but, on the contrary, rely on free space.

Tidy things up that are filled with a pleasant "story" for you to emphasize their flavor.

Focus on objects made of natural materials, perhaps caused by a local craftsman, or objects that speak of your history, something that comes from your hometown.

In life, the wabi-sabi philosophy is expressed in the love for simplicity, for all that is natural. It's about functionality, not a demonstration of luxury. For example, using the wabi-sabi style in her life and work, Jessica Alba founded a company that produces natural cosmetics for children's skincare.

And Robert De Niro, also a follower of Japanese philosophical principles, when he finished the 630-meter Greenwich Hotel, used natural materials for the area in which the building is located: stone and wood. The building has a more captivating and familiar aesthetic.

Another critical aspect of the wabi-sabi lifestyle is that this "path of simplicity" does not require a lot of investment. Almost anyone can implement it in their lives. For example, following this worldview, to cover the floor in an apartment, you can choose not a luxurious and expensive walnut but a more common pine and perceive its natural pattern not as an asymmetry but as harmonious natural beauty.

Also, your favorite knitted sweater can be tidied up with the help of stylish patches, and the cracks in the bathroom tiles can be filled in with beautiful paint. As a result, things will be preserved, you will not have to buy anything new, and their native warmth will warm your heart for a long time.

Learn to enjoy what you have to simplify your life, and you will see that the hustle and bustle will leave you, and you will become much calmer and happier.

CHAPTER 9
WABI-SABI DESIGN

W abi-sabi- style interior initiated the well-known European "minimalism." It will not be easy for European municipalities to get used to such an interior immediately.

The wabi-sabi design trend is not focused on luxury or exuberance; it is designed to seek Truth, meaning, and beauty much deeper than the surface. The wabi-sabi style is often found in Japanese hotels, in the more expensive rooms. This indicates how much the Japanese appreciate the genuineness, sincerity, and simplicity that the wabi-sabi "absorbed" into itself. Now, even in modern European interiors, you can see the motifs of this style. They gladly decorate the whole house with antique materials under wabi-sabi, giving new life to worn-out things with their unique history.

What does wabi-sabi mean?

If you translate the phrase " wabi -sabi," it will sound like modesty, simplicity, and calm. Wabi is unpretentious simplicity, while Sabi is harmony in solitude. This style represents Japanese beauty and sophistication. It is expressed not only in one of the interior styles; it is a whole philosophy and lifestyle of the Japanese.

The peculiarity of the wabi-sabi design trend is to show that chaos reigns over precision and judgment. This is expressed in the asymmetry and irregularity of the lines. Wabi-sabi wants to show us the good side of an imperfect world.

The designers tried to show us the very texture of the materials without hiding them under a layer of unnatural colors. Those internal details that declare their novelty are not chosen; the more "seasoned" things with a long history are preferred.

Therefore, Japanese people value space very much and do not take up all the free space. This is one of the main features of this design.

Wabi-sabi colors

Natural and light shades should prevail. To create an antique interior, it is best to use white, beige, milky, gray, and brown colors. The off-white color is trendy. It is he who can so accurately convey the mood of wabi-sabi design. It is often used to decorate walls, floors, or furniture. The wabi-sabi design trend includes a continuous connection with nature. To do this, dark woods are actively used in the interior, which brightly contrasts against the background of light walls. All materials used in wabi-sabi are tested to be left smooth and unprocessed. The same applies to wooden surfaces, which in no case should be painted in unnatural colors, but only slightly hidden by the paint. This creates a unique interior in your home and maintains a special atmosphere.

Wall texture

As we have already said, the main thing in this style is simplicity, non-invasiveness, and naturalness. This applies to the small details of the wabi-sabi design and the wall decoration itself. The best materials will be stone, wood, brick, metal, or concrete. No matter what it will be, the main thing is that they can "talk" about themselves. A suitable material for wall decoration will be a brick painted in light colors. In no case should the house cry out to its newness and luxury, just restraint and modesty? The stylistic trend is somewhat similar to the rustic style.

Moreover, you can see the clear motifs of its design in wabi-sabi. But, unlike the rustic, the latter is fraught with the philosophy and mystery of Japanese beauty—a minimum of finishing, polishing, varnishing, and a maximum of naturalness and imperfection. Wabi-sabi does not recognize artificiality and elegance: everything should be light and discreet.

Wabi-sabi furniture

Furniture for this style also needs to be selected specially. When choosing it, you should pay attention to natural and natural materials. The table doesn't have to be perfect; it can look unfinished and asymmetrical. Wabi-sabi interior design often uses DIY furniture, which further emphasizes the particularity of the style. The rough stone that covered the fireplace, the rough surface of the wood, the "worn" look, and the strange shapes of benches, chairs, and tables: this is what distinguish Japanese interiors. But, even though wabi-sabi implies old and worn things, that doesn't mean that modern notes can't be added. New technologies go well with the imperfect Japanese style. They have learned to combine modernity with antiquity, adding fresh notices to the classic wabi-sabi style.

Floor materials

The best materials for a wabi-sabi floor would be wood or concrete. There is no fine parquet, carpet, or bright tiles, just restraint and simplicity. If it is a concrete floor, it must be well sanded. The material may look shabby and old - this will be the basis for the entire interior design in the style of wabi-sabi. If you like a tree, it should also show its ancient history with its appearance. Modern hardware stores offer us a large selection of various types of floor coverings made to match the interior of wabi-sabi. They will be good helpers in creating this unique design.

Lighting

Wabi-sabi's interior lighting philosophy is similar to Scandinavian-style interior lighting - soft, muted, and diffused light. The interior of Wabi-sabi inherited this principle from the lighting of the Japanese teahouse - Chashitsu, which was purposely built with windows on the north side and next to which trees grew that spread even more light. (You can read more about the effect of orientation to the cardinal points inside).

Storage spaces

All these things come together, guided by the principle of

"timelessness." It shouldn't be clear from within which century it belongs. Therefore, it is not allowed that a plasma TV hung in plain sight in such an interior or there was a high-tech iMac.

How do we solve such a problem? After all, we are talking about modern interiors and modern people. Now there is no problem; order a built-in wardrobe in the joinery for the entire height of the wall. Raw panels can be taken as facades. Inside there will be storage space and a retractable TV. You can even do an electric drive with remote control. And the cabinet doors will open by pressing them. It is cute simple technology widely used in kitchen fronts. Imagine that not the photo below is not a single block of planks but three doors on hidden hinges—an entirely feasible design.

In the end, if the area of the room allows, you can make a separate storage room for things, which in the interior can be relatively modern.

And as for the computer - remember, this is conscious modesty, so just a laptop that you keep on your knees while you work, and then take it off so as not to be noticeable.

As you can see, even at first glance, the exotic interior of our country can be recreated without special financial or temporary costs. After all, sushi and sashimi have taken root in our country, so why not make Japanese interiors?

The most important thing is that nothing catches the eye with its unearthly beauty and perfection. On the other hand, the surrounding things can be seen with pleasure, thus immersing oneself in the real space around you instead of running somewhere. Part or dig into your phone. The style should be so subtle that it is not visible.

Accessories are simple, modest, and nostalgic elements: ceramics and stones.

Simple doesn't mean cheap, especially for accessories. It is not so easy to choose the correct details for this style in the modern world. Choose the most natural and possibly unfinished. As you know, naturalness costs a lot of money. Various vases, pots, bowls, figurines, engravings, etc., are welcome in the design. The main thing is natural materials, such as clay, stone, metal, or wood. Choose handmade items, especially dishes. The various plants that will bring your home to life are not without importance. Pots for them are also better to choose from clay.

Style wabi-sabi is not governed by fashion but by the ability of things to tell their story. Nothing extra in it that can distract attention. Wabi-sabi was created for comfort and solitude so that a person can put his thoughts in order.

But don't be mad if Wabi -Sabi's inside isn't within your reach. You need to be very creative and resourceful so that the house can be decorated with your own hands. National motifs will add uniqueness to this style. It is not necessary to adopt everything from the Japanese. "Minimalism" can be created on your own. Making rooms with the right colors is half the problem; the important thing is to create the correct details. Try looking for old clay pots, cups, and plates in the attic. They will become indispensable accessories in your home. If you don't find them, you can now easily buy an ordinary clay pot and decorate it with antique spray cans of various colors. There will also be multiple wooden baskets and chests. Turn on the fantasy, and you will be successful!

The beauty of purity, transition, and imperfection of Wabi-sabi is at odds with the definition of classical Western beauty, which emphasizes perfection, durability, monumentality, and materialistic obsession. Incorporating the Wabi-sabi philosophy doesn't mean hiring an interior designer, becoming a Japanese culture expert, or living like a Buddhist monk.

Adopting the Wabi-sabi philosophy requires a shift in your perspective. By removing the obsession with material possessions, you should be able to create a happier home where you feel more satisfied.

You don't have to let yourself be overwhelmed by runaway shopping to decorate your home; you don't need anything new to change your home. Japanese philosophy values nature, so pay attention to the materials you bring home. Wood, stone, and metal elements are predominant, aesthetically pleasing, and age well.

These are some accessories you already own and have never appreciated! Choose based on the principles of functionality, minimalism, and simplicity. Search the kitchen drawer, where it waits to find some old rusty knife or some other iron, brass, or copper object. Their imperfections tell a story of years and years of use. You may come across a chipped vase, container, bowl, or flowerpot in your basement or attic. All the signs of wear or the "wounds of time" are appreciated in the Wabi-sabi. On the other hand, if you decide to buy new home accessories, we recommend choosing sustainable, high-quality, handmade, or vintage products and materials.

Antique accessories and furnishing elements can be perfectly mixed with modern and minimalist furniture. This type of furniture combines the imperfections and asymmetries of furniture and accessories in an attractive and hospitable living space. Wabi-sabi points out that the home must be a comfortable space where one feels at ease. Pillows, for example, add comfort.

During the transformation, you can also decide to refresh the walls; look for inspiration in nature for the choice of colors. This will allow for a wide selection of colors, from soft pink or beige to soothing blue or green. Or, with decorative techniques, you can give the appearance of rusty iron or oxidized copper, obtaining different degrees of rust or oxidation.

Nothing is definitive. All things have a predefined course; they are born, live, and die. This inevitable circle of life forms a vital cornerstone in Japanese aesthetic philosophy.

Not surprisingly, in traditional Japanese architecture, since no building was to last too long, the constructions were made of wood, which has a natural time limit.

Unlike Western architecture, which is primarily made of concrete and carries the illusion of eternity, Japanese temples and houses have been rebuilt many times, even altering the original design.

Translated into a more homely environment, the Wabi-Sabi style means avoiding the shiny, the perfect, and the uniform for an attitude more exposed to use, time, and the elements, and therefore unique.

Remember that there is always ethics behind aesthetics, which generates a feeling of calm, evoked by elements such as light furniture and organic shapes.

Recovery is an integral part of the design. This translates into fewer "catalog" furniture choices to prefer objects assembled, found, repaired, and relocated in the same environment.

Time becomes art. Light is the protagonist, even when it is dark or chiaroscuro. Antique furniture or poor art emerges from nowhere to reinforce the forms of architecture.

Wabi-sabi is the perfect antidote to the rampant pompous, cloying and institutional beauty style that was and is desensitizing Western society.

The choice of materials is an elegant chromatic path that leads from white to black through neutral and natural tones, where the presence of the others enhances the identity of each color. It is a tactile and material exploration: from smooth surfaces like silk to irregular and imperfect ones with natural grain.

The wabi-sabi style "lives" of beauty, that of every day.

As you may have understood, the materials flee from millimeter perfection:

- Gypsum and hand-brushed plaster.

- Rough or inlaid parquet.

- Oxidized metals.

- Pieces of recovered marble form a "background" made of sculptural elements.

Time becomes a place: without a glossy finish.

The wabi-sabi style is not for everyone, and it is useless to delude oneself. It is a design attitude that starts from a place and a specific state of mind.

The wabi-sabi style is not decorative. It left no room for the factory's wallpapers, glass, and mirrors yesterday. It cannot be done for just one room because the others have already been furnished.

Instead, this style:

- Dress the space with charm and suggestion

- It prefers soft textures to the touch and of high aesthetic quality.

- It mixes rusty metals, gold foil, exposed concrete, and textured paints

- Use aged wood, not Ikea lacquers

- Use opaque fabrics and materials, not the glass and chrome steel

• He is not afraid to recover objects and furnishings, even if they are broken or in bad condition

• Use rough concrete

• It does not use stadium spotlights, psychedelic lights, or exaggerated LED cuts.

• Natural light becomes the undisputed protagonist, and the furniture seems to be chosen and arranged perhaps more as a pretext to enhance it.

• Prefers soft fabrics in natural materials (cotton, jute, linen, wool...)

• It does not repaint or clean up after a while, years. Cracks and the patina of time are examined and treated if necessary.

• It generates sophisticated and not at all trivial spaces, albeit minimal.

• In practice, some materials can be used or preferred over others.

CHAPTER 10

JAPANDI, THE STYLE THAT MARRIES HYGGE AND WABI-SABI

Japandi, a word that combines the terms Japan and Scandinavian, indicates a furnishing style that harmoniously blends the characteristics of the hygge and wabi-sabi philosophies.

For several years now, the Scandinavian style has been characterized by warm and welcoming environments where nature plays an important role. Scandinavian furniture features simple lines, natural materials, and great functionality. The philosophy that animates the contemporary Scandinavian style was born in Denmark and is called Hygge.

Japanese furniture represents the essence of minimalism, elegance, and sobriety. The search for aesthetic purity gives life to virtual environments characterized by rigorous lines. Perhaps to balance such rigor, the wabi-sabi philosophy, which seeks beauty in imperfection, introduces handcrafted objects, preferably handmade and described by some defects.

Despite the geographical distance, these two styles have two points in common: minimalism and the use of natural materials. The Japandi style grafted onto these two peculiarities a sober and elegant character, typical of Japanese aesthetics, combined with extreme functionality of Scandinavian origin. Today, the Japandi type is increasingly sought after, but this is not new. It was created over 150 years ago.

The harmonious Japanese style arose from long-standing cultural ties between Japan and Denmark. The unique types of the two countries began to interact more than 150 years ago when Danish architects, artists, and designers traveled to Japan in search of new inspiration. They were one of the first people in the West to come to the country across newly opened borders, as they had been closed for the previous 220 years.

However, the admiration is mutual. The Danish style has been sought after for decades in all corners of Japan. Both types are characterized by respect for artisans, handmade products, natural materials, and a positive approach to simplicity. You will also find similarities in the complete functionality of space and a balanced vision of life.

The colors of the Japandi style are sober and contemplate a palette ranging from neutrals to pastel shades. White, gray, and different shades of light brown can be used without moderation. For accents, green, blue, or yellow, but strictly in pastel shades. Gold to be dosed with caution but essential, perhaps included in complements and accessories.

After all, the notes of color are dictated by the materials used, mostly natural. Wood is the absolute protagonist, both painted and raw, to be chosen in the bamboo, lime, or oak varieties. Metal, fabrics such as linen or cotton, ceramic, stone, and paper are the other materials to be preferred.

Furnishing in the Japandi style means coming to terms with oneself, putting aside the tendency to accumulate objects or fill the rooms with furniture. Provide built-in wardrobes and closets to store the inevitable ballast of unnecessary items unless you are already an expert in decluttering. The Japandi environments are characterized by minimal furniture and a few complimentary objects.

For the essential comfort corner, you can abound with cushions, blankets, and rugs to mix natural fabrics such as wool, linen, cotton, or vegetable fibers.

The importance of lighting and greenery

Lighting and greenery play a vital role in Japandi furnishings. Austerity and minimalism must be dampened on pain of a cold and unwelcoming environment. Warm and differentiated lighting, which manages to create exciting chiaroscuro in the background, can be obtained with different lighting devices.

Suspension lamps are placed on tables and kitchen islands, alternating with countertop lamps for the most intimate corners. For general lighting, choose floor lamps with a discreet design, bearing in mind that the light must always be muted.

Do not skimp on the green to complete the picture: succulents, green indoor plants, and elegant orchids will enliven the environment. Use earthenware pots and handcrafted ceramic pot holders or glass jars to insert twigs, leaves, and bamboo canes.

Combining two very distant styles can offer the opportunity to bring out character and personality.

A hybrid style like the Japandi one guarantees a balance between Japanese elegance and Scandinavian essential modernity.

The meeting point between these styles is represented by simplicity together with certain aesthetic minimalism, for which clean, tidy, and essential environments are recreated while maintaining their functionality.

The colors used by the Japanese and Scandinavian styles differ significantly since the first is based on earthy nuances, while the second mainly uses white.

Japandi style perfectly mixes these color palettes, playing with the contrasts between bright colors and natural colors to create exciting and relaxing environments from an aesthetic point of view.

Japandi -style space, we could put dark accents in a light setting, such as charcoal or dark brown objects.

Or, vice versa, insert lighter furnishings reminiscent of the Scandinavian style, in a dark space, with sage green or gray tones.

These additions can be made thanks to pillows, rugs, and frames; however, remembering not to overdo it to keep a minimalist look.

The role of natural elements

For a Japandi -style interior, one of the essential characteristics is the presence of natural elements, another point in common between the Scandinavian and Japanese styles.

The addition of plants gives the rooms an atmosphere of well-being and tranquility, provided by the shades of green.

The strong Japanese influence in the Japandi style, however, wants the quality of the plants to be given more importance than quantity.

Consequently, selecting a few specimens with distinctive and elegant leaves will be ideal.

The functional furnishings

The furnishings in the Japandi style have essential and clean lines, keeping functionality as a priority aspect.

To create a perfect fusion, it will be necessary to blend light-toned Scandinavian furniture with soft lines and dark and elegant furniture typical of Japanese interiors.

It is a combination capable of balancing rigor and sinuosity, typical of the Japandi style.

The Japanese furniture based on traditional culture is characterized by the low table, which gives the possibility to stay as close as possible to the earth.

To mix styles, you could opt for beds, coffee tables, and low benches, taking care to leave ample free space.

Furnishing accessories and materials

As for furniture, functionality and quality are more important than quantity for accessories and furnishing accessories.

The Scandinavian style focuses on a few pieces which give well-being and are welcoming, such as rugs and soft cushions, while the Japanese style focuses on authenticity.

A perfect fusion knows how to choose functional, simple, and essential accessories.

Think, for example, of adding wooden Venetian blinds, which are beautiful and essential to look at aesthetically and, at the same time, capable of guaranteeing privacy and energy saving.

The materials must be natural and preferably of craftsmanship.

Craftsmanship is one of the most authentic expressions of this thought since the objects are not made perfect in series, but each one is created with its characteristic imperfection.

The selection must include simple and quality materials, such as linen, cork, terracotta, and jute.

All with the typical feature of giving the rooms a welcoming and comfortable atmosphere.

Eliminate the superfluous

The Japandi is the fusion of two interior design styles, based on the concept of essentiality, created by eliminating the superfluous in favor of the functional.

The mix must give life to airy, tidy, bright, and clean environments, capable of having everything you need to be condensed into a few elements.

In short, this style goes perfectly with the need for decluttering at home, making it more essential, clean, and welcoming.

CHAPTER 11
THE KITCHEN IN JAPANDI STYLE

In this chapter, we report tips on creating a Japanese kitchen. This style best suits those who want to approach wabi-sabi design but perhaps do not currently have the psychological or economic force to transform their kitchen. So if you're going to close wabi-sabi one step at a time, this is the easiest way.

Japandi style kitchen is minimal and essential, characterized by furniture with clean and square lines, a few colors, and furnishing elements are chosen with great care and care, in a not unexpected way.

Japandi style of furniture was born as a hybrid style. It contains the best of typically oriental aesthetics - especially Japanese - and the characteristic features of the Nordic Scandinavian style.

Precisely what they are looking for in the Japandi style of furniture. According to the Japandi aesthetic, everything has its function, and, not secondarily, nothing is ever out of place. In an often chaotic home environment such as the kitchen, the Japandi style of furniture is an actual injection of rigor and minimalism.

Japandi style kitchen

Since Japandi is a hybrid style, the reference color palette contains shades dear to both kinds from which it originates. In the kitchen, soft and light shades find ample space, starting from white to the entire range of beiges.

Like in the Scandinavian style, these soft shades - by the way, effortless to combine - are a must when furnishing the kitchen in Japandi style.

Even if there is no lack of darker and more intense touches of color, dark browns and blacks, typical of the Japanese décor style, is equally popular with the Japandi. Depending on your preferences, you can decorate the kitchen with lighter or darker shades.

The ideal is to wisely combine them, creating a beautiful harmony as a whole.

Wood and other materials for Japandi furniture in the kitchen

Japandi-style kitchen. Just as the Japanese oriental tradition suggests, it is wood that dominates. Therefore, the wooden kitchen is the closest to the Japandi style, in which other natural materials also find space.

Bamboo, rattan, and rice paper evoke a strong bond with nature. Just think of the hood or the seats for some accessories or single functional kitchen elements; for example, steel and cast iron are also recommended.

Chairs, tables, and inevitable furnishing accessories

The Japanese-style kitchen is usually characterized by low furniture, and there are those who, by furnishing their home in the Japandi style, follow this rule. Depending on your preferences, insert furniture elements such as more or more miniature low chairs and tables. As for the chairs, there are many options to choose from.

Wooden stools when combined with a peninsula. Alternatively, opt for rattan armchairs with a comfortable and enveloping seat.

As already mentioned, the Japandi style strongly believes in rigor and order. Therefore, there is no lack of cabinets full of doors (preferably sliding) to keep the environment as tidy and "clean" as possible in a perfect Scandinavian Japanese kitchen.

As far as lighting is concerned, the ideal is pendant lamps, with a contemporary and very trendy appeal. Choose them in bamboo or wicker according to the Japanese aesthetic.

The importance of plants in the kitchen according to the Japandi style

Anyone who knows the Japandi style knows that plants play a fundamental role in furnishing the house. These symbolize the bond with nature and with the earth. Place a more or less large plant on the table or the kitchen cabinet, preferring the green and luxuriant ones. Even bonsai is confirmed as an excellent choice.

Alternatively, decorate the room with many cherries or orange blossom branches to dry and store in a vase.

CHAPTER 12

IDEAS FOR CREATING A WABI-SABI LOW STYLE KITCHEN COST

If you do not intend to spend too much and therefore not make too invasive interventions, you can start from the walls, for example, with an oriental wallpaper.

If you don't want to ruin the entire original wall, some stencils recall the Japanese style, depicting peach blossoms, bamboo canes, oriental writings, etc.

Suppose your kitchen is "far" from Japan. In that case, you could cover the furniture, choosing on the internet or in any DIY store models of adhesive paper that, for example, replicates wood, the material of choice for the Japanese.

You can also focus on chandeliers, especially if your kitchen is made up of a peninsula, on which to drop classic Japanese lanterns, in rice paper or fabric... even on a wooden table.

Another touch of style can be given with wooden utensils insight, such as spoons and ladles, or even by hanging Japanese ceramic plates... all simple ideas to make but above all inexpensive.

Challenging and luxurious solutions

The possibility of wanting to renovate the kitchen entirely and the various accessories and furnishing accessories of your Open Space cannot be excluded.

You will certainly start from the kitchen... opt for a simple material: wood and for linear and square shapes.

It will be up to you to opt for the peninsula, table, or both... wooden stools with wicker seats and wooden chairs to combine oriental cushions.

If you have much space in your house, you can find a corner to place that tea service directly from Kyoto, perhaps under a shelf on which you will add your favorite teas and herbal teas.

And those Japanese ceramic bowls, where do you usually serve ramen to your friends on cold winter evenings?

Insert a showcase between the kitchen cabinets; you can store them in plain sight and indoors, so they won't collect dust!

To illuminate by creating an effect of lights and shadows, which are very zen, you can imagine the light that penetrates between one intersection and the other of the bamboo... these chandeliers will float on your table, softening the squares of the surrounding furniture.

Japanese style tableware

A kitchen with a Japanese design cannot fail to be treated in detail, so if you want, you can exaggerate, starting with cutlery, for example.

The time has come to abandon the belief that the Japanese eat only with chopsticks; they use cutlery just like us, different in colors, materials, and shapes but still cutlery!

In Japan, ceramic is used a lot; the difference lies in how it is decorated, the colors, and the elements depicted on the dishes, such as flowers, samurai, geometric figures, and Japanese calligraphic writings.

Of course, wooden dishes are also widely used.

Japanese style dishes

Flat plates for sushi and funds for the food of choice, which in Japan is rice, ramen, and broths based on meat and vegetables, and bowls for sauces that almost always accompany their typical dishes.

Japanese style centerpieces and tablecloths

Greenlight also to grandmother's doilies, doilies, and embroideries that you can use on your kitchen furniture and the table under glasses.

Finally, you can set your table with that hand-painted tablecloth you have kept in the kit until today to make a great impression on your guests.

Otherwise, you can choose Japanese-style tablecloths and napkins, in pure cotton or linen, or for quick meals, some wicker placemats to unroll at the moment and go... more luxurious than that!

Japanese style decor

Finally, we think of further embellishing the environment created so far with plants and flowers. You can think of a bonsai, a succulent plant, as a centerpiece.

Think of orchids if you love flowers with a delicate and exquisite appearance.

Peach blossoms are the must-have of Asian countries like Japan, but it's also true that they are seasonal flowers, so they don't last all year round.

The alternative is that of fake flowers; in this way, they will last and require no care, if not a dusting.

Open space ideas

You can create a living room with fabric sofas, carpets, strictly low tables, poufs, and wicker baskets if the room is enormous.

Imagine a large painting on the sofa wall that perhaps depicts a buddha," the great wave" of Hokusai, samurai, flowers, or a simple Zen landscape.

Tall and narrow glass vases are also preferred. Fill the bottom with stones and stick some bamboo inside them; the effect will be 100% Japanese.

CHAPTER 13
HOW TO FURNISH THE BEDROOM

Wood is, therefore, the material you cannot give up if you want to furnish the bedroom.

This material becomes the basis for the floor, but also the furniture. Lightwood and even raw wood should be preferred.

The actual unique and particular combination is the combination of wood with vibrant materials, such as dark marble, which is also used to create elegant Japanese-inspired coatings.

Another material is paper. Rice paper is used for making lamps or light paintings. He also uses bamboo for the decorations of the environment and rich fabrics that have simple, linear, or solid-colored patterns and embellishments.

The decorations suit this style for your bedroom, trend towards sobriety and elegance. In particular, plants play a leading role; large indoor plants make the environment lively and cheerful.

Secondly, wallpapers are of great importance. Scenographic designs, inspired by pure geometric shapes and Japanese art, are made of natural subjects, leaves, and colors such as gold, black and deep green.

Another element that you cannot give up for the bedroom is the cabinets, bedside tables, or benches with simple lines. In particular, use furniture that prioritizes empty spaces over full ones. Everything becomes light and becomes minimal.

As for the secondary decorations, use a framed mirror and paintings, which reproduce within them simple subjects or drawings inspired by lineart, the art of depicting six subjects, people, or passages using a continuous black line on a white background.

When referring to Japan, a technologically advanced nation immediately comes to mind, at the forefront of most sectors, full of skyscrapers and full of luxury and comfort. These are certain truths that sometimes cannot entirely refer to the style of Japanese houses.

Minimalist and aseptic at first glance, Japanese homes are straightforward and economically furnished, as the inhabitants of this nation prefer order and simplicity. Despite this, mainly because they are very different from ours, Japanese houses are full of character, which is why we love so much to be inspired in design by this Eastern culture.

The Japanese bed stands out from all the others for its shallow height, able to raise even the lowest ceilings. You can either buy cheap or create a bed of this size using thin wooden planks. An oriental-style alternative to the standard bed is the futon, a type of bed that can be rolled up in the evening and rolled out in the morning, which allows the bedroom to be converted into any other room for everyday use. On the leading e-commerce sites, it is also available at 70 euros.

The lights

The lights can increase the oriental atmosphere inside the Japanese bedroom. Usually, the classic Japanese lamps are used, with small dimensions for the bedside tables and high ones to act as floor lamps. The style in question loves square and regular lines, so rectangular and square lights are perfect to be placed inside the bedroom. The small Japanese lamps, mostly made of bamboo, are available on the market for around 20 euros; the floor lamps, on the other hand, start at 40 euros.

Colors

The Japanese style is not very demanding for colors, but the most used are warm tones such as yellow, red, orange, and brown: the latter is also due to the presence of natural wood, a material widely used in this type of design. Among the cold colors, gray, black, and light blue win, as long as it is pastel or very soft.

Plants

Although Tokyo represents the typical metropolis with a western flavor, the Japanese are true to nature lovers. For this reason, they love to furnish their bedroom by inserting some plants, as long as they do not make the air suffocating. There are aloe vera, pothos, peace lily, and lavender among the perfect plants in the bedroom.

Doors and screens

Thinking about a Japanese home, one cannot help but imagine the classic sliding doors. Suppose it is impossible to convert the western doors into Japanese-style ones because the cost can even exceed 1000 euros. You can easily opt to introduce some wooden grids to the walls to give the bedroom that good quality. Squared and geometric effects that would be missing. The slats that make up the grid can be easily recycled from an old bed base.

Japanese screens

Another way in full Japanese style to divide the house's rooms is to insert screens of various sizes. There are all shapes, types, and colors, usually available at an affordable starting price of 30 euros: the screens most appreciated by the Japanese are the simple ones in shades of white or those with floral and fauna textures.

Even in the Western world, the charm of Japanese bedrooms is becoming more and more popular. These are simple yet visually striking and suggest a vast impression of serenity and balance. Japanese furniture today can present itself in various forms, from the hi-tech version to the one that combines the Japanese imprint with the Scandinavian one. The solutions are different, but one of the most popular in any case is the classic one, with fusuma, Tatami, futon, and so on.

Bedrooms need to be functional and elegant, and one inspired by the Land of the Rising Sun fulfills all these characteristics. Some essential accessories are required, such as a Japanese-style bed, a low nightstand, and other elements that we will discuss shortly.

The futon: the futon occupies a special place in Japanese bedrooms. We refer to the traditional flexible mattress, which can be placed directly on the floor or a low wooden bed. Due to its structure, the futon can be rolled up easily and stored in a wardrobe or large drawer in the morning. This allows you to save space and have a completely free and uncluttered floor. For this reason, the futon is also often used in guest rooms: it can be stored without problems and moves easily from one room to another.

In addition, the futon is "green" for the materials with which it is made! The best futons have cotton or wool padding: you can buy both types to alternate between summer and winter. The surface is soft but still able to offer the proper support to the spine. There are also latex futons and futons with coconut slabs to accommodate all needs. As for the coating, it can be either in cotton or zinc oxide. The result is eco-friendly, comfortable, and safe. The futon is a must for Japanese-style bedrooms. And maintenance is simple, as you need to avoid moisture.

The low wooden bed: those who do not want to place the futon on the floor could choose a soft wooden bed to match the traditional Japanese mattress. However, these accessories are perfect not only with futons but also with western latex or memory mattresses. Foam. The most suitable beds, in this context, are the interlocking ones: entirely made of wood, without metal details such as screws and nails. The wooden panels fit together, guaranteeing solidity and stability. A wooden bed is eco-sustainable, spectacular, and very comfortable. Wood is one of the fundamental materials in Japanese furniture, suggestive of its grain, natural, and capable of transmitting warmth and harmony.

The doors: fusuma and shoji - When you need to set up a room, it is essential to take care of the choice of doors. The Japanese ones are called fusuma and shoji. An internal door, which connects the bedroom to the house's other rooms, is called fusuma. It is rectangular panels with a wooden core and a cover of fabric, cardboard, or rice paper. The sliding takes place on wooden tracks. Instead, the term shoji is used for exterior doors. These elements are made of wood and paper and are truly beautiful.

The Tatami - In Japanese bedrooms, you could also arrange a tatami: the classic mat for the floor, in a rush, and rice straw with fabric edges. The Tatami can be of various heights, ranging from those typical of Japan (5-6 cm) to those lowered, more similar to Western solutions, of 2.5 cm. Foldable, rollable, rubber tatamis, and so on. The possibilities are endless, as are the decorative motifs!

Furniture and Accessories: to conclude, what else is missing in a Japanese-style bedroom? A low wooden bedside table, just like the bed, or even a tatami bedside table with a rice straw interior is lovely. To keep personal effects, you need to assemble a wooden wardrobe with a pure and minimal design and some wooden shelves. As for accessories, lamps of wood and rice paper are evergreen. A themed print of a Japanese artist to hang on the wall, and that's it!

CHAPTER 14
THE BATHROOM

The best bathroom color in this style is neutral.

In terms of color, most colors are pretty neutral. Warmer and more earthy colors are ideal; they will calm your mind and create a friendly atmosphere. So choose, for example, beige, cream or brown. To liven up the interior, you will consider the contrast of dark colors - emerald, indigo, or dark purple. But you don't have to overdo them! As for patterns, it's best to avoid them.

Furniture and love for wood

Japandi style prefers low-to-the-ground furniture. This custom promotes people's connection with the earth and their sensory perception of nature. So are, for example, the cabinets under the sink, which also save space. The furniture lines are clean and minimalist. And what material to choose? Definitely wood. One option is to buy furniture that mimics a wooden surface, but you can also look for natural wood. In this case, tropical woody plants used to humidity are ideal. However, expect a higher price.

The furniture must be chosen carefully because it is a distinctive and bold element. Don't forget the quality: always buy only from certified producers. One option is to use recycled older pieces.

Faucet for sink and basin

Another essential element is, of course, the sink. In the bathroom, it will stand out both freely placed on a support surface and classically connected directly to the washbasin cabinet. To emphasize the harmonious atmosphere in the room, you will choose round shapes: both round and oval washbasins are made.

Also, don't forget the basin mixer. It should match the sink, so if possible, choose products from the same series of products from similar lines. Since the Japanese style prefers simplicity to complex shapes, choose between lever taps rather than knob taps. However, you can also select a contactless tap: it is not just very modern but also highly hygienic.

Bath or shower?

In every bathroom, whatever the style, there is an element that will attract our attention at first glance. Most often, it is a bath or shower. The Japanese-style bathroom does not prefer any of the options. It is up to you which option to choose. If the room is spacious, we recommend choosing a freestanding bathtub: it will look truly unique. It compares all the different designs for the shower and chooses the best one. Here too, however, the more the rounder, the better.

Walk-in showers are also an exquisite solution. However, you can also choose a custom-made atypical shower, which everyone will admire in your bathroom. The same goes for the bathtub; in no case can there be limits to your imagination.

Minimal accessories

Don't go overboard in the Japanese bathroom with accessories. In this style, functionality comes first. The decoration will be minimal: it mainly consists of plants, glass products, and handmade ceramics.

urushi wallpapers, shibori fabrics, bonsai, or paper lamps. Even the walls should not be too decorated; we recommend choosing a dominant decoration and adding only a few details. One such dominant feature may be, for example, a frameless mirror, which optically enlarges and illuminates the space. Last but not least, you can use fabrics made from natural materials for decoration.

CHAPTER 15
THE LIVING ROOM

Create a magnificent living room using the Japanese style philosophy. Recreate the Rising Sun atmosphere in the living room by studying furniture arrangements and aiming for a Zen and minimal lifestyle.

Escaping the allure of the Far East appears difficult for some people: once upon a time, it was said that Africa was sick, but today, it seems that Japan piques the interest of many who usually travel to the Rising Sun in search of a modern destination with an exotic flavor. To be inspired and meditate, as prescribed by ancient Zen philosophies.

When you return from your vacation, you should re-propose the series of furnishings that define the authentic Japanese style in your apartment.

Let's try to design a modern living room but, at the same time, is strongly influenced by Japanese culture and its millenary history.

Let's consider the essential points of this style before opening your wallet and wandering around shopping malls and ethnic shops specializing in the furnishings that offer this style.

The dominant philosophy in Japanese homes is based on the search for harmony and lightness, which are essential founding points of the Zen lifestyle.

The apartment, and thus its rooms, are designed and studied so that its coexistence and stay inside the theme is marked by the essential, to the point where it can be identified, in some features, as similar to the minimalist style.

As a result of the success of sliding doors allows you to join rooms with a simple gesture while also allowing light and airflow between spaces to flow freely.

Colors reflect this spirit of life, always harmonious and soft; thus, the prohibition of temptations to overdo it with flashy and contrasting chromatic games.

It is the triumph of different natural materials such as wood, mainly bamboo, which is used to make most of the furniture, and rice paper, which is used to cover the doors of wardrobes, sliding doors, and dividers.

The central station, the sofa, is placed against the wall to keep the passage as straightforward as possible: the table in front will be helpful for lunch or dinner. At the same time, you can sit on the cushions without collapsing or making large movements on the floor.

The Tatami, the carpet used for judo and karate competitions, is the most common surface coating in Japanese homes.

The Tatami is constructed with a wood or other material frame and then covered with woven and pressed straw to provide some resistance to body weight.

The sofa is crucial in the living room, especially in Japanese homes where rest and meditation are an essential part of daily life.

For those who appreciate tradition, the sofa has a distinctive wooden structure and a futon mattress, which can be placed on the floor for afternoon or night rest if you have visitors.

Let us recall that the futon is a comfortable roll-up mattress that is beaten in the morning to allow it to absorb air and be free of dust. Then it was wrapped like a sleeping bag.

The furnishings of traditional Japanese houses are sparse. The Zen philosophy imprints a lifestyle on minimalism; the search for essentiality and, therefore, tinsel and not very functional furniture are not foreseen.

Rectangular or square in shape, entirely in wood, it has accentuated edges while the colors remain on the classic brown of the wood or, in a more modern version, black.

They are used to discreetly divide rooms or create a corner within an environment, as is the case in the bedroom.

They must be easily moved and provide an interesting decorative element.

When you want to decorate in a meaningful way, images of landscapes, volcanoes, and country towns are often drawn on the shutters rather than gardens.

The dividers generally have a height of about 180 cm and have at least 3/4 doors.

Japanese style living room: lighting on the other hand, ceiling chandeliers have a distinct charm, with luminaires that have a simple shape, such as square, rectangular, or spherical, with regular dimensions.

The lampshades have no ornaments or designs, and the colors are dull and monotonous, primarily white, beige, or grey.

CHAPTER 16
THE FENG SHUI

Design rules, materials, and colors to furnish the house with the Feng Shui method for an apartment inspired by the teachings of Taoist philosophy.

How to design a Feng Shui furniture for the home? Before moving on to practical advice, it is good to know that the expression "Feng Shui" comes from Chinese and means "wind and water." It is an oriental discipline that combines practices of reading and interpreting buildings' landscapes, forms, and interior spaces to establish a perfect harmony between people and the environment.

According to this discipline, born about five thousand years ago, the arrangement of rooms and furnishings inside a house affects the energy inside and, consequently, the people who live there. Therefore, the goal of Feng Shui is to create a positive flow of energy in every room of the house through the creation of sober, comfortable, and tidy spaces.

Feng shui in Chinese means "wind and water." The wind is the sky, the air that carries the clouds swollen with rain, the water without which every creature on the planet could not survive. The ancient discipline of feng shui is considered indispensable and is a set of practices of reading and interpreting the landscape, the shapes of the buildings, and the spaces inside the buildings to avoid the negative influences of various kinds that can affect the structures the man.

The practice of feng shui is a five-thousand-year-old Chinese and Tibetan tradition with a Japanese equivalent in Ka-so. Ti-Li, or "blackbird art," symbolized the solar spirit, the god of geography and astronomy, whose teachings served as the foundation for agricultural and land planning practices

in ancient times.

This tradition is still very rooted in China and Hong Kong, so the first expert to be consulted is a Feng master when buying land or a building. Shui; his opinion affects the real estate market. Even when an economic activity suffers setbacks, it is customary to ask him for a response to any hostile energies set in motion by the type of architecture or interior decoration.

The aesthetic concepts of "beauty" and "harmony of proportions" and the economic ones linked to the exploitation of the territory and its characteristics are closely related to the practice of geomancy, that is, respect for subtle balances (earth, telluric, and energy of the sky, cosmic) to make the energies of the place favorable to human settlements.

According to this ancient Chinese discipline, the house-man relationship identifies the vibratory aspect of energy structures in which subtle energy fields are identifiable, recognized as constituting a pattern within which a vital energy flows connected to all forms of life.

FENG SHUI: GENERAL RULES FOR FURNISHING

Feng Shui conceives the domestic space as a container that adapts to our personality and activities.

Below we propose some basic rules of organization of spaces and style for a perfect Feng Shui home.

Feng Shui at home: the position of command

In Feng Shui furniture, it is appropriate to establish the command position in some house rooms. The command position is located at the opposite corner from the door. At this point, you must place a bed, a desk, or a sofa: the aim is to reduce one's vulnerability by assuming a dominant position to control and enhance one's energy flow.

Design spaces with the Bagua map

The practical principles of Feng Shui are expressed through the Bagua, a Chinese term that means "eight trigrams." The Bagua is a geomantic map that matches an aspect of life, such as work, health, and social relationships, to every room in the house.

A Bagua map is composed as follows:

Eight sections (Gua) correspond to the sides of the octagonal map, which represent family, marriage, children, social relationships, career, knowledge, health, and wealth;

every Gua has a number that corresponds to the eight cardinal points, which helps know the personal energy of the inhabitants of the house;

every Gua is followed by a trigram, each with a different combination of lines: the solid ones represent the masculine yang, while the broken ones represent the feminine yin ;

the eight different combinations of the trigrams represent the forces generated by the five natural elements: fire, earth, metal, water, and wood;

the central area is occupied by the symbol of Tai Chi (Ying Yang), representing the balance and harmony of all Gua and, therefore, personal well-being and health.

To use the Bagua map, it must be superimposed on the floor plan of the house by matching the center of the map with the center of the house; it is necessary to make the entry point coincide with the water Gua. To facilitate furnishing with the Feng Shui method, the octagonal pattern can be replaced with a square model divided into nine areas, each marked by the Gua, the characterizing natural element, and the primary color.

Choose colors in a balanced way.

The colors yellow, ocher, brown, apricot, and gold belong to the earth element. They are associated with the cardinal points of the south-west (social relations and marriage), the north-east (knowledge and self-realization), and the center (health). Yellow is associated with patience, control, and tolerance; others have a calming effect and stimulate concentration; a light apricot tint conveys warmth and coziness and is ideal for a bedroom.

Green color belongs to the wood element and is associated with the east (family) and south-east (wealth, prosperity, and abundance) cardinal points. In particular, green favors balance, harmony, and peace. The green decoration for the walls should be chosen only if there are few plants in the room to avoid generating redundancy in the environment.

We are renewing the house with colors: practical ideas for any environment.

In Feng Shui furniture, black, blue, and light Blue is associated with the north direction (career) and falls under the element of water. Black symbolizes work, power, and money and stimulates the imagination; Blue has a calming effect, makes a room with little natural light bright and welcoming, and is suitable for bathroom decor. On the other hand, Blue is ideal for small spaces, helps fight insomnia, and is perfect for furnishing a small bedroom.

White is rarely used in China because it is the color of mourning. It is perfect for illuminating and restoring a sense of order. However, it should be avoided in icy environments and in children's bedrooms. Gray and neutral shades convey balance and stability; they are ideal for the walls and furnishings of a home office or study corner. Both colors belong to the metal element and are associated with the cardinal points west (children and creative projects) and the north-west (friendship and support).

According to Chinese tradition, red is the luckiest color, a symbol of passion, joy, and growth: it is used with caution to avoid making the environment aggressive; it is suitable for a living area, even in furnishing elements. Orange infuses happiness and constructive energy: in less-lighted environments, it helps to create a relaxing atmosphere. Pink refreshes the rooms and makes them more welcoming in the lighter shades. These colors fall under the element of fire and are associated with the southern cardinal point (fame and reputation).

Feng Shui favors natural materials.

Wood, stone, metal, and fabrics are the most suitable materials for furniture inspired by the Feng Shui method. Wood is considered a living material with multipurpose characteristics and can be used for furniture, fixtures, and flooring in any house room.

The stone elements - shiny or porous, even in travertine or slate - must be inserted in a balanced and essential way.

Metals are also crucial in a home furnished according to the Feng Shui method, with different characteristics based on their composition. If the metal furniture elements are shiny and reflective, it is better to place them in environments intended for relaxation.

Finally, fabrics, especially natural ones such as linen, silk, cotton, and wool, must be used in a balanced way in the areas intended for rest since their interwoven composition slows down the flow of energy.

The importance of decluttering

Feng Shui furniture requires careful space optimization: get rid of different objects to make more space available.

The accumulation of unused or disordered objects would prevent the flow of positive energies. The rooms must be cleaned and tidy every day, eliminating unnecessary things, clothing, and furnishings using ecological methods.

FENG SHUI FURNITURE FOR THE LIVING ROOM

In the Feng Shui furniture style, the living room must have a square or rectangular floor plan. The key element around which the entire arrangement of the furnishings revolves is the sofa, which must have a linear and rounded shape, with a high back and armrests. Place it against a wall, possibly respecting the control position described above, i.e., in the opposite corner from the door.

According to the Feng Shui style, the room must be furnished with space-saving elements, rounded and harmonious shapes, and made with natural materials such as wood.

The living room is the environment of relationships and the fire element, so the best choice is to use red or its shades, always considering the geographical position concerning the Bagua map and, therefore, the corresponding colors. Red, in some cases, can be too energetic: the best solution is to include colors and materials belonging to each element to balance the energy.

Plants are full of positive energy and can help balance energy flows. It is better to choose plants with soft-shaped leaves and avoid those with a pointed shape.

FENG SHUI FURNITURE IN THE KITCHEN

In an ideal Feng Shui home, the kitchen is rectangular in plan, facing south, well lit, comfortable, and has extensive work surfaces.

The arrangement of the furniture must take into account the flows of energy and the symbols of nature: stove and oven (fire) must never be placed near the refrigerator and dishwasher (water), or at least they must be separated by cupboards or wooden shelves, element that represents the control over the destructive relationship between water and fire. Arrange them so that you do not have your back on those who enter to control the environment completely.

The colors to choose from are different; each can perform a specific function in the kitchen based on its exposure and the elements that compose it. Generally, it is advisable to take advantage of the lighter shades that reflect the light by focusing on colors such as green, yellow, white, and those of the earth, both for the furniture and for the walls and dividing panels.

Orange represents joy and vitality, stimulates the appetite, and has a regenerating effect on the nervous system; yellow is ideal for a dynamic area such as the kitchen as it has a warming and energizing function; green balances all the other colors recall the plant world and transmits calm; finally, the cleanliness of the white, with cream or butter shades, can also be used for the worktop, to be balanced with furnishings in darker tones to create light color contrasts.

Spice racks, utensils, cutting boards, pantries, and wooden containers also allow you to obtain positive energy. If the house does not consist of a dining room, the table and chairs in the kitchen are also preferred in wood, a symbol of prosperity and family union.

To circulate positive energies while respecting the cardinal points and free the negative ones from the environment where the cook transforms food using the five elements: water, wood, fire, earth, and metal.

FENG SHUI FURNITURE IN THE BEDROOM

On the other hand, if the bedroom is in the front, a mirror hanging in front of the door, behind the median line of the house, will "push" the room back.

The feng shui attaches a lot of importance to the bedroom's layout. The bed should be placed across, with the head facing east. The optimal location is in the corner diagonally opposite the entrance, in such a way that you never have heads or feet pointing directly towards the door to the room.

Inwood or upholstered fabric, the headboard must be placed against a wall to obtain a greater sense of support and protection.

Even the bed height must be chosen carefully: it must not be too low. In general, solutions with integrated containers should be avoided to allow energy to circulate even under it.

On the sides of the bed, it is possible to place bedside tables, preferably round in shape, so that the energy does not flow directly onto the person who sleeps, destabilizing the rest.

On the bedside tables, it is recommended to keep lampshades that give an oriental touch to the bedroom and allow you to create a relaxed atmosphere. Alternatively, you can use lamps with adjustable light intensity via switches, ideal for establishing the most suitable lighting level according to your needs.

In Shui style bedroom, the wisest decision is to use pastel colors or neutral shades.

Green and blue are the colors of nature, therefore very relaxing, associated with care and refreshment. Purple is a balanced color linked to prosperity and financial abundance with its lavender undertones.

Even so-called "skin colors" with shades ranging from pale white to brown are good options for a bedroom: ivory, Pink, beige, chocolate and bronze give the room a calm and friendly feel.

Colors

Green is the color of fresh plants and nature; it symbolizes growth and study.

Red represents animal life and learning; it is a good omen, especially in combination with black.

White is the color related to money and is used in public places to call good luck.

Black is related to rest and settling (of ideas).

The feng shui recommends not placing mirrors in the bedroom due to their ability to disturb the energy field. Covering the mirrors during the night improves the quality of sleep considerably.

FENG SHUI FURNITURE IN THE BATHROOM

The element that characterizes the bathroom is water, a symbol of life and purification. This element can also be reproduced in the furnishings through furniture with soft, twisted, and wavy shapes and colors such as blue and light Blue. Green and white are also suitable for decorating the bathroom with the Feng Shui method as they represent nature and purity, respectively.

To avoid energy dispersion, the bathroom must be balanced with the earth element through different materials, such as marble and quartz, which are excellent for the sink and other surfaces. Even the ceramic tiles, glass, and stone reinforce the reference to the earth and the terracotta, light yellow and delicate beige colors. The balancing of the elements can also be obtained with metals, particularly brass if the bathroom is facing south.

To add elegance and warmth, plants of tropical origin can be used, suitable for hot and humid environments. In particular, if it is lit enough by natural light, the best plants to choose from are aloe vera, begonia, orchid, fern, and bamboo.

The mirror has a reflective ability which makes it an energy amplifier. Since it is associated with the water element, the mirror must have characteristics that make the environment more harmonious: round in shape, essential, and positioned to reflect the wall but not the bathroom fixtures.

Office

To respect the feng shui in the office, the worktable should be placed at the most vital point of the room so that the back is protected and the gaze can be directed at the door and window. What is in front of the workstation is also extremely important as it increases the Qi and is a source of inspiration. Therefore desks with a position facing a wall should be avoided.

Feng shui and architecture.

Western and Eastern architecture have the same basic concept: achieving a balance. However, while Western architecture reaches it through symmetry, Eastern architecture goes it through dynamism: a yin is never the same as yang: they are always in changing relationships now one dominates the other, and the task is balancing these two forces.

The four celestial animals of feng shui

People called feng shui to choose the ideal place to erect the village in ancient times. For this reason, the presence of the four celestial or emblematic animals that we can define as the guardians of the four directions had to be recognized in the landscape: the dragon, the tiger, the tortoise, and the red phoenix.

The feng shui and water

Water is linked to abundance, wealth, money, and communication. Therefore, a watercourse that flows calmly near the house is considered favorable, preferably from east to west, or a small lake to the south, which can enhance its beneficial presence, reflecting the sunlight. Water must always be present in the rooms of the house.

CHAPTER 17

KA-SO, THE FENG SHUI MADE IN JAPAN

F eng Shui is the oriental art of furnishing according to the harmonic canons of human well-being. This particular discipline was born in China at a very distant time, and, recently, it has been observed that already in the Neolithic, the tombs were conceived following an exact layout and construction method.

This doctrine also has its roots in very remote times, and, in 1983, some scholars from the University of Illinois in Chicago translated ancient texts in which all the principles of Ka-So are kept.

BETWEEN SPACE AND TIME

The Ka-So aims to generate a total harmony of the subtle energies within the home. The fourth dimension, time, represents a fundamental variable. In the Ka-So, the time component translates into the period of the year or the season. Therefore the arrangement of the bed or futon within the housing unit acquires a different function also based on this factor.

Lao Tzu, a Chinese sage who lived in the sixth century BC and was considered one of the founding fathers of Taoism, argued that "the essence of the ship is the void within it." The Japanese art of living also took up this consideration. Design is imagined beyond the standard three dimensions and sublimation of time, also understood as space. For this reason, Japanese houses are furnished with the bare minimum, which translates into the use of futons, tatami mats, and a few other accessories.

THE INFLUENCES OF CHINESE CULTURE

Ka-So is the fruit of notions imported to Japan by an itinerant Buddhist monk in the last decades of the sixth century. From that moment, the planning of cities also began to follow pre-established schemes, and actual departments for the supervision of architectural projects were established. Kyoto itself (capital of Japan until 1868) was designed according to the principles of Ka-So.

CHAPTER 18

IKEBANA: THE FASCINATING JAPANESE ART OF ARRANGING CUT FLOWERS

To give a Wabisabi touch to your rooms, you can try Ikebana, an ancient Japanese art for creating cut flower vases.

Japan always offers magnificent artistic ideas, which are always modern and current, although born in ancient times. Ikebana's case indicates the ancient Japanese art of arranging cut flowers, branches, stems, and leaves harmoniously and elegantly. The name Ikebana derives from the union of the word Ike, which in Japanese means "alive," and Bana, which means "flower." Unlike the Western habit of filling a vase with more and more flowers, even of different types, Ikebana art aims at minimalism; a vase will hold a few flowers, the bare essentials to bring out the inner qualities of the flowers.

Given their meticulous artistry, Ikebana compositions can be defined as art installations in all respects.

How to make an Ikebana

These harmonious floral compositions can be formed by different types of flowers, starting from the orchid to hydrangeas, from chrysanthemums to gerberas, and from roses to bamboo branches. The main rule for creating an Ikebana composition is to use all elements of an organic nature, whether they are flowers, herbs, components, or leaves. Branches and flowers are thus arranged to create a triangle: the longest chapter called Shin, the most important one, is considered as the element that extends towards the sky, the shorter branch, the Hikae, symbolizes the earth, while the intermediate one, the Soe, represents the man. We need to balance Shin, Hikae, and Soe harmoniously without too complex elaborations.

Kenzan is the basis for Ikebana, a fundamental element for shaping the course of the composition as desired. Available in different diameters, this heavy support has metal spikes that will be used to pierce the stems of the cut flowers and keep them in an upright position.

Vase: the vase will allow you to create a balance between all the natural elements used. You can choose the vase as you like; some prefer low containers, others tall vases with a vertical trend. The decision will also vary based on the type of flowers selected. Floral arrangements created in flat containers are called Moribana, while those modeled on tall containers are called Nageire.

Scissors will be invaluable for cutting branches and flowers, removing excess parts, or reducing the size. There are no detailed specifications on the scissors; the idea is to use a model with a comfortable handle and made of resistant material to cut even large branches easily.

The courses that allow you to learn how to create your Ikebana are increasingly popular; in detail, they will focus on understanding how to properly cut flowers and branches, evaluate the correct positioning, and preserve living materials for a long time.

If you are fond of elegant flower arrangements, you love everything to do with minimalism, and feel a great attraction towards oriental culture; you will only be fascinated by this beautiful ancient art of arranging cut flowers.

When you find yourself in front of an ikebana composition, do you also feel a sensation between adoration and disorientation?

This Japanese art, so rich in history, exudes a charm that can be intimidating; yet, to practice some styles of Ikebana, you don't need to be an expert.

Like many traditional Japanese arts, Ikebana also asks to be 'listening' to oneself and nature. The composition that Jenny shows us is created according to the Nageire style, characterized by the spontaneity of execution, which emphasizes the natural beauty of the material used. It contrasts with the more artificial and complex techniques created.

The composition consists of three main branches, accompanied by various smaller branches.

Choose a tall and narrow vase and fill it with water; it will lend itself to the horizontal shape we will give. To keep the branches in the desired position, you can build flat forks with pieces of extensions fixed against the vase's edge, forming a cross.

Take the aucuba branches and the stems of the two hydrangeas and remove the leaves from the part that will go into the water. Too long stems and components should be cut diagonally to anchor them to the vase. The stems are always cut underwater to ensure fast absorption and avoid bubbles in the lymphatic channels of the branch.

Now insert the branches into the vase. The Shin branch defines the character and line of the composition. It is one and a half or two times the length of the vase. In the horizontal Nageire, this branch rests on an imaginary horizon. The Soe branch is half of Shin and must be placed on the opposite side; the Hikae addition is a third of Shin and should be positioned in the center, at the bottom.

Lastly, insert the flowers, in our case, two hydrangeas: we have chosen them to respect seasonality and 'zero km. You can spray branches, flowers, and leaves with a vaporizer, especially if it's hot.

CHAPTER 19
HOW TO COVER A FLOOR WITH
TATAMI

In Japan, the tatami floor has spread to almost all homes thanks to its particular characteristics that allow it to be used in the same room for multiple purposes. In fact, during the day, it can serve as the ideal support for the typical Japanese coffee tables and the Japanese zaisu chairs, helpful in having lunch or consuming the typical tea ceremony. In the evening, the Tatami becomes a comfortable bed by simply spreading a Futon, the traditional Japanese mattress, on it. In both Japan and the West, the tatami floor is also used in all gyms where martial arts are practiced, such as Judo and Karate, because it reduces the risk of injury when falling.

What is Tatami: characteristics and composition

The term Tatami indicates the single rectangular or square carpet made of woven and pressed rice straw, and the traditional Japanese floor is composed of several mats placed side by side. Over time, these mats have also been increasingly sought after in the west to create an environmentally sustainable environment free of harmful substances as it consists only of natural elements.

The edges of the Tatami are squared with precision to avoid the presence of gaps when they are placed side by side to create the coverings. Thanks to this possibility of perfectly fitting them, it is unnecessary to use adhesives to fix them to the floor.

The advantages of tatami floors

The materials that make up the high-quality tatamis are entirely natural, making them ecological and perfectly biodegradable products. The woven straw surface gives off a pleasant scent and offers a sense of comfort that massages the sole when you walk on it. Therefore, walking barefoot, without shoes, or with the traditional Zori slippers that can certainly not be missing in an authentic Japanese home is recommended.

Like expanded cork and wood fiber, the natural and organic composition of the straw acts as an excellent thermal insulator. Furthermore, since the air molecules trapped in the straw weave of the tatami floor are insulated from the outside temperature, they can maintain a constant temperature. Precisely for this reason, the tatamis have the advantage of making the rooms cool in summer and warm in winter. In this way, they contribute to creating a healthy environment in the house, purifying the air and mitigating any humid climate in the rooms.

The tatami floors also offer an excellent degree of acoustic insulation, both thanks to the sound-absorbing properties of the straw that allows it to absorb a large part of the sound energy and because the thickness of the weave absorbs shocks and, therefore, noises.

When the individual tatami mats are put together to cover a floor, particular designs can be formed on the floor that strike for their perfect symmetry, creating scenic interlocking effects. Here are some examples of the compositions that can be made by combining tatamis of the same or different sizes:

Any interior floor can be covered with a bit of creativity, enhancing irregularities such as columns or walls with particular angles. Suppose the dimensions of the tatami panels do not match perfectly with the measurements of your room. In that case, you can also make custom-made tatami floors without cutting the carpets because they would almost certainly risk wearing out over time. These frames are usually colored black or wenge to make them uniform to the color of the edges of the tatamis. However, it is also possible to color them with other colors to match the rest of the other furnishings.

With wood, you can also create other additions to the tatami floor that enhance its design and offer practical solutions for the daily use of the environment.

For example, if you want the tatami floor to reach the house entrance, we can create a wooden island in front of the door that facilitates entry and allows you to take off your shoes without stepping on the Tatami as soon as possible enter the house. Or it is possible to create wooden frames that form islands in the middle of the floor, which can serve as a support for oriental vases such as our bamboo vases or suggestive Zen fountains.

Suppose you want to create a tatami floor in rooms where you also want to place furniture, such as a chest of drawers or wardrobes. In that case, you can make elevations of the same height as the carpets (about 6 cm) under the table to allow you to open the drawers or doors easily.

Finally, if you want to preserve an existing door that opens toward the tatami floor, you can cut the lower part of the door to align it with the new tatami floor, which will be about 6 cm higher than the previous floor.

Shoji sliding doors or walls are traditional Japanese room dividers made with a wooden frame on which rice paper is mounted. Japanese. Shoji sliding doors are particularly appreciated for the light and translucent consistency of washi rice paper, which filters the light and spreads it evenly throughout the room.

CHAPTER 20

HOW TO CREATE A TERRACE WITH A ZEN GARDEN

How do you furnish a Zen-style deck? What elements must not be missing? Find out how to design an outdoor space to find balance and harmony. Take a cue from these decor ideas to create a beautiful Zen terrace.

Balance and harmony are two basic principles of Zen art, a word that encompasses many oriental meditative disciplines aimed at achieving tranquility and greater self-awareness.

The style of furniture that reflects this philosophy of life is expressed through modern and essential-looking furniture, few colors and most natural, and the inevitable presence of the four natural elements: water, fire, earth, and air.

Designing a harmonious and peaceful space in your home is not difficult at all, but to create a place where you can relax or where you can meditate, we suggest you consider the idea of creating a Zen terrace.

Not sure where to start? Do not worry: here are furnishing ideas and practical advice to design a perfect outdoor space.

The project must reflect a pleasant and as natural place as possible, where the placement of each element responds to a specific need. Here is what should never be missing in the design of a Zen terrace:

• Minimal style furnishings: a Zen terrace is characterized by the presence of few but essential furnishings. Sofas, a low table, a meditation mat, and lots of comfortable cushions

• Prevalent of neutral and natural colors: beige, brown and black, white, blue, green, and yellow.

• Elements of nature: the presence of nature is essential to create an atmosphere of harmony and serenity. Therefore, plants, stones, and water from an electric fountain must not be missing, but also natural materials such as wood and rattan, flanked by furnishing accessories in sisal, hemp, and jute

• Asymmetries: nature is indomitable and chaotic, so the terrace must reflect this wild spirit through an asymmetrical arrangement of the various elements.

For the flooring, it would be preferable to opt for wooden platforms or interlocking modular tiles to be alternated with bands of stones or pebbles. Sand and gravel also give a decidedly natural look, but it would be better to reserve them for the green corners of your Zen terrace for convenience.

As for wood, you prefer teak, wengé, or wood with more amber shades such as Douglas: in addition to being hard and resistant, they give back a warm, natural and enveloping atmosphere. And walking or meditating barefoot will always be a pleasure.

When choosing furnishings, prioritize natural materials, such as wood or bamboo. Ecological materials are also perfect, such as rattan and poly-rattan, always preferred in light wood shades. The colors tend to be neutral and enlivened by some hints of brighter color and fabrics with optical or tropical prints.

As for the furniture design, I prefer modern low furniture, characterized by well-defined and essential lines. The minimal style is undoubtedly the most suitable trend for furnishing a Zen terrace.

Do not forget to insert a corner dedicated to meditation and tea: place a low table on a round carpet of woven rope and arrange large colored cushions or Japanese poufs in natural straw.

Lighting: how to create zen atmospheres

Lighting is an essential component of the Zen terrace because it recreates a harmonious and suggestive atmosphere from sunset to sunrise. Choose warm and natural lights, opting for lantern-shaped suspended lamps, to give that Japanese-style Zen touch that will immediately make the difference.

Place candles or candles of various sizes on the tables, placing them on a tray or in a glass bowl filled with water. Finally, don't forget to illuminate the plants and the darkest corners of your terrace by installing adjustable spotlights or a modern lighting system built into the floor.

We also offer you an equally suggestive decorative idea, namely the purchase of large outdoor vases with integrated LED: thanks to their soft light, your evenings on the terrace will immediately become more magical.

You can create a karesansui, a term for the Japanese Zen garden, if space permits. You will need to create a flat area enriched with gravel, pebbles, and stones of various sizes.

Alternatively, you can create a vertical one by installing masonry planters on the wall embellished with green leafy plants or the beautiful Japanese maple. On the terrace, it would be preferable to opt for the dwarf variant to avoid problems with space management.

Other plants that should never be missing are outdoor bonsai and bamboo plants. The latter should be placed in large rectangular planters so that their height can be exploited to create dividing spaces between one area of the terrace and another.

To give the last touch in Zen style, insert some decorative details of significant effect, remembering not to overdo it: essentiality is an essential factor, and too many decorations could make the environment anything but Zen!

CHAPTER 21
MISTAKES NOT TO BE MADE FOR A
WABI-SABI DESIGN

T he wrong furniture, the incorrect arrangement of furniture and accessories, and even not choosing the right decorations are just some of the ten mistakes not to make when decorating your home in the wabi-sabi style. So let's see in detail what else we need to pay attention to.

Furnishing in this style is not easy. One must always look for harmony and an outstanding balance in the arrangement of every single object. Furthermore, it is a culture very distant from ours that reflects all its traditions in furnishing the house.

Because of this, it's easy to make mistakes. To help you better follow this trend, we have listed ten typical mistakes not to make.

1. Using too much furniture

Japanese style loves simplicity. Furthermore, a balance must be created in the environments. This means that the relationship between full and empty spaces must always be well balanced.

Considering that there is usually not a lot of square footage available, it would be a mistake to get caught up in the urge to buy too much furniture and fill each room more than necessary with unnecessary pieces of furniture.

2. Choose bulky furniture

If you want to furnish this style, you will have to give up the elaborate furniture full of decorations or inlays.

On the contrary, furniture made of wood or other natural materials with clean lines is preferred. Remember that Japanese houses are tiny, so the table must be as functional as possible.

3. Opt for the classic bed

Today there are many types of beds. We can choose between various materials and also different kinds of heights. So don't choose a classic bed in a home.

In this case, if you want to respect tradition, you have to opt for a futon. It is a mattress wrapped in comfortable blankets placed directly on the floor.

4. Place the chairs next to the table

When furnishing the kitchen or dining room, choosing a lovely large table and then adding matching chairs comes naturally.

However, if you are furnishing in Japanese style, this is a mistake not to make. The Japanese eat sitting on cushions on the floor so that you won't need chairs. As for the table, however, opt for shallow specific models.

5. Arrange the objects symmetrically

Don't arrange the objects symmetrically. Strange as this may seem, the Japanese do not like symmetry because it is compared to stillness.

Arranging the objects not all on the same line represents dynamism. This is good as it helps stimulate creativity.

6. Choose the wrong decorations

As much as the Japanese style loves simplicity, decorations in the home must not be missing anyway. However, we must evaluate which are the most suitable s and try not to overdo them.

Some porcelain may be on display, but nothing too modern. Flowers and candles are also welcome, as all objects contain water, such as small fountains that help you relax.

7. Forget about plants

Among the fundamental decorations when furnishing in Japanese style, we cannot fail to mention the plants, in particular, the bamboo and the bonsai.

They symbolize this culture and are considered real good luck charms. So forgetting them surely would be a mistake not to make.

8. Leave the walls bare

The walls of a house must constantly be embellished, certainly in the right way. Often, panels are placed as decoration, and there is no need to add anything else.

In other cases, however, paintings are welcome as long as they portray natural landscapes, flowers such as cherry trees, or are the typical Japanese prints.

9. Don't design large windows

Japanese culture pays excellent attention to the inside and the outside balance. This is reflected in a continuity also between the inside and the outside of the house.

For this, large windows overlooking the garden are essential. Avoid putting up curtains or anything else that could block your view.

10. Don't do decluttering

We have said that according to the wabi-sabi, one must accept imperfection. So you can leave the house a bit 'in diosrdine, but remember that you must always try to eliminate the extra.

CHAPTER 22
THE DECLUTTERING

Tabi-sabi philosophy, there is no place for the extra. Everything must be functional. Without forgetting that the extreme mental disorder, accumulating things in bulk in a maniacal way limits the spaces inside the house and our minds. So let's see how we can free up the areas outside and inside us.

The KonMari method by Marie Kondo: what it is and where to start

We have already talked about decluttering in the past, but making room in the house also has another famous name! You have often heard about it: the KonMari method, invented by cleaning guru Marie Kondo, has conquered the world.

A bestseller that has only anticipated a real revolution in tidying, or rather the Netflix series "Let's tidy up with Marie Kondo. " Boom.

However, a method promises to restore order, light, and joy in the home (and perhaps in life) through many small tricks applied rigorously.

All very interesting, but in practice… where do you start?

According to the KonMari method, it is not necessary to proceed by room, but by category of objects, strictly in this order: clothes, books, papers, and Komono (or... miscellany).

Everything, therefore, belongs to a macro or sub-category. It is strongly recommended to collect all the objects belonging to the same category and arrange them on the floor - or in any case, on a flat surface, which can be a bed or a table - and analyze them one by one., choosing their fate.

Before deciding what to keep and throw away, and before letting yourself go of the memories, ask yourself: "Does it make me happy?"

We must surround ourselves with beautiful things which remind us of happy moments and which, looking at them, make us feel joy and well-being.

So let's throw away that pair of jeans that we've been promising ourselves to wear for two years when we have lost 5 kg (making us feel inadequate in the meantime), away with those books that collect dust and haven't opened for ten years, out with that box full of notes, ribbons, pens, and objects of various kinds that have been closed for months.

Not everything should be thrown in the garbage; indeed, when possible, we strongly recommend donating, giving away, or reselling what you no longer use, but in some cases, the only possible answer, unfortunately, is the garbage nerd!

Everything at once

KonMari's method is unforgiving: it is best to apply it all at once, even if this means taking the entire day.

Postponing or dividing the method into too many phases would seem the best way to fail. And if Madame Marie Kondo says so, who are we to contradict her?

Clothes

How many clothes have been sitting in the closet for months, if not years? In addition to the clothes, even those socks that have been unmatched for months, the underwear with the now gone elastics, scarves that we last put on back in 2005… everything away.

Only clothes worn regularly in the Spring / Summer and Autumn / Winter seasons should remain in the wardrobe. Everything else must disappear.

How you fold and hang your clothes is also essential,

Books

We like full bookcases and houses overflowing with books. Still, over the years, we risk accumulating many titles that we will never read again, and that only takes away space, collecting dust.

The used book market, for example, is very active, but associations, literary clubs, bookcrossing, and libraries can also be good choices to "free" the books that we no longer need.

Sheets, slips, scattered papers

The great enemies of clutter pop up in all corners of the house, from the desk to the bookcases, from the fridge to the drawers. Old receipts, photocopies, flying notes, and printed lists are all things we haven't looked at for months, making the house and our lives more messy and crowded.

In this case, no mercy; the important thing is to save the essential documents, and the rest must be thrown away.

Komono

The collection is perhaps the most complicated part to fix because it encompasses everything.

Everyone knows what brings disorder into their home; the important thing is to keep in mind another piece of advice that is part of the KonMari method: before putting everything back in order, immediately throw away all the discarded things, avoiding accumulating them in the garage or a box. !

CHAPTER 23
THE RULES TO FOLLOW TO PERFORM DECLUTTERING AT BEST

Have you ever felt suffocated in the house due to all the objects in every room that create disorder?

Do not worry; it is a sensation familiar to many: homes are often excessively full of objects that risk-taking over and create chaos that can generate a feeling of discomfort and throw you into despair.

In a conscious and reasoned way, the secret is to eliminate all we have accumulated over time, which is useless or does not represent something necessary. The way you organize your space can therefore affect, both positively and negatively, your state of mind and your mood. For this reason, it is essential to living in a tidy and organized home, and decluttering can help.

Especially if we want to embrace the wabi-sabi philosophy

BUT WHAT IS DECLUTTERING?

Literally, "to declutter" means "to make an order," so the word "decluttering" is often translated with the definition "to remove things you do not need from a place, to make it more pleasant and more useful." It is, therefore, the ability to make room and get rid of the extra.

It is a powerful weapon to improve your life and well-being and make you master your space and time again: by learning to get rid of the extra, you will immediately feel better and in a good mood.

1. THINGS TO KNOW BEFORE YOU BEGIN:

Decluttering requires a good dose of decision and the ability to live with small moments of melancholy and nostalgia. While you make room and get rid of the extra, you also come to terms with memories and the past. For this reason, decluttering involves not only the physical space but also the interior one.

You don't need to hurry to do everything right away, but proceed step by step according to the time available: you can choose whether to dedicate half an hour a day to decluttering or do everything over the weekend.

Don't move deleted things to the attic or basement - for decluttering to make sense, the things you don't need must be eliminated.

The decluttering process should not be seen as deprivation but as a fun and creative journey towards a regained simplicity.

2. HOW TO RECOGNIZE A SUPERFLUOUS OBJECT?

This is the focal point of the whole process. The first few times, it may seem complicated, but slowly you will be able to recognize different objects on the fly. Look at each item in the room you are tidying up, and ask yourself:

1. if you still like it.

2. if it is applicable.

3. if it has sentimental value.

Any item that does not meet these three criteria must be put aside. Do not keep an object just because your mother gave it to you and you think she would be upset if she didn't see it anymore or because "one day" it might come in handy: if you haven't used it so far, it means that you can make it. Unless forever.

Decluttering means just that: getting rid of the extra and tidying up. The idea of living a simpler life with fewer material things interests many, but they often find themselves not knowing where to start and asking themselves many questions, such as:

"What if I still need this object?". As we said before, if you haven't used it until now, you can do without it.

"Isn't it bad to throw away things that still work?". You don't have to throw them away - you can give them away, sell them or donate them to charity, but more on that later!

The wardrobe is the perfect example: how many useless clothes do we tend to accumulate without realizing it? How many clothes do we wear? Take it all out, choose and then decide what to donate and throw away. Some shops take old clothes back in exchange for shopping vouchers.

Here are some examples of items to delete:

- Dry cleaners hangers

- Sports gadgets

- Tablecloths too large or small

- Mismatched socks

- Unnecessary business cards

- Souvenirs you don't like

- Stained, torn, or frayed towels

- Obsolete video games

- Notebooks that are no longer needed

- Store catalogs available online

- Ruined clothes

- Broken electronic appliances

- Cookbooks you've never used

- Shoes that hurt are old or are worn out

- Broken toys or board games with missing pieces

- Dishes you never use

- Greeting cards, wedding invitations, etc.

- Old calendars

- Empty shoeboxes

- Boxes of electronic devices whose warranty has expired

- chargers and old cables of various types

- Unused or damaged backpacks and bags

- Decorative elements (favors) that you no longer like

- Cosmetics that are out of date or you don't like and nail polishes that have congealed

- Damaged or unworn jewelry (e.g., mismatched earrings, broken necklaces)

And here's why you won't miss these things:

They are old: you will never wonder why you have thrown away all those unused cables or those uncomfortable shoes.

They're broken - if you wanted to fix those things, you would have already done so.

You and your beloved family no longer need - this is the most important thing.

3. HOW TO ORGANIZE THE DECLUTTERING

There are two unique ways you can take, depending on how you are best at the organizational level:

1st method: go to rooms.

2nd method: go for types of products.

Go for rooms

It is the most straightforward system to follow because it allows you to work on something targeted: choose the room to arrange and work on it until you have obtained the desired result.

How to organize the work?

Take out everything you want to analyze (for example, all the clothes in the closet) and place it on a free surface.

At this point, divide all the objects by choosing whether to keep them, throw them away or give them away.

After a thorough cleaning of the spaces, put away the objects to keep organizing them as best suited to your needs.

It is essential to put away everything used regularly and instead set what is used only occasionally in the most uncomfortable places. Using suitable quality boxes and baskets will help keep things clean and tidy more efficiently and put things away quickly once used. Finally, it is beneficial to use labels when storing something rarely used.

To simplify the process, you can divide it into two stages. You'll be sure you want to delete some items, but you may have some doubts about others. Then put all the objects in "maybe" in a box or bag. At the end of the selection and first elimination work, you will have a clearer idea of the usefulness of keeping something of what you have provisionally placed in the box. You will be able to act in consequence.

Proceed in this way room by room until you have completed the whole house.

A little trick: to keep your clothes tidy, buy some fabric boxes (you can buy them from Ikea or online) and put away the clothes. If you roll them up, they won't have creases when you take them out to put them on!

Go for types of products.

It is the most complicated system since not all clothing is in the bedroom wardrobes in the house, electronic equipment is not all in the same room, and ornaments, books, magazines, etc.

Going for products means examining the whole house by focusing on a particular product (example: electronic equipment) and acting on it. The work is undoubtedly more complex, but it offers better results in many cases.

Look for all the objects of a specific category and store them, if you can, to always know where they are. In this case, all the accessories and phone chargers have been kept in small Ikea Godmorgon containers - it's a very clever idea for organizing drawers.

DECLUTTERING: KEEPING THE "MEMORIES" YES OR NO?

Most of the objects we have at home do not serve a specific task but are part of the "memory" of the life of one's family: I'm talking about letters, photo albums, objects dear to our ancestors, and much more. In this case, the choice is personal and must be made after careful reflection on the importance that specific memories can have in family life.

4. WHAT TO DO WITH THE OBJECTS TO BE ELIMINATED?

Donating to Associations: I always recommend donating to local charities and organizations as much as possible. Presenting what you don't need is twice as good: you'll have fewer things in your home, and other people will get the items they need.

A gift to those you know: if you know that relatives or friends need something that you own and no more prolonged use, but it is in good condition, give it to them: from clothes put on once and never again to equipment for children (seats, cots, etc..), anything that can help them will be seen as a very welcome gift.

Resell: if you have any valuables you don't use (jewelry, appliances, silverware, etc.), you can always resell them online or in thrift markets. If you want to get rid of antique furniture, call an antique dealer for an appraisal to know their exact price.

Throw away: Finally, don't feel guilty if many things, especially if broken, end up in the trash. Always remember: your home is not a warehouse. Some things must be thrown away, adopting the most appropriate system from time to time: undifferentiated or differentiated garbage for small and medium-sized objects, while landfills for larger objects and household appliances. Remember to respect the environment!

SPECIAL MENTION: THE DECLUTTERING OF BOOKS

A necessary premise: books should never be thrown away for any reason. So, if you need to make room in the library or your house is too crowded with books, the keyword is: give as a gift.

Among the possible recipients of the books you have discarded: are neighborhood libraries, schools, hospitals, retirement homes, prisons, and other types of communities.

5. THE TRICK OF THE BAG

This is a little trick you can use to keep your house tidy after you have it fixed or before doing an initial roughing:

Get a bag.

Decide what to focus on (Paper? Plastic? Other?).

Take a tour of the whole house.

Throw everything that is too much into the bag without thinking about it so much. Do not put it on hold when it is complete: get out of the house immediately and throw everything away. How do you feel? Do you feel a feeling of relief and lightness?

The secret to the success of this system is only one: zero organization.

It's so simple it can't fail.

It is perfect for giving a packed house a first "blow."

It gives a feeling of relief and success instantly and with little effort.

It is very effective as a maintenance technique.

It can be applied in the vast majority of situations.

The technique has its limits: it cannot take you alone to "solve" an entire house, but to make skimming and set a decluttering that seems stuck to the starting grids, the bag trick is ideal. What do you think about it?

Try to go by material: so you can use a plastic bag for all plastic objects, a paper bag for sheets and documents, and to simplify the recycling of materials!

FINALLY, A TIDY AND LIVABLE HOUSE!

When the job is done, you will be surprised to discover a more spacious house, where everything has its place, and there are no piles of unused objects.

But how do you keep the results over time?

Pay attention to making purchases aware that they do not go to fill your house with unnecessary items again.

To adopt this little rule, one must go out for everything that enters.

Use the bag trick frequently to avoid the new accumulation of items.

But I'm sure that once this hard work is done, you will have no desire to return to your old messy and stuffy house: the satisfaction of being surrounded only by beautiful objects that represent us will be stronger than any form of laziness!

And now, a roundup of ideas for ordering your home after throwing away the extra elements!

Bathroom idea / 1: if you have a drawer, organize it with small boxes to divide the various products: in this way, everything will have its place, and you will not waste time looking for things. You can find dividers online.

Bathroom idea / 2: No problem if you have doors instead of drawers. Store the products in baskets, better if made specifically for the organization than divided internally.

Wardrobe idea / 1: for the drawers, use dividers to find everything on the fly!

Wardrobe idea / 2: instead of folding sweaters and T-shirts, roll them up on themselves so as not to create creases and to optimize space.

Closet idea / 3: To organize the closet, you can use boxes. This will facilitate the organization and the change of season: just swap the boxes with the clothes of the past season with the boxes of the current one.

Kitchen idea / 1: to make the most of the space, use risers.

Kitchen idea / 2: make the most of the space under the sink by using containers for bulkier products and a basket to hang on the door for smaller products.

Kitchen idea / 3: even in the refrigerator, use containers to separate the various products and keep everything in order.

CHAPTER 24

KINTSUGI THE JAPANESE TECHNIQUE THAT TRANSFORMS BROKEN CERAMIC OBJECTS REPAIRED WITH GOLD INTO ART

When a plate, a vase, or a bowl breaks, shattering into a thousand pieces, albeit with regret, we throw them away. However, we should take an example from the Japanese, who practice the kintsugi technique for some ceramic and porcelain objects, a repair system using resin and gold dust that highlights cracks and fractures instead of being invisible.

Kintsugi, the Japanese art of repairing cracks with gold, increasing their value

Kintsugi mean

Literally, in Japanese, it means 'to repair with gold.' The union of the two words kin means 'to reunite' or 'to repair,' and tsugi, which means 'reunion.' It is also sometimes found as kin-tsukuroi.

In practice, this technique adds value to the broken object. But it is not just a repair; it is also a philosophy of life. The underlying concept can also have a profound symbolic meaning.

It is a technique and also a philosophy of Japanese origin. Like other practical forms that hide deep meanings linked to oriental philosophy, such as Ikebana, the art of arranging flowers, ikigai, the search for one's self, or the Zen garden, kintsugi also has a Zen implication.

It means 'to repair with gold' and is an ancient Japanese technique that repairs ceramic and porcelain objects, such as vases, plates, and trays, using gold to weld the various fragments together.

The cracks thus remain evident and not hidden, as we Westerners would be led to believe when it comes to repairing a broken object. And indeed, it increases its value.

Origins, history, and legend of kintsugi

It is a restoration technique devised at the end of the 15th century by Japanese potters to repair the delicate porcelain cups for the tea ceremony.

Legend has it that Ashikaga Yoshimasa, VIII Shogun of the Ashikaga Shogunate, after breaking his favorite cup, sent it to China to have it repaired.

Since the repairs of the time were done with metallic ligatures that were not very beautiful from an aesthetic point of view, Ashikaga Yoshimasa decided to try the repair again by contacting some Japanese craftsmen.

These, surprised by the shogun's tenacity in getting his beloved cup back, decided to try to transform it into a sort of jewel, filling the cracks with lacquered resin and gold dust.

The kintsugi technique

The traditional technique foresees that the broken pieces of the ceramic object are welded together with a thin layer of urushi lacquer, which is derived from the resin of a tree.

First plastered and then sanded, the breaking lines are finished with red urushi lacquer with a brush on which the gold dust is dropped.

The purpose of this type of repair is not to hide the damage but to emphasize it, incorporating it into the aesthetics of the repaired object.

From an artistic point of view, the repaired piece will thus be "better" than the new object and will be considered more precious, both for the presence of gold or silver and for its uniqueness.

The breaking lines joined with urushi lacquer are left visible and more highlighted with gold dust.

The ceramic objects repaired with this artistic technique become true works of art. Their fragility is transformed into a point of strength and perfection. Each repaired ceramic presents a different intertwining of unique and unrepeatable golden lines due to the randomness with which the ceramic can be shattered.

This practice stems from the idea that an even greater form of aesthetic and interior perfection can be born from imperfection and a wound.

140

What it takes to do the Kintsugi

The material used as the glue is urushi lacquer, which is extracted from the native Rhus plant Verniciflua. But rice or wheat flour, Tomoko, and gold and silver dust are also used.

The drying process of the lacquer, used as an adhesive for ceramic, a stucco, and as an adhesive for gold dust, takes place in the wall, in a warm environment (about 25 °) and with a relative humidity of around 70- 80%. The drying time is variable: it ranges from 3 to 7 days.

The philosophy of kintsugi

This is not only a mere artistic concept but also has deep roots in Zen philosophy. The concepts enclosed would be:

Mushin: the ability to let go, forget worries, and free the mind from pursuing perfection.

Anicca or impermanence: the awareness of fate and the transience of existence. All things are destined to end, and we must accept this condition with a calm and conscious approach.

Mono no - aware: a kind of empathy for objects. Appreciating its decadence, one comes to admire its beauty.

This ancient art of repairing precious objects is often used as a symbol and metaphor for the concept of resilience.

Furthermore, it would also represent the concept of fracture in a broad sense and, therefore, the crises and changes that the individual may have to face in life.

The basic idea is that a better and even more effective form of perfection, aesthetic and interior, can be born from imperfection and a wound.

In this practice, the broken vase or object is repaired without hiding the cracks, but, on the contrary, the latter is especially emphasized through a precious material such as gold. This enhancement of the fracture represents the new history of the broken object.

The idea of recovering and enhancing an object that otherwise would have lost its intended use can also be applied to people. Even after a break or damage, it is possible to overcome and 'heal' one's internal wounds and become better.

And again, as the precious metal enhances the fractures, the person can proudly show his scars because they represent his experience in the process of rebirth.

What can it do today?

In this period, in particular, many of us need tranquility, free the mind for a moment from the hectic thoughts of the day, and worry-free. Right now, even very normal activities such as shopping, which we are usually used to doing since childhood, for many bring with it anxiety and stress.

However, a hobby that could be started is that of Kintsugi, albeit in a small way. To glue the pieces together takes a lot of concentration (so much so that Japanese artists who practice this technique sometimes take more than a month to repair a single object), so the mind has to concentrate only on this, letting go of the rest and fixing itself in one dimension of calm.

With what to practice it?

Top-rated is specific kits, which can be purchased in specialized shops for DIY and the restoration of antique objects or online to proceed and practice this ancient technique with the right tools. To learn the method and find inspiration for a new creation, you can consult various texts.

CHAPTER 25

HOW TO DO THE KINTSUGI

T he traditional technique is very complex and challenging to reproduce, especially since it is not so easy to find urushi lacquer.

We can perform kintsugi-style ceramic repairs using cutting-edge materials thanks to modern synthetic resin technology.

Furthermore, to carry out an inexpensive operation, it is possible to replace real gold and silver with metallic pigments that imitate the features of the two precious items.

At this point, it is time to move on to practice. Let's see what we need and how to proceed to repair a broken object with this technique:

- object in ceramic or porcelain

- two-component epoxy glue

- gold or silver powder or simple metallic pigments

- chopsticks to mix the various components

- brush for finishing

Preparation. Mix the two-component glue with the gold powder or imitation pigments in a bowl. Consider three parts of glue for one metal powder.

Assemble the various fragments trying to respect the original arrangement. Spread a sufficient and homogeneous amount of adhesive paste on the edge of the piece. Keep the parts glued in place for a few minutes to facilitate fixing. And repeat the operation with all the fragments.

Using a brush, go over the gluing so that the material expands well, even outside the crack of the break. By doing so, the repair will take on a deep gold or silvery color.

It is essential not to remove the golden glue from the joint. This is precisely the peculiar characteristic of this repair technique.

If some small ceramic pieces are missing, we can fill the gaps with epoxy glue mixed with the metal powder.

Finally, it is also possible to avoid mixing the epoxy glue with the metal powder, simply gluing the fragments only with great glue. At the end of the gluing operations, rain a sufficient quantity of metal powder onto the excess adhesive that comes out of the joints.

What glue to use for kintsugi

Lacquer should be used, but regular two-component epoxy glue to mix with gold powder is fine.

It should be applied abundantly to the ceramic cracks to remain visible along with the damage from the joints.

Also known as kintsukuroi, it is the Japanese technique that repairs broken ceramic objects with gold.

And that invites us to love and show imperfections (even ours)!

REQUIRED

- two-component glue

- golden powder

- some chopsticks to mix the components

- brush for finishing

HOW TO DO

- Mix the two-component glue with the gold powder

- Apply the mixture obtained to the ceramic cracks so that it is abundant and visible

- Hold the parts to be glued in place for a few minutes

- With a brush, carefully go over the gluing so that the material spreads well even outside the crack of the break and the repair takes on intense gold color.

CHAPTER 26
HOW TO RECOVER OLD LAMPSHADES

Do you have a lamp you adore, but whose lampshade you hate? Or maybe you've remodeled a room recently and want the lights to match the rest but don't want to break the piggy bank to buy all new lamps? Whatever your reasons, getting your lampshades back is your best bet. You need an old lampshade, some new fabric, and a little creativity.

1-Take measures

Prepare your work table. It will be better to work on a table because you will need a flat surface on which you can arrange all your materials. Place newspaper on the table and the floor around your countertop, as the spray adhesive can stick to almost any surface and could damage your furniture or beds.

2-Remove the old fabric from the shape of the lampshade. Remove the hem (if there is one) by pulling it. The scissors pierce the old material and cut pieces off the body. Do not cut the lining fabric.

Depending on the adhesive used to adhere the fabric to the shape, you may be able to cut sections and then use your fingers to pull the remaining pieces of material off the frame cord.

3-Spread out a piece of pattern paper and measure your lampshade. Make sure the article is flat and wrinkle-free. Roll the lampshade in the report, tracing the edges it forms with a pencil. To get an exact measurement, it is essential to track where you started on the lamp.

4-Add length to the shape you drew. You will need some extra fabric, so you should add 1.5cm along both long sides of the body you removed from your lampshade and 2.5cm to one of the short sides.

5-Cut the pattern paper along the lines you created. You will use this template as a stencil for the shape you cut from your fabric.

6-Choose your fabric. When retrieving a lampshade, choose the light, relatively thin material.

Consider the design of the fabric. While lamps with a top and bottom of equal sizes will work well with any material, lights with a small shelter and broad base will look odd wrapped in a vertical line pattern (which tends to appear to fall into the back seam).

Cut the fabric

1- Ensure there are no wrinkles or creases and that the material is completely smooth on the flat surface. You need to spread it out so you don't accidentally cut it into a fold and end up with an asymmetrical fabric cover for your lampshade.

2-Spread your pattern on the fabric. Make sure the paper is flat too. You can use pins to keep it snug against the material.

3-Mark the back of the material. Using a suitable pen or some other drawing tool that you will be able to see on the fabric, trace the outline of the paper stencil. Be very careful to be as accurate as possible. You draw on the back of the material to make sure that the drawing does not show on the final result.

4-Cut out the material. Using fabric scissors, gently cut the material along the lines created with the fabric pen. Remove any remaining fabric from the work area.

Retrieve the lampshade

1-Spray your fabric with adhesive. It is essential to do this in a well-ventilated area, as the spray adhesive can be harmful if you breathe in too much. Remember that adhesive spray is incredibly sticky (and permanent), so make sure you don't put it on anything beyond the fabric.

If you bought an adhesive-backed fabric, you do not need to use spray adhesive on the material. Use the adhesive canvas to adhere the fabric to the shape of the lampshade. You must first heat the canvas with an iron, place it in place on the body, and finally cover the canvas with the fabric. Spread the material as you move it around the sides of the canvas and shape it until the lampshade is wholly protected.

2-Place your lamp and add the fabric. To do this, center the lampshade in the material so that the edge of the fabric and the existing seam of the lampshade are aligned. Roll the lampshade along with the fabric, stretching the fabric and removing any creases.

If you are using a fabric with a design, it is also essential to make sure the design lines up correctly when attaching the material to the lampshade.

3-Create a seam with the extra fabric on the short side (the vertical edge). You'll have additional material to roll your lampshade into. Rather than leaving the edge of the fabric visible, fold the excess fabric to create a straight hem. Make sure you only use a little glue - if you use too much, it may come off the hem (which isn't the best to see).

4-To give your lampshade a finished look, it is best to fold the extra material inside the lampshade. Make sure it stays up and down by securing it with hot glue.

5-Add some finishing touches. To make your lampshade look fresh from the shop, add a coating along the bottom edge of the lamp. Simply use hot glue to attach a thicker piece of fabric along the top and bottom edges of your light. You can also add some fringe, a rick-rack hem, or other materials to cover the top and bottom edges of the lampshade with its new coating.

Advice

To make this project even cheaper, look for old lamps at thrift markets.

Things you will need:

- Lampshade

- Scissors

- Fabric

- Tape measure

- Line

- Pencil for fabrics

- Spray adhesive

- Iron (if using material with an adhesive side)

- Hot glue

CHAPTER 27
SHIBORI: HOW TO DYE AND NATURALLY DECORATE FABRICS WITH THE ANCIENT JAPANESE TECHNIQUE

Shibori is an ancient Japanese technique for dyeing fabrics still little known in the West. In shibori, cloths are tied and manipulated or protected in other ways before being immersed in the dye bath.

Shibori is an ancient Japanese technique for dyeing fabrics still little known in the West. In shibori, cloths are tied and manipulated or protected in other ways before being immersed in the dye bath.

In this type of dyeing, very particular decorations are obtained. The parts of the fabric that do not have to absorb the color are protected to make this happen. It is interesting to experiment with this technique using vegetable dyes obtained from plants and vegetables (for example, beet, wisteria, or nettle).

With this technique, very original abstract decorations are obtained. This technique comes from the word " shibori, "which means to twist, tighten and press. Similar dyeing techniques in India and other countries such as Malaysia and Indonesia have different names, such as banda and trick.

Compared to the more well-known " tie and dye techniques, "much more imaginative, rich and varied decorations are obtained with shibori.

- Materials

- 100% cotton fabrics

- Powder dyeing for fabrics or suitable vegetable dyes

- Clothes pegs, rubber bands, office clips

- Twine

- Wooden dowels and sticks of various sizes

- Waterproof gloves

1) Prepare the color in a pot or bucket. You can try experimenting with natural dyes with vegetables, flowers, and leaves. Read here.

2) Cut out a square of fabric from the chosen cotton fabric. Test with a square with a side of 45 cm. Most shibori techniques suggest starting with a square shape.

3) Fold the fabric back on itself to obtain a triangle from your square. Or fold the fabric like an accordion to make a rectangle.

4) Secure the folded fabrics with wooden sticks and rubber bands and clothes pegs, and document clips. Also, place oval and square wooden dowels on the fabric parts you would like to decorate in a

particular way and secure them with rubber bands.

5) Secure folded fabrics very well using rubber bands and clothes pegs. Put on waterproof gloves and dip the materials in the dye bath. The more the fabric remains immersed, the more intense the color will be.

6) For powder dyes for fabrics, a time of 45 minutes can be respected, but always check the instructions on the package carefully. For natural dyes, longer times may be needed. Some powder dyes may require adding calcium carbonate to the dye bath.

7) Remove the fabrics from the dye bath after the rest time. Rinse them very well, and then let them dry.

CHAPTER 28
HOW TO MAKE A SCREEN YOURSELF

W ooden screen for the house: how to make it yourself. Useful DIY ideas.

A practical and excellent idea for furnishing the house and organizing spaces can be to use booths or dividers. There are many on the market, in wood with rigid panels, with slats or shutters, or in fabric, plain or printed, on a wooden frame.

On the market, in furniture stores, there are many. You have to choose the one that's right for you. Or you can make your booth yourself—an opportunity to learn how to create something new and have a lot of satisfaction.

Wooden screen for the house: how to make it yourself

The easiest way to make wooden screens is to get boards that have already been cut or have them cut to size. Or cut them yourself if you are experienced in carpentry. Once you have your panels, you can leave them in natural wood or paint them if you get by with paint. A surefire decoration is the one that involves the use of stencil and découpage techniques. Once the decoration is finished, join the panels of your booth with particular hinges, which you will apply after making small holes in the wood where you can insert the screws. You can let the base of your booth panels touch the ground if it is thick and stable enough, or you can apply feet to the floor.

Instead of panels, you can prepare or have a wooden frame designed, with or without feet. In the empty spaces, inside the squares or rectangles of the frame, insert the fabric of your choice taut, fixing it on the back with wood glue or small staples to be applied with the appropriate stapler.

Screen in Japanese wood

Finally, an original and refined idea can create a Japanese shoji booth. These dividers are widely used in Japanese homes, both as screens and as natural walls, doors, or sliding doors. They have a square frame made of light-colored light wood. At the same time, the spaces inside the structure are covered with fine Japanese paper. You will already find wooden strips and Japanese paper in stores specializing in DIY and home DIY.

Once you have purchased the necessary, mount the wooden strips according to the size of the screen and the number of panels you want to make. The strips of the external frame will be thicker for the stability and solidity of the structure. At the same time, the internal ones are lighter. You can also make a single ample panel rest on wooden feet for stability. Or you can also apply wheels to the base.

To form the structure of the Japanese screen, join the various wooden strips with small nails, the groups to be applied with a not too heavy hammer. Make square frames. Then, in the empty spaces of the squares, use the Japanese paper to be fixed to the strips, at the back of the screen, with glue or staples, as above. Join the panels with the hinges. You can create quadrangular support bases to be arranged diagonally to fold the meetings for more excellent stability. Indeed, the wooden feet or the wheels allow greater mobility to the boards, which you can also tuck into a booklet when you want to put away your screen.

The Japanese shoji screen is elegant and highly versatile. It allows you to hope for the environments of the same room with discretion, without weighing down the furniture, and above all, it gives excellent brightness thanks to the lightness of the Japanese paper that lets the light filter through.

CHAPTER 29

CONCLUSIONS

T rends in interior design are constantly changing. Today wabi design has come to the fore Sabi. It refers to minimalism, vanishing, and a lack of attachment to material objects.

Wabi-Sabi originates in the Land of the Rising Sun - Japan. On the other hand, Sabi is an artistic term that can be translated as covering things with the patina of time. The Wabi-Sabi definition refers to a style philosophy of finding beauty in humble and not quite perfect things.

A reference to nature and simplicity can characterize Wabi-Sabi design. Without a doubt, natural materials are its most essential elements:

- natural wood

- stone

- wicker

It is better if these materials are marked with use. As for the decorations, Wabi-Sabi art is dominated by ceramics, such as small candle holders and vases.

Wabi-Sabi design – colors:

- beige

- dark or light brown

- shades of gray

- white

Due to the colors referring to the earth, the Wabisabi interior looks significantly warmer and more welcoming. Plus, they make the room seem bigger. It is essential for interiors with little space, for example, a small living room or bedroom.

The neutral colors on the walls also promote quick relaxation, for example, after a long day at work. One can calm down and sleep in such an interior.

Wabi-Sabi - characteristic materials:

The meaning of Wabi Sabi also refers to the non-attachment to the quality of the products.

When choosing fabrics, it is recommended to choose linen. This material wrinkles easily, so accessories made with it always look crumbled - it fits perfectly into the Wabi-Sabi design.

The philosophy is also about evanescence and the passing of time - the wear and tear of the furniture used in the interiors.

An interesting effect can be achieved by using a unique method that makes the plaster look like it is falling off.

Wabi-Sabi design - for which interiors is it suitable?

Wabi-Sabi's design looks good in any interior. But you have to accept the passage of time - the gradual damage to furniture and other objects. Lack of attachment to new items is key to this style, so it might be good to look for second-hand furniture with a fascinating history and age. ** Currently, many manufacturers offer custom furniture collections for the Japanese philosophy.

Wabi-Sabi design – accessories:

Wabi-Sabi art and philosophy refer to nature. A piece of bark with some moss and a few small candles could be a good decoration. Even a single flower in a small vase matches this style perfectly.

You can also make perfect decorations using the DIY method - for example, a candle holder.

Wabi-sabi art, fabrics:

Authenticity is also the watchword for fabrics.

Space for natural alternatives such as wool, linen, and organic cotton is even better if with raw and material processing. Greenlight for a thick-weave plaid or tricot to be placed at the foot of the bed, on an armchair, or on the sofa, ready to give warmth and comfort.

On the other hand, unpressed linen sheets are the protagonists of a bed not made to perfection.

Natural and non-ironed fabrics characterize wabi-sabi.

We also find linen in the kitchen. A tablecloth or runner made with this material gives character to a table embellished with a vase of wildflowers and a freshly baked cake to be enjoyed alone or in good company during a sweet afternoon break.

And for a break that involves all the senses, how about letting yourself be enveloped by the soft embrace of an organic cotton bathrobe to wear after a nice warm bath?

Relaxation will be guaranteed.

Wabi-sabi art, colors

The sense of natural imperfection that characterizes wabi-sabi art also influences the choice of colors. Which ones to bet on? Indicate the palettes that run through earth tones, alternating with warm and versatile whites.

But not only that: wabi-sabi culture is contemplation and acceptance of things. Therefore, it is normal for it to be associated with a meditative lifestyle that prefers not very bright shades.

In this sense, the furnishings that include the whole scale of grays and intense blues on cushions, textiles, sheets, and small objects should be enhanced.

To give the house a personal touch of color, we can use floral solutions, such as lavender, placed in recycled vases; a cast iron teapot with an oriental allure is perfect.

Let's not forget, then, to recreate an even more intimate atmosphere with soft lights to be placed at strategic points of the house.

We have seen so far the materials, fabrics, and nuances that characterize the wabi-sabi style, but how do we propose them in various domestic environments?

The common thread is functional and aesthetic essentiality; spaces must be comfortable and sober, transmitting inner harmony.

To embellish the relaxation area or the reading corner, accessories and decorations with simple lines and a recycled look include jute rugs, rattan baskets, and bamboo lampshades.

However, the focus shifts to the mise en place in the kitchen or the dining room.

The table is dressed in delicacy and is tinged with natural shades: a linen or cotton tablecloth, recycled glass bottles as vase holders, and sets of plates and glasses that combine different patterns and materials. And then, a chipped plate can find its place next to a perfectly intact one.

Wabi-sabi touch to the bedroom.

Rattan abat-jour, a set of raw cotton percale sheets, invites us to enjoy a good rest. A pile of books and magazines still to be read can be transformed into an unusual table.

In general, a room must be thought of as a place that invites rest and concentration.

Its essentially minimalist character induces us to dispense with furniture that is not strictly necessary. After all, getting rid of what you don't use is undoubtedly a way of simplifying your life.

The idea of the Japanese style is based on simplicity and cleanliness (there is just a term to indicate a room furnished with the Japanese style: Washitsu).

An inevitable element in the bedrooms and, if desired, in the other rooms is the booth shoji, a folding panel usually made of rice paper and bamboo or wood. It is a traditional element of Japanese culture when it comes to furnishings.

The booths shoji can help hide things and objects that we have in a room, such as the living room, where we usually receive guests, and that we do not want to be in sight, such as, for example, cardboard boxes or gym bags.

But be careful when you ask for shoji: formally, shoji means both room dividers (Akari shoji) and the sliding doors inside the rooms, fusuma (also called kirigami shoji), and the windows made with blown rice paper, lighter than fusuma to allow light to enter (which are called shoji).

If the view from the bedroom window is not to your liking, the people across the street are too close; the shoji panels can be placed in front of the window to protect your privacy while allowing light to filter through. And light up the room.

It is preferable to choose low furniture that allows more significant space.

Of Japanese conception are also zabuton, zafu, and futon. Replacing the summer mattress with a futon is a choice that is economically advantageous and allows you to save space.

The choice of colors must fall on neutral colors. Japanese decoration is based on balance.

Wooden furniture and a slightly brighter color focused on a single point of the room, for example, the bed, are indicated, breaking the neutral colors' motor.

The sheets and curtains could be silk, a fabric that goes well with a Japanese décor.

Finally, always remember the golden rule less is more.